PERSPECTIVE

PERSPECTIVE

A Greek American finding his way in Greece

By Peter Manouselis

ISBN: 9780578718477

Cover Illustration by Andy Bridge
Printed in the United States of America

For Mom and Dad

"I did not know what I was going to do with my life; before anything else I wanted to find an answer, my answer, to the timeless questions, and then after that I would decide what I would become. If I did not begin by discovering what was the grand purpose of life on earth, I said to myself, how would I be able to discover the purpose of my tiny ephemeral life? And if I did not give my life a purpose, how would I be able to engage in action? I was not interested in finding what life's purpose was objectively - this, I divined, was impossible and futile - but simply what purpose I, of my own free will, could give it in accord with my spiritual and intellectual needs. Whether or not this purpose was the true one did not, at that time, have any great significance for me. The important thing was that I should find (should create) a purpose congruent with my own self, and thus, by following it, reel out my particular desires and abilities to the furthest possible limit. For then at last I would be collaborating harmoniously with the totality of the universe."

Nikos Kazantzakis, *Report to Greco*

CHAPTER ONE

For some people, a quarter-million dollars is the seed of their future business empire. For me it offered a new perspective on life.

However, by my thirty-first birthday, a substantial portion of that quarter of a million dollars that had been in my bank account when I left my job as an investment banker at the ripe old age of twenty-six had been depleted, and all I really had to show for the past four years were a number of romances, some travels, and one big revelation. Now, six months after the big revelation, I was in San Francisco, in the finest hotel, on top of the highest hill with the widest view, gazing at the vast, orderly skyscrapers in wonder.

Lying naked in bed behind me was a lovely woman whom I'd had to see one last time. Her name was Francesca, pronounced with a soft *c* as she had been quick to correct me when I'd got it wrong at our first encounter. She lay on her side with her hands underneath her head. She was a brunette, lithe and natural looking, and she had hurt me a great deal.

"Why are you leaving me?" I asked as I turned back to her.

She rolled onto her back and the sheet covered her breasts. "You're the one going to Greece," she countered.

"Just come with me."

Francesca was the image of perfect beauty I had always hoped to find in a woman. Unfortunately, she was also a piece of fabric woven tightly into my American blanket. She was a modern career woman, financially successful. She was on a rocket into the future, on a trajectory marked by opulence, which I feared would leave me insignificant if I didn't participate in it now. She was everything that I had been. She was also my last chance to reverse my decision; yet whenever I contemplated doing so, I was consumed with anxiety and a twinge in my gut that roiled down into the depths of my bowels. I honestly felt that I had no other choice but to go.

The pace of society in the US overwhelmed me. I felt hijacked by my way of life and out of control. No, not even this nascent romance, as wonderful as it was, was going to stop me from going on this quest I had chosen for myself.

Next morning, we left the hotel and took breakfast at a fancy place on Fillmore Street. Afterwards, as we still had some time before Francesca's flight, we went to Lafayette Park and lay on the grass together where we could see the bay. The beach towel I had brought was small; Francesca rested her head on my arm and squeezed close to keep off the damp grass. We remained silent, though I wanted to know what she was thinking.

I was thinking about last night at the jazz bar at the InterContinental hotel; about Francesca's voice when she'd said, "You make me so happy."

She hadn't been wearing a bra because I had asked her not to. I wanted to be able to grab her breasts cleanly and cover them with my palms when I kissed her. We had kissed and touched each other with enough passion that I had insisted we return to our hotel room.

"Not yet," she had said in response, tightening her grip on me.

I pulled Francesca onto my lap, and she draped her arm over my shoulder. When we paused from kissing, we looked out at the city stretching away from us.

"This is spectacular," I said in reference to the entire night.

"You made it all happen," she responded.

I had made this night happen when I bought her a plane ticket to come up from LA to see me one last time. I had booked my flight to Greece out of SFO instead of LAX, so I could spend my last week with Mom who was visiting my two sisters who lived in San Francisco. In hindsight, I should have flown out of LA and avoided the chaos I stirred up with my sister, Toula, that led Mom to break out in tears when she witnessed us spar over my plan to leave a few boxes in her storage room without having asked her and I called Toula a bitch. I was not going to miss my two sisters nearly as much as I was going to miss Francesca.

Now, on the grassy knoll in the park, I thought about how this moment would soon be just a memory, paired with the memory of the night before. I was bothered by this fact, this passing of moments into memories. Because if they were good memories, I knew my oversensitive self would harbor the nostalgia until an onset of sad feelings arose within me. Soon, Francesca would be back in LA, and I would be here, alone. Having her close to me and relaxed in my arms, yet knowing she would soon be gone, was a terrible thing for one who had never felt better.

Though we both insisted we would see each other again, I knew it wasn't true. It was the way we had made love the night before that had revealed the truth: we made the kind of love you make when you aren't holding back for the next time. It was the kind of lovemaking that was guided by all the love we'd made in the past, and the accumulation carried enough weight to squeeze out the space for any more.

"I'm going to miss you," Francesca said.

I insisted I would drive her to the airport. The ride was silent and tense and we arrived at terminal three much too soon for me.

"Should we head back into the city?" I asked, half-seriously.

"I have a birthday party."

"What if I change my flight and we see each other again next week?"

"I'll be in Dallas for work...Peter!"

Francesca had her schedule planned out months in advance. She already had her thirtieth birthday in Cabo organized and that was six months away. She shifted off her seat, her bottom resting on my center console, and kissed me.

"What am I going to do without you?" I asked when we separated.

She gazed at me for a long, silent moment. "You're going to go to Greece, and you're going to be the new handsome face there. In a month, you'll have forgotten all about me."

"Why do you have to say that?" I demanded, taking hold of her hand.

We gazed at each other some more, and she saw that I was deeply hurt by her comment.

"You're adorable!" she said, as if she always knew that what we had couldn't last but had nonetheless enjoyed our time together. "But Greece is where you need to be."

Unfazed, she changed the direction of our conversation on a dime. "What are you going to do today?"

"Write for a while, then wander the city thinking about you…missing you."

I kissed her one last time, tenderly, and, when my lips touched hers, it hurt so much and I felt I would never get over it. The last I saw of her were her long legs, clad in impeccably stylish jeans, striding away.

I drove on to terminal four and attached my Uber sticker to my windshield. Within a few minutes, a passenger pinged me. He was a young businessman. He entered my car with a sense of urgency and a brown leather bag. "Four Seasons, downtown. Thank you," he shouted in a monotone.

The man reminded me of my old self. I had no sooner asked, "How's your day going?" than his phone rang and he told me to turn down the music. *Yes, this had definitely been me*, I thought.

CHAPTER TWO

Growing up as a child of Greek immigrants in the United States, I had always thought of Greece a mysterious place. The culture of my forebears seemed strange, alien, and, as such, I avoided it.

During my childhood I could sense our family lived differently than the neighbors and my friends' families lived. I was only a kid then, so I lacked the insight to measure my difference, but I didn't lack the weight of self-consciousness that kept me feeling inferior.

My self-consciousness with regards to my identity was probably the reason I never boasted about being Greek. I never went to Greek school like my sisters. I never had any Greek friends. As I grew older, I could sense that my sisters felt the same way as I did about our ancestry, and suspected they felt out of place too.

I found the story of how Mom knew Dad for only a week before they married comical. She agreed to marry him based only on a black and white photo of him. She said about the two times they met during that week that he was nice and handsome, and she was excited that he lived in the US. And Mom really wanted to move to the US for a *better life*, she once told me.

Yet by the standards of the time, how they came together wasn't entirely odd. Arranged marriages were common in Greece back then, especially among people from small villages. Mom and Dad grew up in neighboring villages on the island of Crete in the region of Sfakia. Dad was from a village up in the mountains called Kallikratis and

Mom was from a village next to the sea called Chora Sfakion. They were both from poor families of farmers.

Dad first left Greece for the US in 1970. He moved to Canton, Ohio, close to where his brother lived in Akron, and found a job in the local steel works. Mom and Dad's romance began when a lady relative of Dad's, who was also from Kallikratis, told Dad's mom about a pretty lady from Chora Sfakion who was only twenty-one and was a *good woman* and *very kind*.

After Mom agreed to marry Dad, he took two-weeks' vacation and went to Greece to sweep Mom off her feet. Mom moved to America sixth months later on December 6, 1975. Mom liked to bring up the exact date every year on its anniversary. She would remind me of how she cried for weeks once she arrived to Ohio.

Mom always told me these stories in Greek, but I always responded in English. I can remember instances where I shouted and pouted and wanted her to speak only in English. I felt terribly uncomfortable when my parents spoke to me in Greek in front of my friends or when Mom offered Greek cookies to them and I had to say their hard-to-pronounce names, like *melomakarona*. I desperately wanted Mom to bake chocolate-chip cookies like other moms and for our house to look neat and tidy like the neighbors' houses, but, to my despair, neither ever happened.

Dad was embarrassing to have around my friends, or, worse, my friends' parents. To watch him being incapable of speaking a sentence in English was an insufferable embarrassment. When my friends laughed about it, I became even more embarrassed and wondered how Dad could be so stupid. Thankfully for my teenage self, he was always working, so he was rarely around.

As the years passed, Greek culture was slowly drained from me by the experience of day-to-day living. By high school, I had given up speaking Greek with my parents. Being Greek didn't mean anything to me. I was proud to be American.

In retrospect, I can see how being teased about my background intensified my resistance to Greek culture. But I also suspect that it had something to do with my family having been poor; unconsciously at least, I associated being American with being rich. Being Greek, I felt, made me an outsider, and like any kid my age, I just wanted to fit in. It would be many years before it dawned on me that my heritage was something to be proud of.

It didn't occur to me when I was in college. All I did then was study and take on leadership roles to improve my marketability for the job I dreamed of having: moving to New York City and working on Wall Street. It was actually my backup dream job. I was an athlete in high school and I played football and baseball. I was good, but I wasn't exceptional and when the reality dawned on me that making a career as a professional athlete was all but a fantasy, I shifted my focus to education. I wasn't a good student in high school, but in college I got nearly straight As. I'm not sure how I did it, but when I ended up with a job on Wall Street, I realized for the first time that I was smart; that I deserved to be here and it wasn't entirely luck.

I worked four years as an investment banker. The job was demanding, involving at least a hundred hours a week, but I was young and keen and I went at it with a will. Success duly came, but at a cost: at the end of the fourth year I found myself rich, at least by my standards, but burnt out and in need of a change. Idly almost, spurred on by my innate curiosity, I began to wonder what else could be out there for me.

So while my peers on Wall Street took the traditional route after investment banking to achieve fancy MBAs and return to high-finance, I went to acting school. I stayed two years. I found my passion for writing in acting school. It was through writing that I discovered more of my self, more about who my family was and my siblings. This all led to my big revelation when I was in LA, jaded by the same sort of hustle it took to crack Hollywood as it did to make it on Wall Street—except success in Hollywood was often a matter of luck. I felt empty and restless. My revelation provoked within me a need to explore my identity. I felt that I had the Greek language in me, but I didn't know it. I felt that I was Greek, but I didn't know how to prove it. And so when the opportunity came after Dad mentioned to me that he had registered me as a Greek citizen and the Greek Army was looking for me, I took it as an opportunity.

I had vacationed in Greece several times after college, but this left me incomplete, with only a vague sense of the local life. My father had moved back to Greece, to his village in Crete, several years before. Visiting him gave me a slightly better perspective of local life than your average tourist, but my trips were only ten days and so I was loathe to spend more than a day or two in Dad's village. I seemed to spend more time hastily canvassing the land, collecting photographs and videos to show my friends at parties or impress girls at bars, than I did actually living in the country. It took some time but I eventually concluded that the only way I was going to fully appreciate Greece was to live among the people, in the culture, wholeheartedly and without the distraction of an alternate world.

Even before I left the States, I believed that living in another country changes you. The Peter Manouselis who left Greece would not be the same person who had arrived twelve months before, but hopefully a more evolved, dynamic human being. My plan was to embrace Greek traditions, speak the language, and experience the country wholesale rather than simply try to capture individual moments. I felt that I had to be molded into the culture. Only then would I understand it and give it the chance to make me someone I could never foresee.

American friends of mine were shocked when I told them I'd be moving to Greece, to the island of Crete. It was 2015 and Greece was battling with the banks and other EU countries, particularly Germany, for financial support to keep its economy afloat. Media outlets online were declaring Armageddon and worse. There seemed a very good chance the country might have to abandon the euro. It was natural for people to be concerned, but the uninformed and often hysterical attitudes I encountered toward Greece upset me. This was a country, after all, with a rich history and a culture that went back thousands of years and embraced the best of science, literature, medicine, and the arts. I didn't like to think of it faltering so pitifully.

"What are you going to do?" people asked me. "How will you make any money? Is it safe?"

A fellow Greek American recommended I locate the US embassy, as if I was plunging into a land of barbarians who daily chop human heads off.

Naturally I was conscious of what I was leaving behind. As Francesca was forever reminding me, a beautiful future awaited me in America. It was the ultimate land of opportunity, where everything— love, riches, a big home, a fine car—was possible so long as you had money. But I'd tasted that future and knew it was deceptive. I'd also learned that it exacted a heavy price in terms of personal integrity. Forget the missed opportunities in America, I thought. I was aiming for something better.

When the plane descended towards Athens, I caught a glimpse of the regal Acropolis and the vast stretching metropolis—a distinct flat whiteness framed by dry, beige mountains. As I gazed out at the distant mountaintops my mind was carried away. I felt that something monumental had happened here; I didn't need to have read the books or to have heard an account of its history. There was a static aura to this territory, as if the inhabitants had yet to let go of the past, because it harbored too deep a nostalgia.

I admit that when I first arrived in Greece I was filled with a great deal of American idealism and self-importance. I was imbued with Pollyanna-ish expectations that my ideas and leadership would save the country. I wanted to proclaim to the Greeks that the papers were coated with honey to poison the minds of the malleable. It was all manipulation. I intended to voice my opinions to every Greek I met because I feared that otherwise they would fall for the manipulative tactics being used upon them. They would allow the self-righteous bureaucrats of America and Germany to swallow them up and then spit them out processing their functions.

As I waited at the airport for my connecting flight to Crete, I could easily distinguish the tourists from Athenians. The Athenian carried on with an added chip on their shoulder. They walked with a sense of grace and fluidity and the women were exceptionally well put together. Crete I knew was going to offer a different experience than if I'd lived in Athens, but I needed the calmer island life.

On my flight to Crete, I was anything but calm. I read an article in *The New Yorker* describing the Greek crisis. The writer explained how the country needed to "adapt to modern times," and "build tourism and tap into the booming global tourism market," and "stop selling all their olive oil to the Italians in bulk." He concluded, "The Greeks need foreign investors to help build industries and they can't do that with an ineffective and tedious legal and political environment…"

I shoved the magazine into the crevice beside my seat and closed my eyes. I wished I had taken the boat to Crete instead. That would have been more beautiful, more peaceful, and far friendlier. The ship splashing across the deep blue sea. I'd have heard foreign words. I might have even encountered a lady traveling on holiday, open to meeting someone new. She'd have been wearing a floral dress with a floppy hat just the right size to accentuate her delicate eyes. I'd have approached her because she was reading a book with a title that caught my eye. I may have fallen in love—again. Ahhh, the pleasures of traveling alone in another country: nobody knows you, nobody cares about you, nobody means anything to you other than how they appear. It's entirely liberating…. But I'm an American and taking an eight-hour boat ride when a thirty-five-minute flight exists simply isn't efficient.

I was pleased the moment I stepped foot on Cretan soil. Suddenly walking felt easier, as if a bolt of lightning had lifted my soles off the ground. Dad wasn't due to pick me up until the afternoon, so I wandered around the city of Chania, negotiating cobbled lanes between meticulously restored Venetian palazzos, their lace-iron balconies strewn with potted plants and adorned by the occasional dozing cat. I walked slowly, ponderously, trying to prepare myself emotionally for what would be my first encounter with my father in two years. If I was to learn anything meaningful here about myself and my family, the information would be funneled through Dad, and I found this ominous. Patience and self-surrender, I had learned, were the two necessary skills I needed to manage myself in his company. In short, it wasn't going to be easy.

I stopped for breakfast at a roof garden restaurant close to the harbor. I was hungry so I ordered the English Breakfast—bacon, fried eggs, orange juice and coffee, and bread with butter and marmalade. It was exactly what I needed. The owner, Maria, remembered me from two years ago when I'd last eaten here. She asked how long I'd be staying.

"I have no return ticket. Maybe a year or two… permanently?"

"Are you working here?"

"I want to learn Greek."

"What do you do in America?"

This question always caused me to raise my guard. It was as if whatever I said would either begin a great friendship or establish an inseparable distance. I had heard enough of it in LA. Many people were going to ask me this question in the upcoming weeks and months. The only way to handle it was to answer truthfully but at the same time to project the pursuit of my dreams in a confident manner.

"I write," I said. "Screenplays—for the movies?"

"Ah, yes, I know. Are you writing something about Crete?"

"Soon."

"You should. The history… it's beautiful."

I deprived Maria of the chance to probe further by swiftly changing the subject, asking about the life here. She replied, "I have my tomatoes and my bread and my stomach is full. What else do I need?"

"How's the crisis?" I asked.

"The crisis they talk about, it's all in the head. What do you want me to do? To cry and bury myself in my bed? We have the sun. We have the sea. My garden is full of fruits and vegetables. The rich

Germans and Americans come here and shove beer after beer down their throats and they take pity on us? Come on now…"

I pondered this from an American angle, wondering how I could relate. What beauty had I missed by occupying myself with toys? Or with beer? I wanted to think I was capable of finding stimulation in nature.

After breakfast I wandered toward the harbor where I stopped at a café to relax and connect to the Wi-Fi. I checked my emails and read the news headlines and the latest stock market report. I exchanged a few texts with my cousin, Nick, from America, who was in Crete just then with his wife and baby. We made plans to meet up soon.

After I had satiated my internet craving, I looked at the sea. The water rested calmly and a slight breeze came off it, cooling me down. I pondered my life. Money was the first thing to come to mind. The next question was: *Will I ever achieve my dreams?* This was followed by: *Should I have stayed in finance?* It bothered me that I didn't know how I would ever get my writing in front of the right people. At the time I didn't know a single person with whom to share it and who might possibly help me. I had been advised to find a batch of writers to whom you can go for feedback on your work and thereby get better. *But where the hell did I find this batch of like-minded souls?* All my friends were in finance. They were hunters. They didn't understand what I did or what it took to make it as a writer. As for family, forget it! My family was too simple-minded to provide the advice and guidance I needed. I saw myself as a stray pup in search of another of their kind. But then, *Jeez,* I thought, *I shouldn't be having these bleak ideas now. I've only just arrived in Greece.*

CHAPTER THREE

Dad silently inspected me in the parking lot adjacent to the agora. The smoothness of his cheeks intensified the flare of his grey mustache but if you looked only at his eyes he appeared welcoming. He had kind, brown eyes with a slight droop at the corners. Relatives and friends would note we had the same eyes. I smiled and reached out my hand. "Welcome," he said, in a stern tone, in Greek. I stuffed my luggage into his black Suzuki and we left for Kallikratis, in the far south of the island.

I knew very little about Dad. I was aware that he had grown up without a father. And all I could remember about his mother was her beating me with a stick until it snapped when I was four-years-old because I was bothering my sister, Georgia. Dad had never told me anything about himself and, no doubt because I've never felt comfortable enough, I had never told him anything about me. Consequently, our conversations had hardly penetrated the rudimentary crust of our feelings. Dad thought a lot and I was always wondering what he was thinking about. We were similar in that way. You watched him and he was constantly turning things over in his head. Our relationship was also hindered by the fact that Dad's English was, at best, at a prepubescent level while I only knew dribbles of Greek. It was therefore all but impossible for us to hold a meaningful conversation.

"What's new?" he asked, breaking the silence.

"Nothing," I said.

"How was your flight?"

"Fine."

"What did you eat?"

"Chicken…"

Usually our scant conversations helped keep us friendly. On this occasion I was distracted by the landscape which shut out any chance of a quarrel developing. It was marvelous to gaze at the mountains on one side and turn to see the radiant sea on the other. The Lefka Ori, or White Mountains, exude dignity, I thought. The way the sun illuminates and sharpens their contours makes them intimidating in their fine beauty.

After we turned off the national road, we ascended a tortuous road passing unique and enduring villages. The rugged atmosphere nurtured my imagination. I didn't just see flocks of sheep grazing and silly dogs barking. I saw sheep meditating and dogs blaspheming. I watched Dad make the sign of the cross every time we passed a church. I knew we had reached the Sfakia region because all the road signs were riddled with bullet holes.

At the top of the mountain lay Kallikratis. Dad was eager to preach its greatness. "This is the beautiful place," he enthused. "Fresh air! Nature!"

Kallikratis was once a large and bustling village populated by many families, but during World War II the Germans burned it to the ground, and then people moved to the more accessible villages on the coast. Over the years the village gradually emptied out, but Dad remained. He was at home in Kallikratis. This had been his village ever since his childhood. He was damn proud of it.

Dad was hidebound, and skilled in the art of survival. He knew how to live simply. Despite the numerous other vexatious reasons for which I could hate him, I genuinely admired this quality: the ability to conserve resources, to live off the land, and waste nothing.

Kallikratis submerges you in a deep and sudden silence the moment you arrive. You feel an immediate disconnect from modern society. No technology, no grocery store, no water supply infrastructure—there are a few raw cafés, and a restaurant without menus. The one-story houses, built predominantly of rough-hewn limestone, looked ruined or unfinished. I stared in wonder at the formidable mountain arches that enclosed the village. There were hawks floating in the sky. The empty, yet unrefined, landscape left me building a new world in my head, where I could let my imagination run wild.

Next to Dad's home was a herbal café and botanical oils store owned and operated by an elderly Greek man and his companion who was from Denmark. It was the most modern place in Kallikratis. And the only two-story wood-framed house.

"They have internet there," Dad said with great satisfaction.

"Kallikratis is modernizing, who would have thought," I mumbled.

We turned onto the long, rocky driveway, and at once I felt the rugged yet pure lifestyle Dad lived. He had two dogs, a border collie and a brown mutt, that barked as we drove up. The mutt was chained to a cinder rod, its fangs protruding from its snout. Dad's dogs never saw the inside of the home and Dad was bothered if I touched them. "*Vromiko!*" he'd shout. "Dirty!"

I gazed at the animals with sympathy. These dogs had no other choice but to endure the tough mountain conditions, whether pouring rain, blistering sun, or knee-high snow. They never received any love, so they hid their fear by barking. Walking away from them I entered the courtyard. I stood under the large mulberry tree. On my previous visits I had carried a singular focus—to make face with Dad for a short time and then move on to the beaches and gallivant about the island. I had invariably started off tense, arming myself for an attack from Dad. This time it felt different.

"Are you hungry?"

"No."

"What?"

"No! I'm not hungry."

He tried to hand me a plastic bag, directing me with his finger toward the orchard, "Go and pick some pears."

"I'm good," I said, raising my hand at him.

"What?"

"No! I don't want to."

"Go! Pick some pears."

"I don't want any pears, right now."

He dropped his head, huffed and went into the house. I needed to be alone just then to make sense of my new surroundings. Dad couldn't help pestering me, but it wasn't the words he said that got on my nerves. He affected me in a way that had nothing to do with words. I gazed out toward the orchard. *Dad has nothing and everything here*, I thought. *He has his chickens, his lambs, his goats, his garden with tomatoes and cucumbers and peppers, his walnut and fig and berry and pear and apple trees.*

He stood at the doorstep eating a pear. "Organic!" he shouted. "Everything here is organic. Not like America."

He was proud to let me know. I glanced sidelong at him. He was glad to have me here.

Dad lived in the same house he had grown up in. I didn't know when it was built, but it was structurally the same as when the German's set it on fire during World War II. It was a simple cottage shaped in an L with a flat roof and a green metal door and green shutters.

He had renovated a room where I could sleep. It was cool and dark inside. The walls were white and looked freshly painted. The floor was tiled and off-white. The only window looked out at the side of a garage Dad had built. Against the wall was a small square table. I brushed the dust from the plastic cover, then I cleared the cobwebs from the table lamp. There was a bathroom attached and in the corner of the mirror above the sink was a small photo of me as a little boy, smiling from ear to ear.

I retrieved my notebook and pen from my backpack and placed them on the table. I sat down, relaxed. I inhaled, deeply, and exhaled, forcefully. I scribbled a thought that had entered my head in that moment.

Dad shouted, "Come, Panagiotis!" Panagiotis was my name in Greek and he only called me by my Greek name.

I stepped outside the bedroom door that opened up to the courtyard.

"Bring the ladder!" he shouted as he reached for the pears.

I lifted the ladder over my head, entered the orchard, passed by the chickens and the rooster, and stopped in front of Dad.

"No. Go to the other side…"

I turned and reached to grab some pears and from the corner of my eye I saw the rooster trotting toward me and I took a few steps back.

"Don't be afraid of the rooster."

I stared at the rooster as I kneeled for a thick stick, *just in case*, I thought. When I turned to pick a pear it came forward again. I jumped away. Dad smiled.

"He's a good protector."

"I don't want any pears."

"They're good now!"

I back-peddled, keeping the rooster in front of me, and picked the pears.

"Take more," Dad demanded.

"How many pears do you want?"

"Fill the bag!"

The rooster inched forward and I swung at it.

"Leave the rooster alone."

I filled the bag, then walked in a circle in the courtyard; then I grabbed a hatchet and struck a stack of fire wood.

"What are you doing now?"

"I'm chopping wood!"

"Are you crazy? Leave the logs alone."

I dropped the hatchet and gasped.

"Go get dressed, we're leaving soon."

PERSPECTIVE

The dogs watched me closely. The border collie was ready at any moment to uncover its fangs. I returned to the bedroom.

CHAPTER FOUR

I changed into a navy polo shirt and caraway-colored pants and walked out to the courtyard. I stepped toward the border collie and it dashed under the car. I could hear the sound of an electric razor coming from the outhouse as I waited for Dad.

"Come, Panagiotis! *Να μου πάρεις το σβέρκο.*" I did not respond. Dad shouted again, "Panagiotis! Come here."

"What do you want?"

"*Να μου πάρεις το σβέρκο.*"

He handed me the electric razor and I cleaned the back of his neck, then I started to remove the hair in and around his ears.

"Not there!"

"It's done. Let's go."

"We're going now."

Dad was ready to go twenty minutes later. He stopped in front of me and stared.

"You don't have a better pair of pants?"

"Are you serious?"

He tilted his neck and pressed his lips together.

"Open the gate," he said.

The border collie scurried out from under the car when the engine started. I closed the gate after Dad passed through. I took a deep breath before I hopped into the car.

As we drove down the mountainside, I felt excitement welling within me. We were going to a *panagiri*, a religious festival, in a village called Kapsodhasos—the name literally means "burning forest". All summer long villages in Greece hosted *panagiria* to celebrate the name days of saints and other sacred occasions. I always enjoyed them for the good food and excellent atmosphere.

Kapsodhasos lay at the bottom on the other side of the mountain, close to the sea. The road leading downwards was tortuous and narrow. Nothing stood between you and the ravine that plunged alongside. You had to be extra careful of oncoming vehicles to make the proper space adjustment. But when you embark on it in the evening, when the sun is setting, as we did, the view is spectacular. I felt as if this was heaven and God had welcomed us into his home as an honored guest, lavishing us with an indulgent feast for the eyes.

I did not get to enjoy the view for long, however, because Dad liked to press down on the pedal. I tensed in my seat as he sped toward a flock of goats resting on the road, only to stop suddenly when the animals remained unfazed, lethargically moving off to the side. It seemed innate in Dad to make it impossible for me to feel at ease when I was around him. I think he believed that keeping me on tenterhooks would make me a stronger man. No doubt it was part of his own survival instinct to always remain vigilant. He simply wanted to pass this capability on.

We parked under a large olive tree. Many other cars were parked in an orderly row on the roadside. We walked for a few minutes before approaching rows of tables outside a taverna called Vigles. I stood behind Dad like a little pup waiting until he sniffed things out before we sat down. He chose the least noticeable table furthest away from the action. I could see him watching me closely in case I attempted anything that would shame him.

Dad knew the owner, of course. He only went to places in Sfakia where he knew the people. Everyone in Sfakia worked this way. They were comfortable around family or relatives and they did what they could to help them—until a senseless quarrel arose, and because of their stubbornness, they never spoke to each other again. The proprietor of Vigles had the same surname as we did. *Manouselis* was popular in these parts, recognized throughout Sfakia and the wider Chania region due to the many celebrated soldiers of that name who died fighting for Greece's freedom.

We had no sooner sat down than our table was covered with plates of lamb, pork chops, and fried potatoes (or French fries, as we say in America), bowls of wet rice and village salad, and a large carafe of village wine.

The party intensified when the musicians started playing. The oscillating wail from the lyra elevated people's emotions. I felt soft for the stray dogs scattered about sniffing for food. I tossed a piece of meat in front of one of them and Dad snapped.

"What's wrong with you?" he barked. "Don't give the dog that good meat!"

"All this food's gonna go to waste!" I shouted back.

They always served an unnecessary amount of food at *panagiria*. What they did afterwards with all the good meat I wasn't sure. I once saw Dad mix his leftovers in a skillet with the grease in the pan and fill it with water. It looked like diarrhea. But he'd feed it to his dogs for supper. Their tails zipped like string trimmers.

"Take. It's good. Eat!" Dad said, forcing more food upon me.

Even after I had told him I was full, he put a few more pieces on my plate.

"I'm full."

"What?"

"My stomach is *full*!"

He went quiet then, afraid I may cause a scene and embarrass him. It was as if, in his mind, I was still a ten-year-old boy without a clue how to survive.

As we sat there listening to the music, I noticed a pretty girl with dark hair two tables in front of me. I didn't dare approach her because she was a village girl. A girl who was in the safe guard of her brothers and father and was only available to a man who was sure to become her husband. She was tall and lithe, her long legs encased in tight red pants. Her ample bosom overstretched her tank top. Then she got up to dance and my blood froze. I had never seen anything so wonderful. Her rhythm was sizzling. She seemed to fly through the air. She was a master of the *pentozali*, a fast and furious Cretan dance that made her bosom rumble and her legs whip from hip over hip. I stared in awe. I felt good, relaxed. Dad wasn't bothering me. After a while I didn't even think of him. It was a balmy night. I could almost feel the girl lying next to me in bed; my hand pulling down the strap to her tank top, my lips nuzzling her neck. I unbuttoned her pants. My hand slowly moving down until...

BANG! BANG! BANG! BANG! The badass Sfakian, dressed all in black, unleashed a clip of bullets from his .45 into the sky. The music elevated. The dancers' tempo increased. The accelerated pace caused my veins to tingle. My fantasy had evaporated. I watched Dad pick at his teeth with a toothpick, contemplating something. Our table was covered with uneaten plates of food. My glass was filled to the brim with village wine. The dogs had scurried off.

BANG! BANG! BANG! BANG!

* * *

The drive back up the mountain was less of an event. Dad drove silently, his gaze on the road. The mountains were black. You could only see what was in front of you, lit by the cone of your headlights. Kallikratis was speechless and blank. I lay in bed, still unsettled by the impressions of the festival—the music and the girl and the guns going off. The odor of the sheets reminded me of my grandmother who had been dead for ten years now. The night was starkly quiet. I switched off the lights. The darkness invoked a feeling of blindness and I no longer felt part of a physical mass. I occupied no space so I needed nothing.

CHAPTER FIVE

The rooster woke me next morning. I took a few long minutes to shake off the morning stupor before I dressed and slipped on my shoes and walked outside. The purity of the air expanded my diaphragm, reached down into my bowels, straightened my frame. The sun hadn't yet cleared the mountain above the village. The dogs lay peaceful in the cool shadow. The cats that lived next to the outhouse huddled close to each other on the steps. Dad appeared on the doorstep grasping a coffee cup. We spoke in Greek.

"Good morning."

"Good morning."

"Do you want an omelet?"

I looked out toward the orchard, raising my head toward the mountain peak, and murmured, "Okay."

"What?"

"Yes! Fix me an omelet."

"Did you talk to Nikos?"

"Yes."

"And what time are we going to get him?"

"He said eleven in Episkopi."

"He is coming with his wife and baby?"

"I don't think so."

"Why?"

"Why don't you ask him when you see him."

Dad walked into the orchard and retrieved a few eggs left by the hen. He made me a spicy omelet, after I'd told him not to make it spicy, and when I'd finished he asked me to sweep the courtyard. Afterwards I sat outside in the sun and read until we left to get my cousin.

Nikos and I had become good friends when I lived in New York City. He moved there a few months before me and left a few months before I did. I called him by his American name, Nick. It had been a few years since I'd last seen him and the contrast in our lives at this point was as distinct as that between slaves and free men. Now he lived in suburbia Detroit with a family.

He was leaning against his suitcase when we arrived, tanned, six-foot-seven-inches tall, with an unbalanced smile. He spoke in Greek to Dad.

"Thank you very much, uncle."

"Where's your wife and baby?"

"They went to Serbia."

"Why didn't you bring them to Kallikratis?" Dad was seriously bewildered.

"I should've… My daughter would have liked Kallikratis," Nick said. "Next time, uncle."

Nick clutched the arm rest of his seat as Dad weaved back up through the mountains. I relaxed with my window down as we ascended higher and the air grew thin. The aroma of slaughtered lamb that permeated the air failed to bother me. I was occupied with other thoughts. Not even the loud grating of cicadas could bring me back to reality. The final stretch of summer was coming to an end, but my adventure in Crete was just beginning. Hanging out with my cousin was nothing more than a postponement—one day reality would kick in, reminding me I was now a resident and had to get on with things. In our minds, we were traveling to starkly different places. I was on a cloud of my own design, floating into the unknown. Nick was in Dad's Suzuki going to Kallikratis.

Upon arriving in Kallikratis we had a bit of a standoff. Dad, typically, had made plans for us. He expected Nick to spend a few days in the village and meet his relatives. I sensed by Nick's demeanor that he wanted to be by the beach, where there was action, so I told Dad that we'd be going down the mountain to stay in Patsianos, a village next to Kapsodhasos that was where Dad fixed up his father's old home.

"You're not going to Patsianos today," Dad said in a disapproving manner.

"Yes, because we're going to Loutro tomorrow morning," I said.

"What are you going to do in Loutro?" he gasped. "Niko, listen—"

"Nick's on vacation!"

"I wasn't talking to you! Listen, you will stay in Kallikratis for a couple days. See your relatives and after you can go to Patsianos."

"Uncle… we'll see. I have *parea* to meet down in Sfakia."

While Dad prepared lunch, Nick and I went for a jaunt in the village. I brought the *katsouna,* a walking stick, with me. Nick snapped pictures of the landscape—the vineyards and the scattered, broken-down concrete homes, and the lethargic goats under the trees. I led him to a little white church on top of a hill. In the yard outside, I pointed out the tombstone of my Dad's family. Engraved on the white marble slab were the names of Dad's mother and father and his brother, Joseph, while inside a box behind a piece of glass was a picture of the three of them and, next to it, an unlit oil lamp. Dad once told me that Joseph had died from a burst appendix when he was twelve-years-old. I gazed at the stone for a long time.

Standing in the churchyard I looked out over the Kallikratis landscape. I watched Nick scurry down the hill, his trainers scuffing the stones. He moved like a big squirrel from one place to the next. In some ways it baffled me to watch him rush for unnecessary reasons. I mean, Dad had yet to call us to eat. He was racing against time, but time felt static here. As Nick paced further away, I contemplated why it was tough for me to stay in Kallikratis for an extended interval. Here I was, in a valley, surrounded by mountains. All I had here for stimulation was nature, which sometimes wasn't enough. Yet to Dad this was existence. He angered easily when people failed to understand it and was disappointed to see his own son stray markedly from his ideals.

I liked the big cities of America. The elements of artificial stimulation that largely compose them are addictive. Sure, your daily routine remains banal and unvaried. But underlying it, the constant possibility of surprise feeds you the occasional jolt to keep you alive and interested and secured in your daily routine until, for no good reason, the unexpected happens again. My life in big American cities, while stimulating and exciting, also inspired a curiosity within me to feel and experience what a sedate life in a village might offer.

In Kallikratis life is different. Nature crushes artificial stimulation here. People don't bother to dream. Everything just is. God creates new livestock and agriculture each year. He's loyal to the people here, up to a point. All you have are nature and feelings and that's a tough way to live a life if you've lived another way for any extended period of time. There's no forward progress; people yield to the elements. While in cities, simple is served to you, here in Kallikratis simple is the daily chore: from the tanks of water that need to be lifted up the mountains to the animals they slaughter for food to the vegetables and fruits that abound. I don't know how Dad does it, especially after living in America for thirty-five years, but it's where he grew up and it's where his real home is.

I considered the sixty or so inhabitants of the village to be, in a strange way, the most liberated people in the world. They weren't weighed down by the crushing expenses of living in a city. Each family had a vineyard, a vegetable plot, some animals, and an orchard. Every person had a specialty, either as a maker of cheese, olive oil, wine, or honey, or as a restaurant or a café owner, or a homebuilder. Not one of them earned a six-figure yearly income. Yet each in his or her own way struck me as aristocratic. They indulged in nature together with their *parea*, the company of friends. Life was elemental here, stripped down to basics. As I was grasping this, I started to see how it could be a permanent way of life for me.

We returned to the house, where Dad was clutching a shotgun. He cocked it, raised it toward the sky, and fired. The shells spun from the ejection port and the powerful noise ricocheted off the mountains, reverberating around the valley in slowly diminishing waves. The border collie hid behind a rock. Nick smiled.

"Welcome!" Dad said with a smile.

"Can I see it, Uncle?"

Dad handed him the shotgun and Nick handed me his smartphone. I snapped a photo.

"Come on," Dad said, "the food is ready."

Dad served us each a fish called *tsipoura* with wild greens, picked from the fields, called *stamnagathi*. The three of us crowded around the small table in the living room. I stabbed the fish with my fork.

"You don't do it that way," Dad said.

"I know how to do it," I said.

"Look how well Nikos does it. See. You have to do it like that."

He reached over my plate with his fork and knife.

"I know how to do it!"

"No you don't."

"Really!"

"Go ahead. Ruin the fish."

I took a deep breath. I did not mind lashing out in front of Nick. I was only upset that Dad ruined any enjoyment I could have eating the fish. We had quietened down. Nick devoured his food. Afterwards Dad offered Nick coffee, and when Nick politely declined, Dad insisted.

"Yes. I'll fix you a coffee."

"No. Uncle. I'm sure. I had a frappé this morning."

He removed the lid from a Folgers coffee container. "Are you sure?" He pulled out a small revolver and Nick stood up from the table and smiled.

Nick fired a round of bullets into the sky. The day was clear and warm, but not hot in Kallikratis. Dad knew he could not stop us from leaving for Patsianos. Instead he made sure to give us a chunk of *graviera* cheese with a jar of honey and a bag of *paximathia*, the twice-baked barley bread that emerges from the oven hard as a rock.

The temperature rose steadily as we drove down the mountain.

"Your Dad's right," Nick said. "If you take away the beach and the restaurants and cafés, there's really not much in Loutro."

I stalled the car.

"*Malaka*, you don't know how to drive manual?"

"Relax." I stalled it again. "I just need to get warmed up."

"*Malaka*, you don't warm up on this road!"

The car was rolling now.

"Slow around the turns!"

"Okay. Sorry."

"How can they not have guardrails?"

"This is Greece, cuz."

When we reached the part of the road that opened up to the sea, Nick had both hands on the door.

"Have your camera ready," I said.

"Stop the car!"

"What an amazing view, huh?"

"*Malaka*, stop the car!" He opened the door. I slammed on the brakes.

"Are you Okay?"

"I'll meet you down there," he said.

"It's a long hike."

"You don't know how to drive manual."

As I drove away, I watched him in my rearview mirror. His bulging arms made his black tank top appear tiny, trudging down the road like a transformer. He could have carried the damn car if he wanted!

Eventually I made all the turns and got out of the car and waited for Nick. I walked toward the edge of the road and stood on a large rock. My jaw loosened and something went free inside me. In front of me, olive groves reached, in billowing tiers, all the way to the sea. It looked like a piece of work by an impressionist painter, with texture and color and warmth that brought you into it so that all that was expected of you was to let it do something to you.

I saw it as a place of untapped beauty. Why hadn't anybody done anything to bring more people here? I couldn't believe it was the remoteness of the place or the unfriendly roads, as local people said. We all know humans are capable of anything these days. The moment one says, "You can't," is the moment when greatness begins. My mind was spinning with thoughts. I could become a business man and develop a thriving olive oil, yogurt, and cheese factory. A facility that would provide the entire world with the best of its kind. I would brand it *Helios*, after the nurturing Greek sun. This would bring industry here. It would be worth billions of dollars. This would help the economy. *There!* A large patch of level terrain, ideal for an airport, caught my eye. My mind kept turning: investment… people… growth… money… life… My American mentality was humming now.

I paused. It occurred to me that I didn't want to be a business man. I came here to write. Swiftly, I shifted thoughts… when I sold my next screenplay and it became a blockbuster and I was worth millions of dollars, I would invest one million to build a beautiful research center for all aspiring creative types. I would make that place for them. They would have access to all the necessary books, a creative courtyard to wander by the sea. They would spend late drunken nights with other brilliant creatives with whom they could exchange thoughts to help ease their pain. This would be just what this region needed. I'd keep it remote, keep the roads rough, so only those who truly wanted to be here, who truly wanted the jagged path of life, would journey here to become amazing.

I came out of my manic daydream, just as the sun seemed to pause in the sky. The world was calm. No humans. I shouted. I heard the echo come back. I shouted again, with more power, raising my voice until I reached a crescendo that left me gasping for breath.

CHAPTER SIX

In the morning, we caught the ferry to Loutro. Next to us two girls in their early twenties were reading books in French. I found it impossible to take my eyes off them.

The girls were wearing dresses. One had a red floral pattern and the other was dark green with yellow dots. Nick elbowed me. My hand fidgeted as I watched them, hoping for a signal, but they remained ensconced in their books. I flared up. I might not interest them, but the landscape was intoxicating. It seemed criminal to ignore it for the sake of a lousy book. Books were better to be read when you were lonely. When you had nothing better around you. How many times would they have this view? *Put down your damn book*, I thought. *This experience is fleeting.*

"Talk to them," Nick whispered to me.

To my surprise, just then the blond girl laid down her book and walked toward the edge of the ferry. It felt a bit odd, as if I had implanted the suggestion in her mind just by thinking it. Excited, I froze. *Give me a look, at least a peek, so I know you find me a little interesting.* I stared at her firmly. If anyone noticed how I looked at her they may have felt frightened. In truth, I was ready to devour her.

I approached her, staggering from two benches away. The timing was perfect. She wouldn't look at me, though. *I'm a good looking man*, I thought. *How can she not?* The moment was scripted like a film. Handsome American meets Beautiful European off the south coast of Crete on a ferry gliding over the tranquil blue sea. I suspected she was in some fantasy of her own and I was not part of it. She was probably already in love and thinking of him. *What do I have to lose? Even if she does have someone. What do I have to lose?* I was so lost in my head that by the time I made it through the maze of hesitation the moment had passed. She walked away. I felt Nick's disappointment as I wobbled back to my seat.

I hoped to see them at the beach. The water was a full, intoxicating blue. The temperature cooled when I swam toward the bottom of the sea and it relaxed me. I scanned the beach, carefully, but the French girls were nowhere to be found. It was a cozy beach, with sunbeds and umbrellas. The entire village was visible from the sea. It was all white, striking against the blue sea and the dun-colored cliffs against which it was set. There were no cars because the coast was too steep. You visited Loutro either by boat or you hiked; this was its charm. I also liked how you could jump from the hot shingle beach to a restaurant in seconds, or sip a cold beer at a café, which was exactly what we did.

The restaurants were aligned on the edge of the water. We picked a table at the end of the dock, near the ferry port. Nick was Skyping with his wife and baby and I kept my head on a swivel. To my despair, everyone was with a companion. I wished to have a pretty lady friend with me to share this moment. Someone who would laugh at my silly thoughts, while I listened to her aspirations.

* * *

That evening we took the ferry to Agia Roumeli so we could hike the Samaria Gorge the following morning. We found a cheap room for thirty-five euros. Nick paid. I felt guilty that he kept paying for everything. I admired his generosity not only because he was paying for me, but also for his awareness of the financial situation of others and readiness to fill the gap to keep the day enjoyable for everyone. We had planned to explore the village that evening but, exhausted after our day in the sea, we conked out.

We woke early in the morning and hiked up the Samaria gorge, which is the reverse of the conventional way. Before the entrance, we passed a flock of lambs huddled next to each other under the sun and a donkey inched for shade under a disproportionately small olive tree. I trailed behind Nick while he rushed ahead. The aromas of thyme, lavender, and mint set me at ease as did the sudden coolness when we entered a shaded passageway. After some time, we reached a point on the trail where we hiked along a stream. The water accentuated the contours and colors of the stones beneath it. I'd never seen such diaphanous water in my life. It was fresh and you could feel the coolness of it, distinct in the heat, on the breeze that wafted sporadically between the towering walls of the gorge. The sounds of nature were singing me tunes and it set me in a trance as I moseyed along. I watched the stream. What splendor on a hot August day to see a flow of water pouring down a mountain.

When I caught up to Nick, he was ready to turn around. We'd been hiking for a couple hours. The allure of the stream became more and more inviting as we descended. My impulse was to jump in and allow it to carry me down the rest of the way to the sea. It was prohibited to bathe in it, though. Yet with each step I contemplated jumping in. Nick felt the same urge. "*Malaka*, that water looks so good," he said.

It was mid-afternoon and the sun was scorching. "Stop," I said. We reached a deep part of the stream. Nobody was around. I removed everything but my briefs. Nick did the same. My testicles shriveled to raisins the moment I plunged in. Seconds later, my legs went numb. I re-emerged into the hot sun feeling as if I'd been baptized. We were standing there, in our soaked briefs, when, suddenly, a pretty brunette passed and smiled at Nick and said, "Hi!"

Nick smiled back. I raised my eyebrows at him.

"Holy God and Jesus! Was that real?"

"*Malaka*, let's go!"

I paced right behind Nick down the gorge. Where the hell was that acknowledgement I had desperately needed yesterday?

We ate quickly at a taverna then went straight to the beach, found a spot under a tree, and relaxed in the shade. After we settled, I noticed a woman in a bikini walk by me and lie down next to an older man behind us. To my amazement, I realized that it was the woman from the gorge. Up close, she looked sexy rather than pretty and more woman than girl, I thought.

"I'm going for a swim," Nick said.

He stood up and stretched his ginormous frame. It was inconceivable to believe she didn't notice him. He swam far enough out to isolate himself. I was sipping on a Greek beer called Mythos, scanning the beach for pretty ladies. I spotted quite a few good ones—all, unfortunately, accompanied. Then the sexy woman sauntered into the frame and I watched the round cheeks of her ass, accentuated by her thong, disappear in the sea. Again to my astonishment, she swam straight to Nick. I lost my breath. What a wonderful moment for Nick…

I watched them closely, as if I was a lifeguard ready to rescue Nick in case he started to drown. At the same time, I couldn't help wondering who the older gentleman lying right behind me was. Certainly not her father.

Nick and the woman were out there for some time, before she made her way back to shore, while Nick remained in the sea. She emerged with a shine that was accentuated by the bright sun and she appeared to be moving toward me. I did not believe it. I straightened my posture. She smiled at me, certainly approaching. Initially I pretended not to notice.

"Are you from LA?" she asked, making it impossible to ignore her.

"Yeah… I used to live there," I replied, my skin prickling with nervous excitement. "You live in LA?"

"I live in Ventura. I'm here with Spiro. He's like my second dad. I work at his restaurant in Ventura."

"How do you like it here?"

"I love it!"

"It's beautiful."

"Autumn," she said and reached out her hand.

I went limp.

"It's nice to meet you!" she said.

"You too…"

It was all I could manage. My insides were churning. I took a deep breath as the woman returned to her sunbed, stretched her lithe brown body upon it and, saying something to Spiro, closed her eyes. Moments later, Nick came marching towards me, ready to report his findings.

"*Malaka!* You won't believe it!"

"Did you at least get a hand job?"

"She works for that guy she's with. She calls him her second dad."

"That's exactly what she told me!"

"She's so fucking hot."

"Why would she be so forthcoming to call him her second dad?"

"Because she wants *poutso!*" *Poutso* was Greek for cock. Nick laughed.

"If we don't claim the elements to be in our favor today, then they're never going to be in our favor," I said. "What do you do in this situation? *Second Dad?* You should get her number? Or I should get her number. You're married."

"I'm married… that's just it. *Malaka,* he's just some rich Greek dude who's paying for her trip to Greece."

"Yeah. She's probably an aspiring actress or was an actress whose career fell apart. Now in her mid-thirties, she has a sponsor. Spiro! Hairy, fat, old Spiro!"

"*Malaka,* stop looking back!"

"God! She's beautiful. She's all woman."

"Yeah. She's a *mounara,* a very hot woman."

We spotted her one last time on our walk back to the ferry. She was talking with a young couple, being absurdly friendly with the poor girl's boyfriend. We walked past and she made no acknowledgement.

I took one last peek. Nick looked over his shoulder too, then back to me.

"*Malaka,* I'm going to be thinking about her for the rest of this trip and she's already trying to bang some other guy."

"She's a tease," I said. "That's what she is. A social climber and a tease. The kind who fawns over you at first sight only to shut you off like a clam after learning your plight."

"That was poetic, cuz."

"We're going to miss the ferry."

The ferry back to Chora Sfakion was crowded. A line of passengers, waiting to buy ice cream, snaked through the rows of benches. The Scandinavians were tomato red and tired-looking. I wandered toward the end of the ferry, away from the people.

The energy changed suddenly when one of a bohemian set of Greeks, returning from the little island of Gavdos, serenaded the crowd with a beautiful melody on his lyra. It was the type of music that calmed and charged you simultaneously. I stood at the tip of the ferry gazing out to sea. My hands grasped the white-painted, thick steel railing. It was a clear, mild evening. The sun was behind me. Tightening my grip on the rail I whispered to myself the line from the film *Titanic*: "I'm the king of the world."

I hesitated… no, that felt false. It was barbaric and dated. I eased my grip. There came another feeling, as if on the salt-smelling air, that was far more advanced. Awe! "I'm at one with the world!"

CHAPTER SEVEN

Yiannis, our second cousin, texted Nick to meet him in Chora Sfakion for the 1st Annual Sfakian Pie Festival. The people in these parts honored the Sfakian Pie—a doughy, pancake-shaped dessert filled with mizithra cheese drizzled with honey. Eight hundred people packed the harbor.

Yiannis escorted us to his table where I encountered a band of distant cousins I had never met before. They greeted me warmly, but I soon began to feel disconnected, as I didn't know Greek or have anything much in common to talk about, so I turned my attention to the Cretans jumping and twirling in the air on the dance floor. I wondered if the tourists who had rooms tonight were upset or got any sleep with the loud music and the bullets fired into the sky.

The party was still going strong and it was past three in the morning. I yawned loudly and straightened my back. There were so many chunks of goat meat covering the tables that I ate my Sfakian Pie from my lap.

Nick looked possessed, with glossy eyes and a tough Sfakian demeanor. Another Sfakian challenged him to chug a glass of wine, called a *koupa*, to test his alpha male credibility. Before he downed it, Nick raised his glass to a third Sfakian man, at another table, challenging him to down a glass, after he downed his. This man had rugged features and a thick black beard that matched his black clothing. He nodded his head, then Nick swallowed his full glass of wine in a single gulp.

"These guys think they're so tough," he tossed off.

Something inside me felt shoddy hanging out like this with Nick. I could feel I was not on vacation and so I was in no rush to seek indulgence. The indulgence would find me. It wasn't about spending money to be serviced. My stomach turned. Nick was having a very good time, but as I watched him lick his fingers, I hungered after something else. Yet while my mind resisted, my body kept submitting to these pleasures. I can't be this way, I thought. I knew I was foolish to mentally reject this time together. In a few days, I would be alone. Loneliness scared me, too.

Again, a Sfakian in all black raised a glass to Nick. He nodded.

"Give me the *koupa*," I said.

"*Malaka*, you're driving," Nick said.

"Give me the *koupa*, *malaka*," I said.

"You know this wine is very strong," Yiannis said.

"I have what feels like a baby calf digesting in my stomach right now. I need it for my health!"

Nick poured wine into my glass.

"Fill it to the brim," I said. I held out my glass. "*Yeia Mas!*" I shouted in Greek. To our health!

* * *

Next morning, Yiannis joined us at the beach. It was very hot. Nick was hungover, appearing almost dead on the blanket. We were lying under umbrellas having a discussion about the Greeks, the Americans, the Germans, and so on. Who was doing it right? It was the type of discussion that raised all sorts of questions, the answers to which we'd never know until many years later. I practiced my Greek and Yiannis corrected me, having me repeat words until I pronounced them right.

As we talked about the Greek "brain drain", a goat appeared and startled me. She had found the bag of biscuits inside my bag. I offered her one and she ate it. She was light brown and down her forehead she had a patch of white fur while dark brown hair hung from her chin. I fed her another biscuit. She reached over my shoulder for more. I placed my arm around her neck and Nick snapped a picture of us. I played with her swollen udders. Nick snapped another picture. She only left after my entire bag of biscuits was gone.

Yiannis and I returned to our discussion. He was an orthopedic surgeon who had left Greece for Germany. Many Greeks had left Greece. Many smart and ambitious Greeks were building a life elsewhere in the world.

"Do you think you'd come back to Greece and open up a practice here?" I asked. He was puffing on a vaporizing device.

"I want to... I'm at home here. I'll always be the foreigner in Germany," he said. "This place is precious but the people aren't so precious."

"What do you mean? What does Germany do so much better?" I asked.

He took a deep breath; his mind was inflamed and his mouth couldn't support all the ideas at once. Slowly, he spoke. "They respect Germany... the rules... the laws. You don't have people shooting street signs."

Nick who was now attuned to his smartphone, would partake in the discussion intermittently. "Yeah! You don't have them shooting bullets into the sky at a festival with kids."

"Greece has mastered the simple life, made it an art form," I said. "Greeks understand how to live. And it hasn't changed for over two thousand years."

"Exactly. We're not living two thousand years ago."

"Life is not all about money," I said.

Or is it? I wondered. The nature of America was to never present life in its raw state. Instead the myth of the *American Dream* was used as a disguise to represent a life spent working to accumulate money. I could not handle this. A pang of sadness seized me. I could rally behind mottos like "In Money We Trust," or "God is Money," if they were blatantly coined and I was medicated with enough drugs to blow out my consciousness. But instead I heard messages of love and freedom and hope and a better life and I wasn't so sure if that was what I lived for.

But maybe this was only me and I'd only assumed the rest of America was the same. And if this was true, was I really an American? I was born and raised in America. I lived my entire life there. I didn't feel Greek. Heck, I couldn't even speak the language. Well, at least I wasn't Greek, yet.

I went into the sea to cool off, devouring all that was around me. Money was important. And Greece had no money and no industry or technology, either. They needed to cut back on the restaurants and cafés and build a product, something they could sell to the whole world, where people could receive it on their doorsteps, or, even better, through the cloud. Or else they needed to be *the* premier travel destination for the world's wealthiest people. Greece needed to be the first destination people thought of when they wanted to travel. Not Italy or France or Spain.

Rationalizing as an American was easy for me. Stepping back and reassessing was the troubling part. Thinking: when you predicated a way of life revolving only around money, eventually the money wheel was going to reach an unsustainable pace and swiftly burst from its rotors. As a former investment banker, I'd built valuation models and forecasted growth and all it showed you was a theorized metric that assumed the business operated in perpetuity. Of course, if somehow earth was joined to an entirely new planet filled with resources that made what we had pale in comparison, we'd simply continue to feed the juggernaut.

I wasn't yet sure if I was a hypocrite. I had wanted to put aside my American ideals in order to find a new way because I did really want the new way. I had no idea how to bring my desire for a better, more refined self in line with the values of my respective heritages, American and Greek. A part of me feared that now that I wasn't a player in the profit wheel anymore, I was jealous of all the people living financially successful lives in America. And for this reason I had to attack the American way of life and leave it behind to discover a better way for myself to abide. I hoped this wasn't the case, for it was a tragically flawed conclusion.

I smiled at the friendly sea, hauled myself out onto to beach, and settled back down on the warm sand.

"There's a spirit here and it's very precious, Yiannis. I can't say that about America. Can you say that about Germany?"

The doctor in him was precise and deliberate. "Greece has always been known for its spirit. But there is a balance. And if you want to have a share in the improvements in the world you have to contribute."

"I'm going to get to see it all firsthand. I'm tired of reading the papers bludgeon Greece for its laziness and profligacy. I need to experience it for myself."

"You will. You'll see. It's good that you're here."

"You know what it is with me, Yiannis. I'm anxious."

"About what?"

"I'm anxious to squeeze the juice out of this country… that's what it is."

Yiannis did not respond. I watched him huff and puff on his vaporizer. Maybe he thought I was naive or, who knows, an imbecile. Maybe, too, my thoughts were badly flawed. Maybe I was too critical.

CHAPTER EIGHT

Nick had one final night left in Crete so we left Sfakia early in the morning and drove over the mountains to Chania. I felt invigorated as soon as we arrived. Traffic streamed from all directions. Cars were parked on the wrong side of the road. We passed down a narrow road that ended in front of the central agora. We turned right and then made a left onto Daskalogiannis street and parked.

The day was sweltering hot. The old town was crowded with people. We checked into a cheap, dumpy hotel because it was the only one in the old town with vacancies. The room made us look like giants. Nick's head could almost touch the ceiling.

"Yiannis is going to be here in thirty minutes," Nick said. "I'm going to take a shower... I say we hit up the beach."

"The beach? I don't know."

"Let's go to the beach!"

"I'm gonna check out one of those cafés at the square across the street."

I found a table shaded by a large tree. I ordered a bowl of yogurt with honey and walnuts and a Greek coffee, double, no sugar. I said my order in Greek. The waitress corrected me; I smiled. I opened my laptop and wrote down some thoughts. Then Dad phoned.

"When are you coming to Kallikratis?" he said.

"I'm not sure," I told him.

He slowly layered the cushions, making the village sound attractive, until somehow he induced me into looking forward to returning. In my mind, it would be better this time.

"I'll be back tomorrow," I said.

I returned to writing. Then Nick and Yiannis joined me before I could fall deeply into it. They asked me again if I wanted to join them. Nick was eating a Greek pastry called *bougatsa*. Yiannis was sucking on his vaporizer.

"You guys go ahead, we'll do it big later tonight," I said.

"You're going to miss out, *malaka*," Nick said.

"He's in writer mode now. He wants to write. The next Bukowski!" Yiannis said.

"Bukowski! *Yeah*, sure," I said.

"Truly, he's a great writer," Yiannis said. "I love his dirtiness."

"He's highly entertaining, that's for sure," I said.

"You got to write like Bukowski, you got to be a dirty old man."

"For you, Yiannis, I'll sprinkle in some dirtiness."

"You got to have experiences to write about, though, and you have to write and write. Truly, you have to be passionate about it."

"Thank you for the advice," I said with a wry smile.

After an hour, the heat caused me to break into a sweat. The shrilling of cicadas had reached a deafening pitch. I stopped writing and I wandered. *I have to find a place to live here*, I thought. It'd be perfect. My breakfast had cost me only four euros. The food was tasty and healthy; the waitress was sweet and dainty. Everything you needed was a short jaunt away. The atmosphere nourished my imagination. A strong artistic vibe warmed me. The colors were real; the people were peaceful; the nature was mystical. The movement was free and rhythmic.

Personal time cures a man's soul. While Nick and Yiannis rested on the beach and burned their bodies in the sun, gawking at the ladies, I was gawking at my new life here. The feeling found a comfortable spot in my stomach. I was going to live near the Venetian fortress so I might wander through the narrow alleys, my imagination finding new surprises with every twist and turn. This wasn't a vacation. I was on a journey, an odyssey that would arouse feelings of anger, despair and joy, but surely not regret. *Strip me naked, oh lord, so others may see me as strange.* Upon catching sight of me, others would perceive that my uniqueness was submerged fully in its environment.

As I rejoiced in this new-found strength, I inquired at the municipal office about a school that offered Greek lessons to foreigners. It was a completely free service available to anyone who lived in Greece. It sounded like a perfect way to learn the language. The woman behind the desk looked at me sternly. I had barely finished two words in Greek before she spoke to me in English. Her reply was sharp and peremptory. It seemed that my inquiries about the program were an inconvenience to her. To my disappointment, she informed me, in the same grim tone, that everything was on hold until the election in a few weeks' time.

I had heard about the referendum, which had been called by the current prime minister to affirm his power and thus help facilitate future political decisions. So as anxious as I was to start learning Greek, politics halted me.

The lady asked where I was from. I told her that I was born and raised in America but my parents were from Sfakia. When I mentioned Sfakia and said that my last name was Manouselis, her demeanor toward me drastically changed. She even offered me a number to call.

"What are you doing here?" she asked. "Everyone else wants to leave."

"Somebody's got to save Greece," I said.

"*You're* going to save Greece? Yeah, right," she said with a wry smile.

"America is all just work and money."

"All we're doing here is working and not making money."

The lady wished me good luck as I waved her goodbye. Outside a café next door, in attitudes of overpowering ease, elderly men sat watching me with the same intensity as I watched them. To think that these men needed saving was plainly ridiculous. It was the delusion of a lost soul who fails to realize that the purpose of his endeavor is his own well-being rather than that of others. I didn't really believe I had come here to save Greece. It was more that I was still unconscious at that stage that I was here to save myself, which made the idea of saving someone else, or even an entire country, an admirable notion. Sure, it was egotistic and unrealistically grandiose.

* * *

I was on the balcony reading when Nick and Yiannis returned from the beach.

"How was the beach?" I asked.

"Fucking awesome! So many hot chicks," Nick said. "I have to take a dump."

Yiannis removed a joint from his bag and joined me.

"Truly you should've been there. Truly."

I took a drag and handed the joint back to him.

"Did you find any schools?" he asked.

"I have to wait for the free school, but there's another across the street I'll check out."

Yiannis bent his elbow and clenched his hand and said, "You got to start from a strong foundation. You have to know the fundamentals. When you learn Greek, I'll help you perfect it. I'll be like your coach in a boxing ring. I'll help you once you're in the fight. Right now, you need someone else to put you through all the grueling training."

His lips parted and he clenched down on his teeth and imitated a growling dog. I chuckled and smiled and looked closely at the shiny top of his head where there were only a few short strands of hair.

"I'm going to get some water. Anybody want anything?" Nick said.

We waved him off.

"Did you do a lot of good writing? Did you write a lot? You got to write a lot."

"Yeah. I wrote as best as I could."

"Good. That's what I want to hear. That you wrote. That it was a successful day. 'Cause you missed out on a good day at the beach. We had good *parea*."

"I'm going to shower," I said.

It was nice to wash off the sweat that had moistened my skin all day and change into my freshest summer clothes. Nick hadn't returned by the time I was dressed. Yiannis was snoring, conked out on the lounge. I grabbed my book and walked out to the balcony. It occurred to me that Nick had been gone for forty-five minutes now. I didn't think anything of it, except maybe he wanted some time alone. We'd been together every day for several days now and he had the wife and baby with him for a week. I guessed he needed some personal time to walk freely and soak in the atmosphere. I understood that, certainly.

When Nick returned, he came out to the balcony and sat down next to me. He was looking at his phone and I could see he was anxious to tell me something.

"Where'd you go?" I asked.

"*Malaka,* you won't believe it."

"What happened?"

"What if I told you I got laid by the hottest girl in Chania for the price it cost to do my laundry?"

"Did you roofie someone?"

"I just banged the hottest chick in the red light district." He turned his head at me and grinned.

"The what?!"

"They have a red light district here."

"How did you find it?"

"*Malaka*, are you serious? It's called Google… *Red Light District Chania*… A hundred results."

He tilted his head down to his phone, appearing satisfied.

I moved to the bed. I felt I needed to hold a woman in my arms right now and sweetly kiss her while she ran her hands through my hair. Suddenly, I missed watching Francesca's face drop after she orgasmed. I couldn't resist. I sent her an iMessage: "I miss you. :-)"

* * *

The three of us strolled around the harbor after a casual dinner at a *psitopolio*, a place that specialized in meat grilled on a spit. All the girls wore their best, most revealing summer clothes. Nearly everyone we saw sported an opulent tan that spoke of days in the sun. People had a sparkle in their eyes. It was as inviting, in many of the female faces, as the sunset.

We went to a café on the west side of the harbor that I had discovered earlier. Nick was like an untamed terrier released from his cage. He was incapable of having a normal conversation without stopping intermittently to ogle passing women.

I could have stayed all night at that café watching the crowd drift past. I particularly enjoyed seeing the dazzled expression that came over people's faces as they emerged from the surrounding alleyways and caught sight of the sea. But after a while Yiannis and Nick, becoming restless, insisted on moving. Reluctantly, I followed them toward the east side of the harbor where the Greek-Americans hung out.

Nick's friend, Stelios, who lived in Chania, joined us. We found a table with a good view of the passersby. The place was fancy and our table was next to a mega yacht where a family was having dinner on the second deck. Nick snapped a picture and googled the yacht's name. It turned out the vessel's owner was a billionaire who owned a shipping container company. Many tourists stopped and snapped a picture in front of the yacht. It was longer than the pier it was docked to.

The place was filled by Greeks who were drinking frappés or fredos or colorful cocktails; the music was loud and nobody danced. Greek-American friends of Nick's stopped by and said hello. I tried to make eye contact with the Greek girls but they never looked away from their *parea*.

We did not have good conversations. Nick continued to say, "*Malaka!* Oh my god!" every time he saw an attractive woman walk past. Somehow this always led to a change of topic. Stelios asked about America. America alarmed him.

"What's up with the police in America?" he said. "They're shooting black people?"

"Last week we had a black guy shoot a white newswoman on TV. If that had been a white man shooting a black newswoman it would have been chaos. Chaos!" Nick's protruding eyeballs revealed the jagged veins attacking his irises. "America is fucked up! Oh my God. She's a *mounara*."

"We have racist police officers," I said.

"You have civilians killing police officers, too," Nick added.

"Just because you have a badge and a gun doesn't mean you can abuse your power and intimidate citizens."

"You are such a liberal."

"I'm not a liberal. I'm only saying that people should feel safe around police officers and that does not happen in the US for some people."

"Oh my god! That is a super *mounara*."

"You're like a wild beast," I said.

"Pete's right, Nick," said Yiannis. "You need to relax."

"I'm on vacation. When I go back, I'm inside a control room down in a basement with no windows, every day."

"Yannis, you think I should go talk to those girls over there?" I said.

"Yes, *malaka*, you should," Nick said.

"If you would like to," Yiannis said.

"If they're not from here you have a good chance. Otherwise, they won't talk to you because they'll be afraid of looking like a slut in front of their friends," Stelios said. "Those girls, I think, are locals."

"They'll probably think I'm a Syrian refugee," I said.

"You tell them you have Greek roots and you're from America," Nick said.

"You don't look like a refugee," Stelios said with a chuckle.

"You're tanned and tall and you look like you could buy the place," Nick said. "Go talk to them."

"Not worth it," I said. "Not one of them has looked over here for one second."

"If I wasn't married, I'd be throwing my *poutso* all over the place."

Stelios grinned. "How many hours do you work a week?" he asked Nick.

"I've been working seventy hours consistently for the last year."

Stelios raised his eyebrows.

"Pete was working like a hundred hours when he was in finance."

"At least in America you work and you make money. In Greece you work and work and if you work a lot you're the *malaka*," Stelios said.

"America has the opportunities if you are educated or if you have a good financial situation," I said.

"We have millions of illegal Mexicans working and they're not educated," Nick countered.

"They're not making a respectable wage for a laborer."

"Twelve dollars an hour is a good wage in Detroit."

"That sounds like a lot," said Stelios.

"It is!"

"I couldn't disagree more with you," I said.

"People who work in tourism here make only three or four euros an hour."

"Yeah. And people in China make two dollars a day."

"You're so Californian ultra-liberal," Nick said.

"I'm not a liberal! I'm not a Californian. In fact, I think the liberals in California are delusional restless souls. I'm telling you facts, Nick! Here let me give you an example. My mom was making twenty-five dollars an hour and that was in the nineties! In Ohio. Working at a sweeper manufacturing company. She made over forty dollars an hour during overtime and she worked a lot of overtime. She had a pension. Full healthcare coverage. On that, people with unlucky circumstances could live the American dream. You could buy a home. You could save money for retirement. You could give your kids the proper necessities to succeed. It was real then. Today, twelve dollars an hour with no health care coverage or IRA is a survival job. And the Mexicans are being exploited by wealthy liberals in California. So you can take your liberal notion and shove it back to Detroit!"

"Dude, relax! *Jesus, malaka.*"

The anger seethed out of me. It contaminated the rest of the evening. I had a lot of anger within me, and I wasn't sure where it came from or how it had accumulated to the level it had. Growing up in Ohio was no doubt one reason. Another was the feeling I had that it was impossible to do anything but conform to the system. Moreover, I was perplexed by how Nick could so quickly forget about his own parents who immigrated to the US in the seventies with no money or education and made a success of themselves.

More morbid thoughts seized my mind and suddenly I felt enervated by our discussion and filled with despair. I looked up at the mega yacht wondering why anybody would ever want to own something like that. The yacht shadowed our table and blocked the glimmer of the lighthouse that was at the end of the pier. It wasn't aesthetically pleasing, or perhaps only in the most basic, vulgar way. It was a monstrosity that offended the eyes.

Some of Yiannis' friends from Athens arrived and he went to talk to them. A friend of Nick's sat at our table and I got up leaving Nick money for my share of the evening. He handed me back the money. I left it on the table and went back to the room.

Francesca texted me: "I've really been missing the feel of you touching my body. Kisses."

As quickly as I lifted off, I popped. I let out a long-drawn sigh. I closed my eyes and I thought of her straddling me wearing only a light blue blouse that was unbuttoned and hanging half open. Her breasts fluttered underneath the blouse and this made her scintillating.

* * *

Nick zipped up his suitcase. Yiannis slid on his shorts and grabbed his keys. I lay on the bed watching everything happen. With their departure imminent, the reality of my journey officially began to hit me. A feeling of deep loneliness struck me. I climbed off the bed and hugged Nick and Yiannis.

"Have a safe flight, cuz."

"Take care, *malaka*. You're living the life."

"I'm living the dream."

"Now back to America where I'm going to lose my tan and realize how fat I got from eating a *bougatsa* every day."

Then they were gone and the room was suddenly a claustrophobic, dark box. I gathered my stuff and left for Kallikratis, but not before I'd messaged Francesca back. "I'm thinking about you… the sweet love we made in SF. I wish I could have you next to me, right now."

CHAPTER NINE

The sun had disappeared leaving only the remnants of its flames. Dad insisted I come with him; he only said we were going to *panorouga* and I had no idea what that meant. I heard faint sighs from the trunk. I looked over at Dad. He kept driving.

"What's that noise?"

Dad didn't respond. The sound was too soft to be squeaky brakes.

"Do you hear that noise?" I asked again.

Dad stopped the car next to a trash container. "Throw the trash away," he said.

I grabbed the black trash bag from the trunk and there was movement inside and the faint sighs were clear now. I quickly dropped the bag onto the ground.

"What the hell is in there?" I shouted at him.

"Throw it away!"

"No! It sounds like a cat. Are those kittens!?"

I stepped further away. The bag wiggled like it had a heartbeat.

"Throw it away!"

"You do it!"

Dad stepped out of the car and launched the bag into the trash container.

"I can't understand," he said.

I returned to the car. I clenched my jaw. I mumbled to myself, questioning why I came back to Kallikratis.

"Where are we going?" I said.

"*Panorouga*, I told you!"

"What the hell is *panorouga*?"

He only lifted his hand off the steering wheel and shook his head in disgust. Shortly afterwards we arrived in the village center of Kallikratis. Dad turned then reversed then moved forward then reversed again, eventually parking the car so close to a galvanized mesh fence that I had to squeeze my way out.

We entered the *kafeneio*, or coffee house, the same cautious way we had done at the *panagiri*.

"*Kerase tous!*" shouted a burly man sitting at a corner table with three other men. "Get them drinks!"

We sat down at a square wooden table against the wall. The cement room was rectangular and naked except for the furniture. There was a single painting hanging on the wall. It depicted ragged kids playing poker; one of them was using his toes to sneak a card along the floor to another player. Everyone in the *kafeneio* was *parea*.

"What would you like?" asked the proprietor.

"A beer," I said.

Dad looked at me strangely. "No," he said, looking down at his *komboloi*, worry beads, as he spoke. "We'll order *tsikoudia*."

The proprietor served it to us in a tiny carafe. Dad raised his shot glass to the burly man. I gulped mine down. Dad sipped his. I filled my mouth with the olives and chips from the small bowls the proprietor left us as a *meze*.

The proprietor and his wife sat down next to us. They asked me how I was and how long I'd be staying. I tried my best to answer them. When I told them I was going to live here now, they wanted to know what I'd be doing. I told them.

"He had a good job at a bank," Dad interjected. "He worked in New York… with stocks."

I stared at him, stupefied, while the three of them segued into a conversation in Greek I couldn't follow. My gaze shifted to the men seated at the table in the corner. I tried to imagine what each one's life was like. One of the men was wearing camo pants with a camo T-shirt. The others were dressed all in black. All the men had thick mustaches and full heads of hair, grayed through age. They wore no accessories. Dirt was built up in the cracks at the corners of their eyes. Their chiseled jaws gave them a mighty look, like ancient sculptures of Agamemnon's army suddenly brought to life. One of the men, with thoughtful brown eyes, had a protuberant belly that pushed up his tight black shirt.

Cracked walnut shells littered the table. I watched their history being revealed one *tsikoudia* at a time. I saw four men who toiled in the fields during the day and spent their evenings together without a care in the world. What were they saying? It didn't matter. Even a simple conversation about the weather, a common topic in these parts, was biblical. In my eyes, the men took asceticism to a supernatural level.

For Dad this was the proper way. More friends would arrive and he would shout, *"Kerase ton!"* "Get him a drink." These were locals born into the tough and exacting fabric of his homeland, men with whom he had lost connection when he moved to America; these days of old age were the re-stitching period to set him right. I was drinking a beer now and it was okay because Dad paid for it.

Soon the mystique of the locals and my fascination with their naturalness turned dull. I watched them for hours and nothing I saw embodied forward thinking. I felt insecure as everyone knew who I was but I didn't know who they were. It seemed to put me at a disadvantage. Dad wanted me here though, to show me off, so people would know who I was; he wanted them to know that I was his son.

I'd have managed myself better if I had my smartphone with me and there was internet. As it was, sitting there for several hours, at the same table, I reached a point where I was filled with rage whenever I looked at Dad.

CHAPTER TEN

The morning was crisp and clean and authentic. I did not have the urge for much of anything. I wanted to slowly proceed. Even a simple question from Dad felt arduous. There was the border collie watching me closely, resting her chin on her paw. I cautiously approached her and she stood up, unsure what I would do. I reached my hand out and whistled. I took short gentle steps until I was able to dig my fingers into her fur. She closed her eyes and wagged her tail.

"Don't spoil the dog," Dad shouted in English from the doorway.

When Dad returned inside, I picked away at the balls of dirt bunched in her fur. I peered over at the front door ready to pull my hands away if Dad appeared. I named her Spirto after the Greek word for "match"—the *match* used to light a flame.

Suddenly she streaked toward the gate where an old man appeared, holding a chunk of what looked like white cheese in an air-sealed plastic bag. He stared at me for a long moment, as if he wanted to see my soul, then he reached out his hand and said, "Welcome." His name was Eftíxis, which meant "happy" in Greek. I remembered him from my last trip.

"How are you?" he said.

"I'm good."

"How long are you going to stay?"

"For a time…"

I couldn't muster up anything more substantial in Greek, so I told him Dad was inside the house. I watched him go in and resumed my game with the dog.

Later, as we were eating breakfast, Eftíxis randomly started to pontificate from the couch.

"The first language was Greek and you can't speak a word. What a shame… You are a Greek and you can't speak it. What a shame."

"I'm trying."

"He went to college," Dad said, pointing his finger at Eftíxis while holding his spoon.

"I know. You told me this last time."

"Drink the milk—it's good," Dad said, turning to me.

"I don't want it."

"It's from the goat!"

"I told you I didn't want it to be spicy."

"I didn't add a lot," he said, as he sprinkled more red pepper flakes onto his oatmeal.

"I don't like it."

"It's good for you."

I grabbed the salt shaker and sprinkled salt onto my eggs.

"Don't put salt," Dad said.

"Will you leave me alone!"

"You don't know how to eat."

The door was open and the sun, having broken the brim of the mountain, shined brightly into the house. The light beamed onto Eftíxis' face and you could see countless dust particles floating in the air. Eftíxis was too old to hear what Dad and I were saying, especially since I was speaking in English. He stood up and Dad encouraged him to stay and have some *tsikoudia*.

"No," he said. He didn't want any breakfast either. Not even a walnut to crack. "My teeth hurt," he said.

I dipped a piece of *graviera* cheese into a jar of honey. Dad gnawed on a *paximathi*. I felt as if Dad was a bossy general who hovered over me ready to oppress me with overbearing words.

"Do you want me to cut you a piece of the *anthotiro* cheese that Eftíxis brought to eat with the *paximathi*?"

"No."

"It goes well."

"I don't want it."

"It's good."

"I'm good," I said with a gasp.

I wanted to engage in a meaningful conversation. Only I had no idea what to ask him in order to establish some common ground.

"I want to go to Chania, tomorrow," I said.

"To do what?"

"I want to find an apartment and live in Chania."

"We have the house in Patsianos," Dad said, shaking his head. "Why would you go rent an apartment in Chania? HAH!"

"There's nothing in Patsianos."

"What are you going to do in Chania?"

"I want to go to school there and learn Greek. To be around people."

Dad swished a shot of *tsikoudia* around in his mouth, then swallowed it in a gulp.

"You can learn Greek here, in the village."

"No!" I said. "I'm not staying here. Are you crazy?" I looked away from him.

"We have work to do!"

"What work?"

"The grapes."

"You said there aren't any grapes this year."

"We have some grapes."

"I have work to do, too."

"What work?"

"What work? I have work!"

"What work?"

"To write!"

He grabbed a walnut and cracked it open with his pocket knife. "Hah! You want to go to Chania. What are you going to do in Chania—Hah! I got the Wi-Fi in Patsianos for you."

I left the plate on the table and walked outside. I grabbed the *katsouna* and walked toward the herbal café that lay a stone's throw away.

A tourist couple were sitting relaxed on the porch drinking lemonade in large clear glasses. I poked my head inside the small store and noticed the owner's selection of products had expanded from botanical oils and traditional marmalades and soaps to include jewelry and postcards of Kallikratis.

I rested at one of the stone tables out front. Vases filled with white and purple flowers stood in the center of each table. They attracted yellow jackets so I moved my vase to the table alongside.

Yianina, the owner, earthy in appearance and tired by age, remembered me. I told her I'd be staying here for an indefinite period. "I'm going to learn Greek," I said.

She smiled. I asked her for a Greek coffee. She smiled again. She answered the French tourists in French before she returned inside.

Two years ago, I remembered, I was enjoying a Greek coffee here, the scene practically the same, when Yianina asked me the most unsettling question I had ever been asked in my life.

"How do you have an emotional connection with your father?"

"What do you mean?" I had replied, taken aback.

"You don't speak Greek and he doesn't speak English."

Never had something so obvious affected me as powerfully as this question.

"We don't," I remembered telling her.

When I had pushed those words out of my mouth, I'd felt undone. The question haunted me for many days. I was only able to forget it once I had returned to America and resumed my ordinary life there. Subconsciously, though, the starkness of the issue stayed with me. It was at the back of my mind now, every moment I spent with Dad. Coming to Greece, I knew, was about more than wanting to write and leave my American behavior behind. I also wanted to establish a genuine connection with Dad.

The question Yianina posed inspired my quest to rectify the disconnect with my father. How could I be so stupid as to not recognize the obvious? I couldn't answer. Of course, I never dared to mention our disconnect to Dad. After all, what would be the point? He wouldn't be able to change his ways or do anything else to correct it. I was the one who was going to have to extend myself in order to try and understand him and thereby deepen our relationship. The first big step to help me do this was to learn Greek.

I neared the last sip of my Greek coffee and the hurdles that stood before me appeared monumental. However I had to take it easy and believe with full faith that if I gave my best effort good things would come to me, both with my father and my understanding of myself.

As I was dwelling upon all this, some German tourists arrived and Yianina addressed them in their native tongue. She was an impressive lady who spoke five languages and lived in the remote village of Kallikratis. I stared out at the calmness of the magnificent landscape. Two goats resting on the road stared back at me, as if we'd met before.

CHAPTER ELEVEN

It was the middle of September and the weather was beautiful; one large clean cloud had covered the sun and its rays spilled over the perimeter creating a bright lightness in the sky, allowing us to work in comfort.

As we went along the rows of vines, Dad occasionally pointed out the grapes I'd missed but this wasn't enough to anger me. We spoke few words. I felt decent in what I was doing.

He wanted me to be proud of this moment. "You have to appreciate it," he'd say. It was the same thing about the weather. He felt good working next to his son in the vineyard he cherished. My feelings toward this experience had evolved to embrace the work as a necessary ritual. I could remember on a past occasion visiting Greece at this time of year and picking grapes, and I had dreaded it and cursed myself for coming to see Dad during this period. It was different now. I now could accept it for what it was: a ritual with Dad.

I loaded the garden wagon with six crates of grapes. Then Dad and I chased the flock of lambs into the field to eat the leaves. The lambs struck me as unique creatures. I had to wonder what their purpose was. The more courageous ones shot into the field as soon as Dad peeled away the wire fence. The others huddled, terrified, next to each other in a corner, escaping to the next corner when I approached them. I felt a human emotion. Dad didn't see them this way, though, I thought. To him they were nothing but lambs you slaughtered and ate.

Back at the house, we dumped the grapes over a large fishing net that was laid inside a spacious black plastic tub. I slipped on white rubber boots and, under Dad's watchful eye, stomped on the grapes. I stomped and stomped while Dad used a shovel to move the grapes around.

"Bravo. That's how you do it," Dad said.

When I had finished, the juice barely cleared the brim of my toe. Dad turned the spigot in the tub and filled two glasses with grape juice the color of ink. We raised our glasses but we didn't clink them. Dad took a small sip from his glass then he handed it to me.

"Drink it," he said.

"You drink it," I said.

"Too much sugar," he said.

"I don't want it," I said.

Dad tossed what was left in his glass back into the tub.

"Well… we'll make *tsikoudia*."

We wrapped a black fishing net over the top of the container.

"Until next year," he said in a hopeful way.

Then he retired inside and prepared lunch. I rested under the mulberry tree watching the grey spotted kitten chase a butterfly. The tiny yellow butterfly danced about the courtyard while the kitten, adorable in its clumsiness, repeatedly crouched down and sprung, catching air every time. It was almost as if the butterfly was deliberately teasing the kitten. They were playing a game of tag and the butterfly was more graceful. I watched the kitten fail, again and again. But who was to tell the kitten he had no chance? For all he understood, he too had wings. The kitten never gave up and the butterfly continued to show off. I thought the kitten foolish. I knew his quest was hopeless. Every attempt to catch the butterfly was a big whiff. This kept me entertained, though, and it was a good way to pass the time.

There were two other kittens, and they clung to their mama by the outhouse, watching their brother's foolish ways. I thought the butterfly was arrogant now. It was practically dancing on the kitten's head. But this didn't stop the kitten. His attempts at snaring his prey grew more accomplished; once or twice, as he sprung into the air, he reached out his paw and almost tagged the butterfly. I grinned. Arrogance versus perseverance. For me to intervene as if I was God, sending an earthquake to scare off the kitten, felt unnatural. I wondered why the butterfly just didn't leave the courtyard, to play on top of the roof or in the garden or even in the apple orchard; the kittens didn't play out there for it was too open a field for the dogs. The butterfly was unrestricted as to where it could go, yet it continued to dance in the courtyard.

It was a tranquil afternoon. The autumn air was percolating. My mind drifted. I wondered what would become of this village in twenty years. It would sadden me if it became desolate. I imagined rebuilding the village into a utopia for artists. I'd recondition the farm land to allow its inhabitants the pleasure of living off it alone. You would know what you ate and drank because you'd be growing it yourself. An organic label would be blasphemy. I'd develop an honorable infrastructure that would house over a thousand families of artists and farmers. We would construct an exceptional library three stories high with all the worthwhile materials at the inhabitants' disposal. We'd have sessions where philosophy would be taught together with medicine, architecture, poetry, and economics. Evening entertainment would consist of films shown over a grassland with a large screen elevated against a mountain. And if a film didn't do it for you, there would be another venue in which to soak up sublime theater performances. This would all be free, of course. You would be able to stroll along welcoming pathways where artists would gather to share thoughts at cafés and restaurants that'd offer you first class meals at honest prices. Afterwards, you'd proceed toward the grand courtyard where you'd find children frolicking and unassuming mothers relaxing in an aura of security and freedom. Dogs would run up to you and roll on their backs for a belly rub. Everyone would be welcome, from all parts of the world, and while they would all know English, Greek would be the paramount language.

All that would be required to enter this world would be compassion and a willingness to discover enchanting points of view. Opinions would be welcomed. The only doctrine that would be professed would be the idea of the unknown; as a result, all prevailing paradigms would be open to reform by the open-mindedness of its inhabitants. No one would stretch the limits of their ideas in a sinister way, to obtain power or popularity, because deep within an honesty prevailed…

Dad shouted from the kitchen and I snapped out of my reverie of an unrealistic utopia, just in time to see the kitten soar into the air and bat the butterfly to the ground. The butterfly fluttered for a few seconds before it was gone. I became angry with the kitten and chased it straight into the chicken pen.

* * *

Dad sat at a small table next to the stove. He had prepared *horta*, wild greens that he'd picked from the hillsides and boiled until they were soft. I doused mine with olive oil and sprinkled salt over my plate.

"I already added salt," Dad said.

I added more salt. Dad gasped and lowered his head. We ate quietly for a bit, then Dad asked, "Do you like it?"

"It's good."

"What?"

"Yes! It's good."

When I had to repeat myself to him, I wasn't sure if it was because Dad couldn't hear me or whether he didn't understand the English word I used. However it was enough to irritate me, which I knew was ungenerous; I was aware that my behavior could be improved in this regard. I stabbed a piece of goat meat. "The meat is tender," I said.

"It's good meat. Finish it," he said.

Dad filled his glass with more wine. He gulped a mouthful and gasped. He was tired. His arms were still and glistened in the sweetness of the day, with flakes of bush stuck to his forearms.

"Do you want more wine?"

"No."

I pushed my plate away from me, leaned back and rubbed my belly. What little Greek I knew, I liked to speak. "It was very good."

I glanced at the wall tiled with photographs. He had photos of all his kids. There was me in my baseball uniform, another in my football uniform. There was a photo of Toula when she was tiny, holding a shotgun in one hand and a dead rabbit by the hind legs in the other. There was a photo of Dad as a young man in his army uniform, and a good black and white photo of him with his mother and brother. He had photographs of our cousins. There was a photograph of Mom holding up a sweater I'd bought her one Christmas, on which was stitched, "Ohio State Mom." She looked very proud and happy.

There was a picture of his Dad looking very serious and stern. I knew his name was Nikos. I couldn't remember grandmother's name. I almost asked Dad but I was afraid it would start an argument.

Dad peeled an apple after his meal. I watched him turning thoughts over in his mind. We looked like father and son, only I was several inches taller and I didn't have a mustache or gray hair like him. He looked remarkably healthy for seventy.

A good son would've offered to clean the dishes, but I knew Dad liked to do it all himself. Inside his home he had to control everything. It was better this way, as I knew Dad would fuss if I tried to do things differently from the way he knew.

"You shouldn't rush to find an apartment," Dad said. "I'll ask around."

"I want to find one soon."

"I need to go to Chania tomorrow, if you want to look then." Dad grabbed another apple and cut around the brown spots. He handed it to me. "Eat it. It's good."

"I'm not hungry."

"It's an apple."

"It's not food?"

"It's a fruit."

He shook the piece in front of me, showing me what an apple looked like. I grabbed it.

CHAPTER TWELVE

During the drive to Chania, Dad suggested I go to the army first before I signed up for Greek classes and lived in Chania. The situation was complicated. I had been registered as a Greek national after Dad provided the necessary documentation to the authorities. This allowed me to live in the country for longer than the three-month tourist visa granted to Americans. The only hitch was that a spell in the Greek Army was compulsory for all male Greek citizens. This meant I could not leave Greece until I had served in the Greek Army. I had been aware that I would have to join the army when I moved here, but I wanted to improve on my Greek before I enlisted.

"You'll learn Greek better in the army," Dad said.

"I need to learn Greek first. I need to go to school."

"What is the school going to do for you?"

"It'll teach me Greek!"

It was inconceivable to him to think school would be useful for me. Basically he didn't believe that I would be able to learn Greek in a school setting. I could understand why he thought this way as he had never attended school himself.

"It's better for you to have a Greek girlfriend who will teach you," he said.

"You have no idea," I said. "Let's stop talking about it."

Dad dropped me off next to the agora while he went to pay his bills. I walked to the municipal office to inquire again about the Greek school. The free program was cancelled.

"Why?" I asked. "Did we not just re-elect the same prime minister?"

"Check in next year and see if things change."

"Next year?"

"No program exists this year. What can I tell you, sweetie? They have private schools here in Chania if that interests you?"

I knew of a private school near the local courthouses that offered classes. The director and instructor, Angela, was a towering figure of a lady, standing only half a finger length shorter than me. She asked me how much Greek I knew. I told her I was a Greek American who knew a tiny amount. When she learned that my parents were both from Crete, she wondered why I didn't know the language.

"Your parents didn't speak to you in Greek?" she asked.

I shook my head, making the same puzzled face I always did when anyone asked me this question. I explained that my parents had worked all the time. I added that neither of them was educated. All my friends, I said, were American. She remained baffled.

"I don't know what to tell you. I just don't know it. Maybe I'm just stupid."

"My lord! Don't say that…"

"I'm a beginner. I need to start with the alphabet."

"We have a class that starts in two weeks, with a group of students around the same level as you, if that interests you?"

"Yes. That interests me."

I paid her cash on the spot.

"Wait, let me give you a receipt," she said.

All over the old town I noticed signs saying, "APARTMENTS FOR RENT". Accordingly, I thought that finding an apartment would be easy, but when I went to inquire it turned out they were only hotels renting rooms by the day. After several failed attempts, my initial optimism quickly turned to frustration. Suddenly it felt like the whole town was out of my reach. One of the hotel owners told me to check in the local newspaper. I bought a copy from a kiosk and found a trendy café across from the municipal building. Here I encountered my next hurdle. I was familiar with the Greek alphabet, but I could only read a handful of words in Greek at best. To translate a sentence proved exhausting. I made a couple of phone calls, but each time I only got in a few words before the person hung up on me.

Dad arrived at the café while I was gazing at the paper. I explained to Dad that the newspaper, the *Chaniotica Nea*, or "Chania News," listed apartments for rent in the classified section and I needed someone to help me with it. I lay the paper down and sighed.

Dad grabbed the paper and scanned the listings. He read a listing aloud. My eyes widened. He read out another. My jaw dropped. It was as if I had witnessed tomatoes blooming from a garden in real time and, as if that wasn't enough, a rabbit appeared and started juggling them. Dad could read! Sure, it was only the classified section, but he managed it easily. What an oversight on my part, I thought, to have assumed otherwise. He didn't have a single book in his home and I had never before seen him read a newspaper. Now, suddenly, he was like any ordinary person in America who read the morning paper along with their coffee.

What he was actually saying meant nothing to me, as I understood not a single word. And to ask him the meaning in English would only have been foolish.

"Call this number and ask about the apartment," I said. It was a number I had called earlier.

"This is close by," Dad said.

"I know. I googled it."

Dad had no idea what that meant.

The lady told Dad the apartment was available to view tomorrow evening. Hah! He called about a half-dozen more numbers and each apartment was either rented or, strangely, unavailable for viewing until the next day.

"You need help," Dad said. "I'll talk to someone."

"I don't understand how people list apartments for rent yet won't let you see them until tomorrow. What kind of procedure is that?"

"That's how it is…"

"It's only three o'clock in the afternoon!"

"People sleep now. What did you think, you'd find a place right away?"

"Why not? Why are all the shops closed now? Three o'clock is a normal time for a store to be open. I need to add minutes to my SIM card and the Cosmoté shop is closed. That's not how you run a business."

"You're not in America, OK?"

CHAPTER THIRTEEN

I wanted to live at the house in Patsianos rather than in Kallikratis with Dad for two reasons: one, it was next to the sea, and two, I could keep Dad out of my personal space. The house at Patsianos was quiet. It was a one-story cement rectangle with a flat roof. The veranda was the best part. I rested there and noshed on a piece of *graviera* dipped in honey as I watched the white glow from an almost full moon burnish the sea.

At that moment, I wished to have Francesca next to me, burrowed in my arms, saying nothing, because we'd be gazing out toward the sea. We'd breathe in the fresh air. Music would drift faintly from the living room, Van Morrison maybe, or jazz, maybe Billie Holiday. I'd kiss Francesca at precisely the right moment, so she'd never feel alone. Like this, nothing could go wrong. And when the moment was ripe, I'd rest her over the bed and blanket her with my body to keep her warm.

"Where are you?" I texted her.

I could hear music coming distantly from the castle in Frangokastello. They were having a *glendi*, a party, down there. I was alone with my thoughts and ideas. My laptop. Wine and cheese. The sea. The view. I had books to read. I could cook a decent meal. Life was fine, if one was capable of managing isolation and tranquility; however, I wasn't capable of that and so I was restless in Patsianos.

The taste of Chania I'd experienced had unsettled me. The thought of living there was far more alluring than here with its limited human life. Staying here would also leave me helpless, as I'd have to sit around waiting for Dad to direct my life; him moving me this way and that way, like a piece on a chess board. I would sink into despair, I thought, if I continued in this way. On the other hand, I knew that I only had to be patient and things would turn. Even though the apartment search in Chania had stalled, it was only a temporary setback.

I knew instinctively that, until I started learning Greek, I would continue to feel helpless, an outsider in this new world I had entered. And Patsianos felt like another Kallikratis, only beside the sea. I worried I was missing out on life's great joys.

But I also wondered: *What are life's great joys?* I had the sense that I'd experienced most of them and they'd failed to move me or, at best, had amused me for a little while before leaving me feeling empty and unfulfilled. Great plans, successful people, beautiful women, wealth, ambition, love—to me, right now, these things seemed to offer few answers. *Isn't that why I'm here, in Greece?* I suddenly asked myself. It was the million-dollar question.

My best remedy for alleviating my restlessness and taming my fear of missing out was to write. Whether or not what I wrote was any good or sensible didn't matter, although it was better when things worked. Since arriving in Greece I had written a lot. Interestingly, as long as I stuck to keeping notes of places, people, and the things that they said, I felt reasonably calm. When I tried to put it together, and give it some meaning, my burden of thoughts was unloaded and I felt lighter. The practice of writing made me feel something about myself that gave me hope for my life here.

Swimming in the evenings was the best part of my day. I splashed around like a little kid, shoving water all around me and up toward the sky. I'd try and stomp on the little fish swimming around my feet. Some nights I'd have a quiet dinner at a taverna. For under fifteen euros, I'd eat sea bream, *tsipoura* in Greek, with fries and a glass of wine. Or I'd eat *tsigariasto*, lamb slow cooked in wine and olive oil, for ten euros. The people at the taverna always served me a complimentary dessert. Nothing was tastier than *tsigariasto*.

One night, after dinner, I walked to the seashore and stared out at the darkness. A cool wind blew off the water, chilling my bare skin. Behind me I could barely hear the noise from the waterfront bars and tavernas. As I looked out, I strained to grasp what creative powers I could ignite within me to send the right signals to my brain and bring forth new ideas for my writing next day. Yet even watching the illuminating power of the stars, which sparked my imagination, left me without ideas. Times like this, though, I wasn't concerned about my lack of creative genius. I felt that it would come, and I'd be okay.

I felt good when I returned to the house. I was lying in bed in my briefs, clutching my iPhone, and I received a text from Francesca showing a lovely photo of her in a bikini in Thailand with a "kisses" emoji. I smiled with delight. It was the perfect remedy for my loneliness. I messaged her back, "dream dream dream… dream a dream… of meeee. :-)"

Next morning there was no Francesca, only Dad who arrived unexpectedly and shouted at me to get out of bed.

"Wake up!" he said. "Get dressed. You have to go to church."

"Church? Leave me alone."

"Today's the day of the Angel Nikita. Get dressed! We don't have time."

"It's nine o'clock!"

I had developed a daily rhythm of waking up slowly, then making a Greek coffee and relaxing on the veranda before I did anything else.

"Come on, let's go!" Dad shouted. "We're having *parea* today."

"*Parea?*"

We drove to the church in Frangokastello. Dad forgot his wallet at the house so I lent him twenty euros. The church was tiny, built of white-painted cement with an orange tiled roof. Everyone gathered outside to listen to the priest inflame them with messages from the bible. I followed Dad inside to light a candle and kiss the icons. He put the whole twenty euros I gave him into the money box. I had intended to leave a euro but changed my mind.

Back outside we stood underneath a large olive tree. Dad held his *komboloi* in front of him as he acknowledged friends. The people looked weathered, hardened. Poor in material circumstances, they nonetheless impressed with their respectable demeanor. I turned my head up and looked with mouth agape at the colossal mountains. There wasn't a cloud in the sky. I was seeing the same beauty that had existed three thousand years ago and this thought excited a feeling of time travel and, suddenly, my life felt less complicated.

They handed out pieces of *tsoureki*, sweet bread, after the service ended. I took one after Dad insisted. We walked toward three of his friends. They each shook my hand. Each man's hand was thick and rough and hard. Dad excused himself and left me with them to return to the house to prepare an afternoon feast.

One of the men was named Grigorios. They called him "the dentist." He was short and skinny with a moustache and a few strands of black hair on top of his head and he wore thin-rimmed spectacles. He invited me and the other two men to his home, where we waited until it was time to head over to Dad's house.

I sat with them on the porch eating apples and drinking *tsikoudia*. His home stood next to the sea. There was a pleasant breeze. As we sat there I felt tongue-tied and stymied. How I wished I could engage in conversation with these older men and ask them questions about their past. Everything they possessed was precious, yet I didn't possess the tools to excavate the gems. I listened quietly as they conversed amongst each other. But what I imagined them saying was fraught with too much logic to do them justice. We left when Dad called Grigorios and told us to come over.

Dad was still frantically preparing as the *parea* arrived. I set the table. He didn't have enough knives, but it didn't matter. This crowd would be content tearing the meat with their hands, I figured. Grigorios helped him slice the tomatoes. I brought the food outside.

On the table was a village salad, a plate full of boiled goat meat, a plate of smoked pork called *siglino,* a large bowl of wet rice, and bread. Dad grasped a large jug of village wine and filled everyone's glass to the brim.

There were eight of us at a large table under the white umbrellas on the veranda. The Libyan sea glowed in the distance. Yellow jackets swarmed the meat, so Mixalis, the auto-mechanic, lit a pile of Greek coffee grinds on aluminum foil. In the absence of knives, Sifis, the farmer, used his pocket knife to cut the meat before handing it to Grigorios so he could cut his.

Hearty conversation revolved around the table, but, again, I was not part of it. I devoured my food and sat quietly. Every time my glass emptied, someone filled it. Nobody ever sat with an empty plate or an empty glass.

At some point the subject of my apartment-hunting in Chania came up. Yiannis, the engineer, lived in Chania and he offered to help me find an apartment. Mixalis, who's automotive shop was in Chania, mentioned a lady across the street from his shop who was renting an apartment.

"Don't worry, you'll find an apartment," Yiannis said.

"I have an old bicycle to give you so you can move easy around the city," Grigorios said.

I was in the presence of farmers, a car mechanic, a hotel owner, an army major, and a dentist. Dad was the *Americanos.* This was the nickname Greeks gave to all their compatriots who left for America. We feasted effortlessly. In its simple grace, the meal was far beyond the strategic occasions I was accustomed to with people plotting and scheming and ingratiating themselves. Moreover the men's generosity toward me was not to please Dad. They behaved that way because they believed it was the right thing to do.

There were no women present and this made the atmosphere overwhelmingly macho. Especially when Dad suddenly broke out in song. They called it *rizitika*, a style of singing done in western Crete, where one man sings a verse and the group repeats it. Each of them sung in a deep and passionate voice. Their eyes blazed; it was their souls delivering the words. It didn't matter that I only understood a few words. The emotion on each man's face was palpable. I got chills. Everything moved in slow motion. The emotion rose to an almost unbearable level. Each man poured out his own individual struggles through these *rizitika* songs and his dear friends repeated the verses in a show of empathy.

As I listened, my skin tingling, I realized that Dad was teaching me the way he knew best. It was the traditional way upon which mankind had depended for survival ever since a chicken was discovered to taste better cooked over a fire. The experience he had introduced me to in this moment, on the veranda of the little house at Patsianos, lay far beyond anything words or a text book could have ever told me. Dad communicated through moments. He showed me things. To show a man was the Sfakian way. You earned your honor through time and patience.

The atmosphere was grandiose, but it was missing one last Sfakian element; only when Dad pulled out his pistol and fired a round of bullets into the air was the mood complete. I was the only one who flinched. I covered my ears, grimacing.

The energy soared to a new level. A fresh jug of wine was passed around the table. Each man saluted his compatriots with a *koupa* before passing it on to the man beside him. There was something sacred going on here. Individual images intensified in form and color as I settled my eyes upon them, as if God had touched each man individually and made him holy. It felt, quite simply, sublime. I looked at the sea, gleaming in the westering sun, and knew where Elysium lay. I was surrounded by men as I expected them to be—dignified, natural, courageous, full of spirit. Three hours went by and I never once looked at my phone.

CHAPTER FOURTEEN

I met up with Yiannis at Mixalis' auto shop. He was sitting outside with two other men reading the newspaper. I saw he had circled apartments listed for rent in the classified section. He offered me coffee and *tsikoudia*, but I politely declined. He only spoke Greek and I was pleased to realize I understood most of it; having lived in Greece for almost a month now, I had imbibed the language at a faster rate than I had expected.

Mixalis appeared from the garage and greeted me with greasy hands. He told me I could take a look at the apartment across the street if I was interested.

Yiannis and I went to look at the apartment. It was dirty and the furniture was torn. The once white walls were tanned with yellow spots. The tiles on the floor were cracked. The natural lighting was poor. The owner was a plump, middle-aged Greek lady.

"I'll paint the walls and clean it up," she said. "It'll look like a doll."

I tried to imagine how she might improve it in a way that would make it livable. She continued to sell it to me and I believed nothing she said. She offered me the place for only one hundred and fifty euros a month, but she could have offered me it for fifty and I still wouldn't have taken it. Apart from its obvious faults, I did not like that it was far from the old town and across the street from the automotive shop.

We had no luck all morning. There was one more apartment to look at in the evening and it was in Nea Chora, just west of the old town. The apartment was on the second floor of a pink house that was tucked away along an alley. It stood next to the sea and was a five-minute walk to the harbor. The owner's name was Giorgia and she looked in her fifties, with bleached blond hair and a lot of make-up. She led us through the gate into the courtyard where there was a large tree in the middle. At the top of the steps I could see a woman changing in the apartment on the other side of the courtyard. I saw her breasts and I looked away and walked inside.

The apartment was renovated and furnished, with a large veranda that overlooked the sea.

"It's three hundred," Giorgia said.

"Does it include utilities?" I asked.

She puckered her lips and lifted her head, leaning against the wall with her left knee slightly bent, clutching her Louis Vuitton purse. I stared at the word *Love* bedazzled across her black shirt that was tight enough to reveal the low mounds of her slumping breasts.

"With utilities it could cost you another fifty euros," Yiannis whispered.

The place was a bargain if you compared it to L.A. If only it wasn't so feminine, I thought. I asked her if she could lower the price. She puckered her lips and lifted her head again. I realized that this was the gesture for *no*. There was another person looking at the place, as we negotiated. Giorgia made a cringing expression. She looked at me, waiting to see what I'd do. Something felt set up about the situation. I asked her if I could think about it and let her know by tomorrow. She said that would be fine.

When I returned to Patsianos that evening, I was more comfortable about taking the apartment, and I was likely going to tell the woman I wanted the place. In the morning, Francesca had messaged me. "Have you forgotten about me already?" she wrote. She sent it along with photos of herself in her hotel room. Behind her was a great green expanse and a body of water. I messaged her back three smiley-faced emojis.

We confirmed to FaceTime the following morning, but this did not help allay my anguish. To know she was in Thailand and I was here and to wonder when would we hold each other again was deeply unsettling. I sat on the veranda, in bright sunshine, sipping my Greek coffee and feeling maudlin. Life could be fixed well if only she was here now. If I was rich, I could fly her here or fly to her.

I wondered if having an apartment in Chania would help calm me down. Dad was against it. He thought I was rushing into things. I could live here in Patsianos for free, he reminded me, again and again. I knew that he would like me close by to help him out. Yet in the end my urgency to learn Greek made the decision easy.

I called Giorgia. She asked me how long I planned to stay. I told her at least six months, probably a year. I asked her again if she'd lower the rent and she wouldn't budge.

"I can come to Chania tomorrow and sign the contract," I said.

"Let me call you back," she said.

I anguished some more, as I had thought the place was in the bag. I did some writing. I went for a swim in the late afternoon and I read in the evening. My anticipation of the morning was high. I couldn't wait to see Francesca's face. I set my alarm for thirty minutes before my FaceTime call with her.

The moment she saw my face on the screen she said, "You have so much hair?"

"I haven't found a barber."

"It's so puffy."

"I know, it's like a 'fro. How are you?"

"I'm good. How are you?"

I told her about my frustration in finding an apartment. I asked her about Thailand and she gave me quick, automatic responses. We spoke few words, repeating trivialities as we stared at each other's beauty. The internet connection would flutter intermittently and the screen would go black. Behind both of us was a scenic expanse and, as we gazed at each other, we finally realized that our relationship was on its way to an end, that it was easy through a text to say, *I want you naked next to me*, but now, as her face glowed in my screen, I could say nothing that would alleviate the unbridgeable distance that separated us at this moment.

"I miss you," I said.

"I miss you, too," she said back to me.

"You're so pretty, have you just been bathing in milk the entire trip?"

"Nooooo…"

She perked up and showed her delightful smile and her only dimple made me soft. We promised to FaceTime again later in the week.

In the afternoon, I went to Chora Sfakion. I found a spot along the harbor where I could write and ordered a fruit smoothie. The weather was abnormally hot for late September. The sun was electrifying the sea and even under the shade I felt uncomfortably hot and sweaty. I tried to write, but my mind kept wandering. Chora Sfakion consisted of little except half a dozen tavernas and a couple of cafés that were best enjoyed with someone next to you whom you adored. Five minutes passed, then an hour. I returned home. I wrote some more. I paused after finishing my first sentence, staring out with a glazed look at the garden. The peppers looked ready to turn over. Two hours passed. I deleted what I'd written.

It doesn't matter, I realized, where you are; you can't write well if you're not in control of your inner emotions. The day dissolved and nothing was complete.

I spent a restless night. I persisted in conjuring up feelings that created anxiety. As a result, sleeping proved difficult. I tried to watch Greek TV, but the language sounded like one oscillating noise. Eventually, I was so inundated with worry that I tired myself out.

Next morning, I left for Kallikratis. When I arrived, Spirto charged toward me and rolled onto her back. I stepped around her and she slid in front of me again. She wiggled, whimpering, on her back. I almost stepped on her the third time. Dad was relaxing on a plastic chair in the courtyard. He was very happy to see me come to Kallikratis of my own accord. He was having *tsikoudia* with apples with two Albanian electricians who had just fixed the power line connected to the wooden pole next to the outhouse.

"They're good apples, you just need to cut around the bad parts," Dad said to the Albanians. "What happened with the apartment?"

"She didn't call me back," I said.

"Don't worry. You'll find one."

"Do you know any apartments available in Chania?" Dad asked the Albanians.

"Not now. For the winter, yes. You can find a furnished studio for two hundred."

"I need an apartment now because I start class next week," I said.

"You can live here and go to school in Rethymno," said Dad.

I sat down next to them.

"It was a good apartment, too."

"It was expensive. You'll find something cheaper," Dad said.

"How much was it?" asked the Albanian.

"Three hundred."

His eyes widened.

"Are you in love with the apartment or the lady?"

"What do you mean?"

"Did she have blond hair?"

"Yes."

"Did she tell you that you're a good kid."

"No."

The Albanians left and I rested in the courtyard and watched the mutt catch flies that hovered around his face. I was still downtrodden. I watched Dad move about the courtyard. He swept up the leaves. Organized and arranged tools.

"Panagiotis, come here."

"What?"

"Bring the corn here."

I helped him pour the bags of corn and seeds into a rusted barrel, then he told me to carry the water jugs inside the house. Then I went back to sit down.

"Come here—Panagiotis," Dad shouted. I went to Dad. "Grab here," he said.

We lifted up an empty water tank and moved it to the side of the house. Just then, my phone went off. It was Giorgia.

"You're a good kid," she said. "I will give you the apartment. There were others, but my husband wanted me to give it to a Cretan. When can you come to pay the rent?"

"Tomorrow?" I said.

"*Malista*," she said. Certainly. "And when are you going to move in?"

"I'll pay and move in tomorrow. Is that okay?"

"*Malista*."

CHAPTER FIFTEEN

Dad didn't agree with my snap decision, but I didn't care. Getting to Chania was my only consideration.

The drive was fairly quiet, except for the few times we argued because Dad disagreed with observations I made. When I said Greece was living backwards, he retorted with, "Your brain is backwards." Then we were quiet until I said, "Ohio is a terrible place to live," and Dad replied, "What do you know, you lived in New York City with the trash—the *vroma!*" So it went on, all the way over the mountains to the verdant north coast, the gentle slopes softened by billowing groves of olive trees as they dropped down to the white concrete sprawl of Chania.

People were taking their naps when we arrived and the roads were quiet. Dad, abruptly, pulled off the main road and stopped at a supermarket. I gasped. He sat there.

"Get what you need," he said.

My first thought was condoms and sparkling water. Instead, I grabbed some Dove soap bars and candles. Dad had in the cart two containers of bleach, paper towels, two packages *tsipoura*, a bag of green beans, a pot for boiling things in, and a dozen eggs. With my luggage, the only space left in the car for the bags was on my lap.

Giorgia was waiting for us when we arrived. She was dolled up like the last time. Dad perused the apartment as if this was still an unfinished deal. He opened the cabinets to see them filled with plates.

He looked inside the stove. He tilted his head and tightened his jaw and nodded his head.

"This is a clean apartment," he told her.

"Of course! I lived here. I renovated the entire kitchen for myself. Otherwise, I wouldn't have done it."

"Outside the house needs to be painted." Dad addressed her as if he was negotiating.

"Yes… it needs to be painted."

Dad looked at me and said, "You will take care of it," as he pulled out his wallet. "I will pay the first month's rent."

He laid three hundred euros on the table. I handed Giorgia another three hundred euros for the security deposit. Then I signed the contract.

"You're a good kid. We had kids from Athens but my husband said to give it to you because you were Cretan."

"Where do you live?" Dad asked her.

"Akrotiri."

"And you're Cretan?"

"My husband is Cretan. I'm from Rentina."

"Rentina?"

"Close to Thessaloniki."

"I know Rentina," Dad said. "I was in the army there for six months." I watched as something seemed to come over him. "Ahh, you're from Rentina…" he continued. "First I was in the Megalo Pefko in Athens for six months and then I went there. We hiked up the mountains through snow that was knee-high in Thessaloniki." He reminisced with his head tilted down. "Twenty-four months I was in the army. I left home when I was twenty-one years old. Afterwards I went to America."

"What work did you do in America?"

"I worked in factories there for fifteen years and then I had a restaurant."

"Your parents stayed here in Greece?"

"It was only my mother. I didn't know my father. He died when I was a baby." He paused. "He had pneumonia during the war. I had a brother who died when he was twelve from a burst appendix."

We stood quietly. I had nothing to add that could encourage the situation. Giorgia looked too overwhelmed to react. It got quieter. I could hear the shrill from a pair of cats scuffling outside.

"Here are the keys. On the first floor lives my niece. If you need anything you can ask her, too."

"Okay. Thank you," I said.

I moved my clothes into the bedroom. Dad commandeered the kitchen area. He supplied me with the essential products of Kallikratis: pieces of frozen goat and rabbit meat; an entire cleaned rabbit, including the head, stuffed into a ziplock bag; a large plastic jug filled with olive oil; a bag of oregano; and, finally, *tsikoudia* and village wine in two-liter plastic Coca-Cola bottles.

Everything was local, fresh, and organic. As I watched him stash it away, it occurred to me that if he'd done something like this back in the States when I was in college my roommates would have teased me mercilessly and I would have hated him for it.

He pulled an assortment of spice shakers from a plastic grocery bag and arranged them on a shelf. I crumpled up the plastic bag and tossed it in the trash bin.

"Don't throw the bag away," Dad said. "Put the trash in there."

"It's a plastic bag. There's more…"

Dad retrieved the plastic bag from the trash bin. Then I watched him put a large piece of vacuum-sealed *graviera* cheese into the refrigerator. He removed all the dishes from the cabinet and began to wash them. At my age and with my experience, this moment with Dad helping me evoked a different set of feelings that could not compare to the feelings I'd have had if this had happened in a much earlier period in my life. Now, I realized Dad cared for me a great deal.

"Why don't you just put them all in the dishwasher?" I said.

He paused for a second and then, without responding, put them in the dishwasher.

"I'm going to buy sheets," I told him.

"What are you talking about? I gave you sheets."

"They're too small. And you can take the blanket. I don't want it."

"What are you talking about, you'll freeze here at night." Dad went to bedroom; he grabbed the blanket. "This blanket is brand new."

"No, it's not. It's old."

"Your brain is…" He grabbed the sheets.

"The sheets are too small—I'm telling you."

"You don't know how to do it."

"This is a queen bed."

"Pull—"

"They're too small, can't you see."

"Pull! God damn it!"

"You're old and you've lost your mind."

The sheet covered half the mattress.

"I told you!"

"I'm sorry," Dad said. "I grabbed the wrong sheets."

"I'm going to buy some sheets."

"The sheets are expensive here."

"Well, I need sheets."

"I have sheets in Kallikratis. What do you say, you can sleep in Kallikratis tonight, then you can take the car back here tomorrow."

"For sure, no way!"

He opened his hand and pushed his arm down. "Do whatever you want."

Dad returned to the kitchen. I followed him.

"You don't have to stay here and help," I said. "I can organize the stuff myself."

"This meat… keep it in the freezer. When you want to eat meat, put a couple pieces in the container the day before and leave the rest in the freezer, because it will spoil if you leave it in the refrigerator the entire time."

"Okay."

"Tomorrow, you can take the bus to Episkopi and I'll give you sheets. It's not necessary to spend money on sheets here. I have a lot of sheets at home."

He had a sullen look.

"Okay. We'll see."

My bedroom window was open. A slight breeze from the sea carried through and the red ornate curtains waved from the hanger. I poked my head out the window and watched Dad drive off. The sun shone over me softly. The atmosphere was serene, the sea effulgent. Below, two old ladies rested outside their home doing nothing except devour time.

At bedtime, I fell asleep to the sound of waves crashing off the rocks. The bed was comfy. I felt rich in solitude.

CHAPTER SIXTEEN

On my first day of class, I wore my caraway-colored pants with my favorite autumn sport coat. The instructor had told me the other students were all girls from various parts of Europe. I hoped they'd all be pretty and single and attracted to me, even though experience had taught me it never worked out that way. The boy meets perfect girl only happened in the movies, at least where I was concerned.

As it was, I walked into a lovely green courtyard, with a waterless fountain, and at the bottom of the steps leading up to the school met a pregnant lady. The building was in the neoclassical style, the sort of place that invariably housed some dignitary during those times when Crete was occupied by Ottomans and Nazis. I approached the woman and held out my hand.

"Panagiotis." I said, speaking as if I was in command of the language.

"Lila," the woman replied. She spoke softly, in proportion to her tiny frame.

"Where are you from?" I continued in Greek.

"I'm from Poland," she said in Greek.

"Where?"

"Poland," she said it in English this time.

We spoke in slow-paced intervals using a mixture of Greek and English. The conversation proved difficult and we soon stopped talking and greeted two other students who arrived: Karina from Romania and Hanna, another Polish girl.

Karina was mysterious with cat-like eyes and she had thick brown hair that extended past her shoulders. From the start she dominated the conversation, obviously keen to show us how good her Greek was. But I had eyes for Hanna. She was a lengthy figure, quiet and calm, with a natural, innocent face and short, blond, wavy hair.

The room was small and intimate. Angela commanded the end of the table next to the whiteboard. To kick off the first class, she handed each of us copies of the Greek alphabet.

"Who would like to say the alphabet?" she asked.

Karina quickly uttered it. Everyone in the class knew the alphabet. We started with simple words. We learned the vowels and the five different types of e variations: ι, οι, υ, ει, η. Throughout the lesson, I wanted Karina to shut up so watching Hanna in flashes would look less obvious. Hanna and Lila were quiet and they sat next to each other on one side of the table. On the wall facing me was a large framed map of Greece which I pretended to watch with interest as I peeked at Hanna.

Halfway through the class I thought to slide Hanna a note saying I liked her emerald earrings. Yet it was only the first day and maybe that would be too presumptuous. She could be married and then we'd be forced to endure ten more weeks of class together. I did not see a ring, though. All I knew was that she was from Poland and for the last two years had worked as a bartender at a hotel in Kissamos. This I had learned during our brief conversation outside.

I considered a more ambiguous way of showing an interest, one that left the door open for another interpretation if she did happen to be married or just wasn't interested in me. The traditional elementary school idea popped into my head. I could tell Lila that I liked Hanna and ask her to mention it to her and, if possible, gauge her reaction. A terrible idea, I thought. The note was better. Although it required a soft touch. Umm. I would have to utilize Lila in some way. She could act as a conduit, because she was married to a Greek man.

I walked back home alone after class feeling like I was twelve again. We had lessons to complete for the next class. The experience of learning to read and write again piqued my curiosity and helped settle my loneliness. I slept well that night.

* * *

My classes were only twice a week for two hours each time. I felt this was inadequate if I was going to learn Greek quickly. Mastering the complexity of the language was going to require significant time outside the classroom so I devoted a couple of hours each day to reading, writing, and speaking.

In the mornings, after a light breakfast, I'd be on my veranda with a Greek coffee and a children's book of Greek myths. The intricate tales of a long-ago and perhaps imaginary world enlivened my spirit. The story of Odysseus and his ingenuity in rescuing Eleni prompted me to ask myself if I could ever be that type of man. And reading about Poseidon while staring out at the electrifying sea made me realize how natural it must have been, for people of a different time, to imagine this type of god.

The Greek text cleared the vague and cloudy images that the English language created. The language was thrillingly specific. Each word meant exactly one thing. I only appeared foolish when I tried to use an English word equivalently. Take the definition of "painter". In English, this had variations, so that while in a place like Berkeley, California, mention of the word would cause folk to smile and rest closely by you with intrigue—maybe even offer to buy a piece—in Youngstown, Ohio, they'd ask, "How much to paint my kitchen walls?" In the Greek language, the guy who painted your kitchen walls was completely separate from the genius who dazzled on a canvas. The intense nature of the vocabulary provided me with much-needed moisture for the cracks left hardened and empty in the drought-ravaged passageways of my mind. The Greek vocabulary overwhelmed me in such a way that I needed a spigot to keep me from drowning in it.

The motion of Greek letters when handwritten and spoken demanded an acrobatic performance as each multi-syllable word required you to dot a vowel to stick the meaning. The verb to "use" in Greek is a five-syllable word, χρισημοποιώ. If you didn't add extra emphasis to the vowel with the tone mark above it you sounded silly. When said properly it elucidated a feeling of grace. The word "bus" was an important one for me. It was a five-syllable word, λεωφορείο.

When I wasn't immersed in Greek, usually I'd spend the afternoons at a café, contemplating existential stuff both abstractly and concretely and working on a screenplay. The old town was full of cafés. Walking through it soothed my soul. They were jaunts, precisely, lacking any real destination. The mom-and-pop shops and the general stores gave you the impression of life as it was many years ago. There were no cars because the cobbled lanes were too narrow. Stray dogs and cats roamed freely. Gypsies stood on corners shaking cups for coins. It was the tail-end of the tourist season so the harbor was lively, but not crowded. I always spoke Greek when I interacted with the locals. The Greeks liked to speak back to me in English, but I continued, undaunted, in Greek. The restauranteurs who solicited tourists would address me in English and I'd say, "Hello, good evening," in Greek.

Some evenings, I'd go to the movie theater. It played all the newly released American films with Greek subtitles. Autumn was my favorite time of year to see movies because it was when films that had Oscar potential were released.

Some mornings, I didn't have the energy to make breakfast, so I'd stop by one of the bakeries and have a croissant. The smells from the bakeries set me easy. I'd slow my walk and linger for a couple of seconds by each bakery and inhale the aroma of fresh-baked bread. Some of the bakeries employed pretty girls and I'd ponder a serendipitous occasion that would bring us together.

I had lived in my apartment for a couple weeks now. I hadn't spoken to Dad. Mom had called me almost every day since I'd arrived in Greece. We had substantially trivial conversations. Sometimes I'd share my frustrations about Dad with her and I learned more about her frustrations with him as well.

"He thinks the world is Kallikratis. He can't see anyone else's point of view," I'd say.

"Now you see what I had to deal with. It's everyone else's fault," she'd vent to me. "Stay in Chania! Don't go to Sfakia!"

"Relax, Mom—you don't need to yell."

"I'm not yelling, I'm just telling you."

Her big concern was my decision to join the army. I was having trouble gathering the necessary documents. I had lived all across the US and the Greek consulates in the US needed me to file a heavy dose of documents to each consulate, one each in New York City, Chicago, and Los Angeles. The fact that I couldn't handle the process with one consulate was a testament, I thought, to Greek inefficiency. The mere thought of paperwork enervated me. Moreover, I was so consumed with learning Greek for half the day, then writing a screenplay in the other half, that in the evenings I just needed to unwind.

I didn't have any friends in Chania, but that changed when I received a follow-up email from a fling I'd had here several years ago. I had approached the girl on the bus. Her name was Viktoria. She lived in Holland, but she was Hungarian. She had sent me an email this summer in which she'd said she would be coming to Crete in October for a little work and a lot of vacation.

"I will be there in October, too!" I had written.

"I would love to see you. It will be fun!" she had written back.

The tone of her email suggested she wanted to rekindle the romance we'd had. At the time, I'd been obsessed with Francesca so the idea of a relationship with another woman could not exist. Even when she'd emailed me a second time I hadn't responded. Now, though, I hadn't spoken to Francesca since our disappointing FaceTime chat and, since starting Greek classes, she had slowly faded from my memory. For some time I had thought about Hanna, but then I gave up on her after learning from Lila one night that she lived with her Greek boyfriend.

Viktoria wrote me again: "You probably didn't come to Greece at the end as you wrote me earlier, right…?! I guess you have your reasons for that and I was probably naive to think that you would be still interested to see me after such a long time… Never mind… I hope that life treats you well and you enjoy the journey to your 'Ithaca.' Perhaps our paths will cross someday."

I wrote back, apologizing, and insisted we see each other when she arrived. We arranged to meet at the same place where we had our first meeting, Alcanea, a corner hotel with a café outside where you could enjoy a view of the harbor. We set a nine o'clock rendezvous. My beer was half empty before the rain forced me inside. By then Viktoria still hadn't arrived. It was inconceivable to think she would have stood me up. Anxiously, as I grabbed my glass, I spilled a gulp of beer onto my lap. Sitting inside, uneasily fidgeting, I watched the entrance closely as the rain splashed the threshold.

It wasn't till thirty minutes later, when I was on my second beer, that she wandered through the door with a carefree smile. She embraced me warmly. We sat down and before either of us said a word we stared at each other to be sure this was real. She was wearing a skirt and tank top. A different look than what I remembered. She was thinner, too. I waved down the waiter.

"How long has it been," I said.

"Paris was three years ago in September."

She looked straight into my eyes, forcing me to turn away.

"You're a half hour late," I said. "What if I'd left?"

"I didn't want to rush. I'm on vacation," she said.

I gave her a brief update on my life. She appeared joyful, happy, passionate about her job as an environmentalist. When the rain had subsided, we walked along the harbor. She gushed about Crete. "It's such a magical place!" she said. "Precious!"

The way the words rolled off her tongue, in her Hungarian accent, sounded naughty and I couldn't help from chuckling. How would the night end? Would I sleep with her? I knew it was virtually guaranteed. Sex—if I wanted it—was more guaranteed than a US treasury bond.

We stumbled upon a bohemian-type bar just off the harbor. We ordered a carafe of *tsikoudia* made from blueberries. As our conversation evolved and we became more comfortable, I was able to see through Viktoria the type of person I had been three years ago. It struck me vividly how my finance-self had billowed out from me during our first encounter. Back then, my urges had been lustful, hedonistic, almost instinctively raw, as well as insensitive and impatient. Now, I was no longer seeing her with the urgency of sexual desire.

"You moved to Greece to live your dream," she said.

I sipped the *tsikoudia* in deep thought, wondering what she meant. Right then, I believed that people change. How wrong I was as a nonbeliever. People change for the better if they have allowed themselves to journey honestly through a multitude of experiences involving the likes of travel, literature, trades, and languages. Otherwise change or, more specifically, perspective, from a younger self to an older, wiser, better self remains stultified. Certainly, I was at the bottom left on the spectrum of change, but the seed of it, I sensed, had just cracked within me.

Viktoria was a strong woman. In ancient times, she would have been the wife of a king. She was too tough for me now. Her words opened my pores. And while my ego still dominated me, I could see how much Viktoria was concerned only for herself. She had a pathos of dated beliefs cemented in her mind. She was a descendent of Hungarian aristocracy. She had been brought up to expect a higher and more certain range of accommodations and luxuries than the common man. I, by contrast, was feeling ever more common and it wasn't such a bad thing, for like this I could relate to more people.

We were drinking strong. We'd each taken back four shots of *tsikoudia* when Viktoria invited a bald bohemian dude sitting at the next table to have a shot with us. His name was George and he was a musician. Viktoria was thrilled. He only had eyes for her.

"What do you play?" she asked.

"The guitar," he said. "I teach at the music school here."

"Can you teach me?" Viktoria straightened in her chair. "Come sit down at our table."

We all took another shot together. "Are you visiting?" he asked her. Then he turned to me. I told him I lived here. "What do you do here?"

"I'm going to school to learn Greek. I'm a writer, too."

"What do you write?"

"Screenplays."

"I'd like to read some of your stuff," he said.

"Screenplays are boring to read. I'm not a *writer* writer, I guess."

He invited us to join him and his friend inside. Before I could say a word, Viktoria accepted his invitation. We sat at a round table. Viktoria was between George and me. George ordered another carafe of *tsikoudia*. His friend Kostas had an untamable beard.

George spoke often and kept Viktoria engaged. She listened avidly as he expressed flowery ideas about love and music and said how, when he plays, his affection for his audience brings him to tears after every performance. "I have a savage pathos for my audience," he said.

He commented on the clarity of her green eyes. Viktoria was smitten with him. We finished the carafe and I hinted to Viktoria that we leave. George insisted we stay and ordered another carafe. His arm grasped the back of her chair, almost touching her back. As the night continued, everyone except me was building energy. Viktoria tilted her head back and grinned when George talked more about love. The conversations were in English, but I wasn't following them. It was past three in the morning and I was fading. George had smoothly executed his plan to extract Viktoria from me. He was only twenty-seven years old. And he exuded a presumptuous aura because he was a musician and thus could get any woman he wanted. I admit that from the way Viktoria and I acted even a blind man could see we weren't a couple, but that did not matter to me.

"Love is all you need," George said.

I turned my head away and furrowed my eyebrows, embarrassed to be part of this conversation. George was an obvious fraud talking about love to Viktoria, who swooned for him. *How simple it was*, I thought, *to win a woman over by laying a melody around the word "love"*. I reclined deeper into my seat and observed.

It was a perfect time to excuse myself. I could leave Viktoria with them. I thought about it but I decided I didn't want George to have her. I wanted him to know that he could entertain her to his heart's delight, but that it was gonna be my cock in her at the end of the night. She was going to be squeezing my body tightly against hers, gasping.

After the second carafe emptied, I demanded we leave and waved down the waiter. The bill came and a curtain closed over George and Kostas. I handed him the bill.

"You can pay for the other half," I said.

I grabbed Viktoria by the hand and we passed through the entrance and when we were outside she said, "They were so much fun!"

I continued to hold her hand as we passed down the brick-laid slope. The old town was deserted. We didn't say a word. I thought how terrible a person you'd have to be to want to work all night to try and take someone's girl. Even if the woman virtually gave herself to you. There's got to be a man code, a mutual understanding that you don't try anything funky with another man's girl. And if a woman did want to abandon her man for you, was that the type of woman you really wanted?

Viktoria led me to her hotel that was tucked away in a small alley in the Jewish quarter. We paused at the entrance, beneath a pair of lamps attached to the wall, before I followed her inside. Her room was on the second floor. The bed had a thin white net wrapped around it to keep the mosquitoes out; it was as if she was a black widow who had lured me to her nest. Somehow, the moment felt wrong. However, it was impossible for me to leave now.

"I'm claustrophobic," I said.

"It's romantic!"

Viktoria removed the tacky net. I lay on the bed and she removed my shoes and socks. She told me not to do anything. Then she removed my pants and in her naughty Hungarian accent, rolling her r's and extending the vowels, she said, "Just relaaax... Looove... Just relaaax... This is gooud... yeees."

I helped her pull off her shirt. I unstrapped her bra and grabbed her tiny breasts. She rolled her lips down my chest, stopping to press her tongue to my belly. I chuckled and fidgeted. She continued kissing me on and around my belly, down to my waist, until I grabbed her firmly by the hair and put her mouth where it was non-negotiable.

She insisted on shoving her long tongue in my mouth, when I wanted gentle kisses on the lips. She liked weird, contorted positions whereas I just wanted her missionary or on top so we'd be holding each other as we made love.

Our last sexual encounter in Paris had worked because we had fucked like dogs. I had a twenty-four-hour layover. She was only a train ride away. When we had met at a hotel, we were faster to tear off each other's clothes than to switch off the lights.

We'd been going for over forty-five minutes now. The bed sheet was moist. She pleaded for me to climax. I closed my eyes and imagined someone else.

I had no sooner finished than I was swamped by thoughts of Francesca. Suddenly I felt deeply, inexplicably, guilty and unfaithful for what I had just done. The hormones that had kept me remotely attached to Viktoria had vanished. Now I longed only to disappear from her sight.

"Lie next to me," she said.

I handed her a towel to clean up, but she wouldn't take it.

"I'm European," she said.

I clenched my jaw and dropped my head before *I* wiped down her body. I envisioned her pregnant. She'd have my baby and we'd be forever linked. I splashed water on my face.

"Come to bed," she said.

"I'm so sorry to do this. But I have to go," I said. "You have every right to hate me."

"What's wrong?" she said. "Come let me love you?"

I twitched my head from left to right. "This was a mistake."

"What is it?" she asked, imploringly.

"There's someone else... I've been seeing someone else in America."

I struggled to release the words from my mouth. She lay naked on the bed and I stood leaning against the wall in my briefs.

"What did you expect. We haven't seen each other in... in three years!" My tone rose.

"I don't want anything," she said, coldly.

"I need to go home and sleep in my own bed. Please understand that."

"I don't care... if you love somebody else... fine. Just don't leave me like this. Just stay the night and hold me. Then we never have to see each other again."

She spoke desperately, unraveling before my eyes, while I stood atop the throne.

"I may kill myself!" I snapped back, then I slowly disappeared out the door.

CHAPTER SEVENTEEN

I apologized to Viktoria via text, intending never to see her again. However, a few days after the incident, she invited me out for drinks with some new friends she had met and the idea sounded good. Or perhaps the thought of declining only made me feel more guilty.

They were at a bar called Fagotto, which lay in an alley close to the harbor. I arrived to find them gathered at an outside table against a rough stone wall. Viktoria was accompanied by three men: a German, an English, and a Swiss. They were halfway through their second round of drinks. I asked the waitress to bring me a Mythos.

This crowd, I soon discovered, travelled frequently. All, with exception of Viktoria, had hiked the nature scene in the US. The Englishman had hiked Kilimanjaro and K5. He spent six months of the year traveling and the other six months in New York City where he lived in Williamsburg. He was an older man in his fifties with a thick appearance and scant hair on his head. His name was Matthew. He was the rich one in the group, but nobody except myself probably thought that way. They all seemed very pleased with their trip and I asked them if they would visit Crete again. They nodded unanimously with conviction.

Henkel, the German, was forty-seven-years-old. He had visited forty-five states in the US and had hiked from Mexico to Canada. He talked his head off. He shared random stories and made funny remarks. He was a nurse who spent his holidays traveling to different parts of the world, always without a cellphone.

The Swiss had long blond hair and didn't say much, and so I thought maybe his English was bad, but after I listened to him make a salient comment on nutrition, I realized he was just the quiet type.

More drinks arrived. Viktoria was drinking mojitos. She was in her laughing mood again, enjoying Henkel's witty remarks. She liked humor, especially the kind directed at one's own stupidity or physical limitations. She was sitting close to me as if we were a couple. "How precious," she said, after a black and white spotted mutt approached us and rested right next to her. She stroked him with the palm of her hand, saying how precious he was. The dog moved closer and laid over her foot as we continued the conversation.

Matthew had a PhD in mathematics. He was writing a book proving mental illness through mathematical equations. He had begun to explain a theorem to us but before we were punished the gods intervened sending rain. The dog scurried away. We went inside and gathered around a wooden table with wooden chairs. Our server arrived with shots of *mastika*. The minty taste of the drink cleaned out my insides, restoring my spirit much as the stories shared by the backpackers lifted my mood.

Henkel had lived in a cave for four weeks in a place called La Corvera. Fifty euros a week was all he needed, he said, to make the occasional trip to town and gather the necessary provisions. We all concentrated on him as he told a story about the wild berries of La Corvera. A Buddhist monk advised him to stay away from them because they were hallucinogenic.

"He told me, with calmness and prudence, as if he had arrived at this moment with perfect understanding, 'This is something you can take once every seventy years.' Then after I'd left him, I climbed down a slab of rock to the cave and the first thing I saw was a blond, naked French girl shoveling a handful of berries into her mouth. There were very few sane people there. The monk was one of the few."

Henkel's animated expression, with his German accent and thin-rimmed spectacles, sent us into a roar.

"People came and went. Many traveled to live there during the winter because the weather behaves warmly to the humans," he said.

It was well past three in the morning when we left Fagotto. The rain had stopped. Henkel and Matthew were staying at hotels by the harbor, so we left them and walked with the Swiss toward his car.

As we were leaving the old town, Viktoria spotted the black and white dog. It was resting in front of a restaurant, under a table tucked away beneath the awning. As soon as she spoke, the dog approached her and she embraced him. The Swiss and I smiled.

"We can't leave the dog here, he's so precious," she pleaded, looking at me. "Do you have any food at your apartment?"

"I have leftover chicken."

"Can he have it?"

"I can't have a dog at my place."

"He's just hungry."

The dog followed us until we reached the parking lot. He wavered behind as we moved further and further away. Viktoria snapped her fingers to draw him on. He wouldn't budge, so she grabbed him and cradled him in her arms. We said goodbye to the Swiss.

"Lucky," he said.

"It's not what you think," I said, glancing at Viktoria.

"You should name him Lucky—the dog," he said.

"Ohh, yes!" I said. "That's an apt name for him at this moment."

Viktoria held the dog in her lap on my steps. When I dropped the chicken on the ground Lucky devoured it.

"Can you give him some water?" She caressed his head as he rested his chin over her knee. I placed a bowl of water next to him. "Look, he's so hungry and thirsty," she said.

"I'm not supposed to have a dog here."

"Can't you leave him outside?"

"What am I going to do with a dog?"

"He's so precious." From the way she spoke, I felt like I was negotiating with a little girl over a pack of skittles. "Do you have an old towel, that he could sleep on?"

I found a pink towel in a trash bag that the owner had stored under my bed. Viktoria set up a space under the awning just outside my front door. Lucky was attached to her, resting next to her. I was impressed by how she had been able to lure him so quickly. Then she looked at me and I stared back at her. She stood up. Lucky rested on the towel.

"I'm going to go now," she said faintly.

"No, you're not!" I told her. Then I hugged her, and we walked into my apartment. I had to block Lucky from getting inside. He raised his paws onto the glass door and pouted.

"He just wants love," she said.

"Leave him alone," I said.

We lay on my bed. Lucky was quiet now. Then my pants were off. Viktoria didn't want me to move, so I watched her. I found it relaxing. My mind was empty. There was nothing but the sensation and the sight of Viktoria performing, with great effort, a good job. I fell asleep shortly afterwards.

I woke up early in the morning when Viktoria rushed from the bedroom and went after Lucky who was barking. The sudden commotion made it difficult for me to fall back to sleep. I slipped on my khaki shorts and walked outside. Viktoria was holding Lucky. She was feeding him cookies she had found in my cabinet.

"Biscuits?" I said.

"He's hungry."

"Dogs eat meat."

"Your neighbor tried to hit him with a broom."

"She's the niece of the owner! And she's probably going to tell her now!"

"He's so precious," Viktoria said. "Do you have any more chicken?"

"I have chlorine under my sink."

"You're going to take care of him, right?" she implored.

I went into the kitchen, but there was no more food for him. The sun shone powerfully through the window. I stopped and glanced toward the sea. The day was glorious. The sky and the sea were the same color. It was a stratospheric blue that overwhelmed my eyes.

"I'll go to the pet store and buy him food," I said.

"Thank you."

"It's a beautiful day today," I told her in Greek.

Viktoria stared out at the sea and repeated in Greek, "It's a beautiful day today."

She smiled, tender and gentle with her stately frame. She wanted to step forward and kiss me, but she was too timid. What a huge difference a few days make. She could see I was tormented and restless. She was a far better person than I was, I thought, to want to see me again after what I'd done on our first night. She was returning to Holland the following day, and to ask her if she wanted to spend one more night together was a risk I didn't want to take.

"What a beautiful day it is today!" I said, looking out to the sea again.

"You can have it all, it depends what you pay attention to," she responded.

"That was beautiful." I gazed at her.

"What?" she asked, lost in thought.

"You said it perfectly."

"What did I say?"

"See you're a poet and you don't even know it."

"I have to go," she said. "I'll leave it up to you to decide what you do with Lucky."

And before this moment could be ruined, she was gone.

CHAPTER EIGHTEEN

Lucky sprinted up the steps as soon as I appeared. He followed me down the steps and tried to force his way outside my courtyard, but I only opened the gate just enough to squeeze through myself. Lucky barked at me. "Wait, I'll be back," I told him in Greek. He ululated when I turned away from him.

It was a lovely autumn day. The town was humming with movement. *What the hell am I doing right now?* I thought. A dog with Viktoria around sounded like a swell idea. But now she was gone it felt terrible. The pressure of responsibility was asphyxiating. If I domesticate him, Lucky will depend on me. *Gosh!* I thought, *I've never had anybody in my life ever depend on me.* The right thing would be for me to at least buy him a dinner. Yes. I'll buy him a bag of doggy food with treats and then he can be on his way.

The clerk ended up convincing me to buy a dog bowl, a pill for worms, and a leash. *What a waste of money*, I thought on my way back. *I can't even have a dog at my apartment! And what makes me even think this is what Lucky wants? How rude for Viktoria to force this dog into my life. Even if I was lonely, it wasn't a dog I needed.*

Lucky was resting on the towel when I returned; he looked awfully bored. I filled his bowl with dog food. I hid the worm pill in a soft piece of dog bacon, then I went inside to study Greek.

I read an interesting text about the Greek landscape and its inhabitants. I learned that Greeks are known for their *philotimo*.

Philotimo? Google translate said it meant "honor". There was another Greek word that I knew meant honor. It confused me.

I went to check on Lucky. He had eaten all the food and looked the same. I took him to a viewing area of the sea near my apartment. I couldn't figure out how to tighten the leash, so he followed me. When he strayed I shouted his name and he caught up. I settled on a bench. I watched him take a sizable shit. I had nothing with me to pick it up, so I left it there. An older gentleman who was cleaning the area saw it happen, so I told him, "He's not my dog." Lucky was trying to sniff the butthole of a domesticated dog at that moment, but the owner kept yanking her dog away from him. He followed me on his own accord back to my apartment.

I wrote nothing all day. Lucky stressed me out. The Greek grammar exercises had fatigued my mind. That night, I watched a movie and contemplated. I was tired from the little sleep the night before and I fell asleep early.

Lucky's food bowl was empty in the morning. I filled it up. I gave him a fresh bowl of water. He must have been very bored all night in my courtyard, I thought. I was fortunate there wasn't a problem with my neighbor. He was unhappy when I left him to go to the harbor to eat something. He barked at me longer than the last time. I planned to take him for a walk when I returned.

I took a particular interest in all the stray dogs I caught sight of at the harbor. They didn't appear sad to me. A few were weak and tired, but most of them looked relaxed, chillin' by one restaurant or another observing the tourists. After I had finished my omelet and was sipping an espresso I observed a hairy, dirty mutt writhing on his back, with his paws bent, under the sun. At that moment a conscionable thought came to me and I realized it was the only decent thing I could do for Lucky.

The food bowl was empty when I returned home so I filled it up again. Lucky didn't approach the food and sniff it like he did the other times. He lay listlessly, even though he was fed properly and was kept dry from the rain. I felt a twinge of guilt as I stared into his soft eyes. It was indubitably wrong to keep him in my courtyard. He no longer had the freedom he was used to, like his friends at the harbor. I could see that now. Viktoria had judged poorly in thinking the dog needed me. I shook my head, saying, "Stupid, girl."

I left the gate open, then walked up the steps to my apartment. Lucky waited down by the gate. He looked up at me. I said to him, "This is your life, Lucky. You decide how you'd like to live it. I welcome you into my life if you'd like."

I went into the house and took a long cool shower. I didn't think of Lucky until I was dressed and then I went to see if he was still in my courtyard. The moment I couldn't see him I was struck with a twinge of distress. I hurried down the steps and sped around the corner. I asked the kids playing soccer if they'd seen him. I walked down to the viewing area. No Lucky. I sat on the bench and stared out at the sea. I scratched my head. I had not thought he would actually leave. I still had a large bag of dog food.

During class that evening, all I could think about was Lucky. We were reviewing our homework and I was anxious to go home to see if he had returned to eat the food I had left for him. The moment class finished I abstained from the usual chit-chat and swiftly walked back to my apartment. I passed through the harbor paying particular attention to any stray dogs. My heart ached as I thought I may never see Lucky again. He may well be dead and it was all my fault for abandoning him. The whole time I couldn't get the memory of his precious pout out of my mind. But then I was halfway along the harbor when, gnawing on a large lamb bone with his cronies feasting beside him, I saw that *little shit,* Lucky. I whistled and he jerked his head up and saw me. I smiled and he went back to gnawing on the bone. Relief flooded over me and I chuckled and murmured, "Lucky… you little shit."

CHAPTER NINETEEN

A week later, on a Thursday evening, I was summoned to Sfakia to help Dad harvest his olives. He had phoned me when I was on my way to the movie theater and in good spirits, as my writing was moving along better and I was gaining a clearer understanding of particular Greek concepts. Dad did not ask me to come, rather he told me to come. He wanted me to take the bus to Patsianos the next day because we were going to harvest the olives on Saturday.

The thought of spending all weekend toiling with my hands perturbed me, as I had hoped to carry the momentum from the week into the weekend. Coincidentally, I stopped in front of a James Bond poster; he was in a pristine white tuxedo and holding a pistol, looking as charming and dashing as ever, and as I inched a little closer to examine his irises the shadow of my head overlaid his and I thought I could not defy my father.

Next morning on the bus, I jotted down many thoughts in my little book as we proceeded over the mountains through the rugged landscape. The angle at which the sun lit each village we passed set me easy. November was a beautiful time of year to be here, I thought. We reached the top of the mountain and the vast Libyan sea and the tiny villages on the coast appeared before me. The sea possessed a lovely crisp color and it paired well with the pale land that in turn accentuated the green trees and to see it all as one picture was mesmerizing.

We slowly descended the tortuous road (supported by guardrails) and a cloud suddenly dispersed, canvasing the landscape with a bright, transforming light. The divinity of this region lay in its impracticality. And every time I travelled this road to Sfakia, each and every moment elucidated my sense of a life beyond my comprehension.

I arrived at the house early in the afternoon. I phoned Dad, to notify him, and he demanded I water the garden. While I showered the garden from the veranda, I found myself staring at the big olive tree next to it and wondering about the olive trees we'd be picking from. Crete was filled with olive trees of different sizes and varieties. Over the centuries, people had planted them in just about any place humanly accessible. Olive oil was omnipresent in the life of Greece. People wore it in the cracks on their hands, in the follicles of their hairs; it quite literally flowed in their veins. For a farmer every single olive mattered. Most every family here owned at least one small olive grove. Dad had a dozen little trees in the space behind the house, but they weren't ready to be harvested. I imagined a clear and open field with rows of orderly trees of just the right size. I imagined eating an olive for every handful I picked. I imagined a regal and enchanting experience, then I snapped out of my reverie and the garden was flooded.

* * *

At six in the morning Dad phoned me and shouted, "We're coming now! Get ready! Eat breakfast—eat a *paximathi* with cheese." Then Dad was in the house shouting, "You're still sleeping? Wake up! Get dressed! Kanakis and the kids are waiting."

I dressed at my own pace and ate a piece of cheese, gulping it down with a glass of water before we left. Dad told me to drive the Suzuki because he was going to drive the Chevy truck. Kanakis followed us in his Toyota truck. He was a close friend of Dad's. He was bald on the top of his head and had a mustache and a belly and was slow getting around. I could not look at him without thinking of the actor Michael Gazzo from the *Godfather Part II*. I was glad he brought his two kids, George and Little Kanakis, to help out.

We passed the villages Kapsodhasos and Skaloti. At the next village, Argoules, Dad drove off the paved road and stopped just before the dirt road started. "Leave the car there," he said. I parked the car and we drove down the road in his Chevy, Kanakis and his kids following behind. The dirt road was carved down the sharp slope of a cliff. I clung tightly to the arm rest as we bumped and rattled downhill. Dad rolled down without a care. We reached a gully that I thought was the definite end.

"Get out of the car," Dad said.

Kanakis' two kids stood by me as we watched the Chevy dip at a forty-five-degree angle, then rocks and earth whip from underneath its tires as Dad inclined over the sheer lip of ground. Then Kanakis revved his engine and charged across. On the other side of the gully lay Dad's olive grove. On first sight I swallowed my spit and stared at the several dozen trees, some of which jutted from the cliff. These trees were the size Cretans had hid in during their wars. From these kind of trees they had ambushed Turks and Germans, spilling their blood into the roots. How, I wondered, did our family have such great fortune as to own a parcel of land in this cruel and jagged terrain? Whom did we not kill? Dad shook his head and murmured to himself as we unloaded the equipment.

"What happened?" Kanakis asked.

"I forgot the olive sacks in Patsianos," Dad said.

"We'll go get them," Kanakis said.

"Go, Panagiotis," Dad said. "They're underneath the *souvla*."

"How did you forget the olive sacks?" I said.

"It's your responsibility to remind me—I'm seventy years old!"

"Are you kidding me?"

"Go! We don't have time."

I climbed up the mountain to the Suzuki. When I returned, having retrieved the bags from under the big iron spit, the fishing nets were outspread on the ground and Dad was perched in a tree cutting branches with a chainsaw. George and Little Kanakis were striking the branches with an olive stick. The boys were twins adopted from Russia when they were babies. They looked nothing alike but they were well-matched with the hardened environment and they were smart and fun to be around.

"*Ela*, Panagiotis," Little Kanakis said as he tossed me a stick.

I hacked away at the branches, knocking off every olive. We took turns using the electric "pummel stick" (or so I called it) that helped bring down the pesky fuckers hanging from the highest branches. "Watch out!" Dad shouted at me after a thick branch almost struck my head.

"Look! Why are you standing underneath when I'm sawing off a branch?" he said, blaming me. Then when olives bounced off the net, Dad would shout, "Gather them all! Don't leave a single one," and, of course, as many lay in the dirt, Dad never stopped; after he had climbed down from the tree he rushed to where the olives had escaped the net shouting, "Look! You left most of the olives in the dirt."

We ignored him and continued striking the branches. But he continued to shout, ordering, "Give me the chainsaw!" and "Lay down the net!" and "Stand up!" and "No, you're not hitting it correct, (Little) Kanakis!" and "Bring the bags—hurry! We're not going to finish."

The fact that Dad didn't say "thank you" or "please" or "great job" didn't matter to me. I knew he wasn't the type to express sentimental emotions, and at that moment it would have felt contrived anyway. I had slowly grown accustomed to his callous behavior, accepting that his principles were rooted in a different era and a different upbringing. However it frustrated me greatly that I was unable to make a suggestion or pass a comment that we could agree on or, even better, laugh about later after finding out we were *both* wrong.

Gradually my patience withered and I yelled back at him in Greek and, as my words dropped like duds, I shouted F-bombs in English. I couldn't ascertain if it was Dad I was impatient with or if the job had got the best of me. Physical labor, anything that required a substantial effort with the hands and legs and up and down movement, required a mindless meditative technique I couldn't endure for long. *I'm far more polished and stately and I should not deign to undertake any sort of sweaty industrious work*, I thought.

This was a monumental flaw of mine. Even as I shouted, I knew I was in the wrong. I was disappointed I couldn't handle the job with respect and composure as if nothing more graceful or worthwhile existed. And in antagonistic situations, this can be a difficult mindset for a man to overcome.

"He yells for the good, not for the bad," Little Kanakis said as I was hacking away viciously at a branch. Above the little boy's top lip was peach fuzz and below his chest a healthy belly. He was a precocious fifteen-year-old, understanding things well beyond his years. He wanted to tell me about Dad. However, he didn't know Dad like I did. He never could. His filter was virgin and the image he saw wasn't cluttered with disappointing experiences.

Kanakis had a heart condition and he watched us all day with his best work being the occasional one-off comment. Every time before he spoke he took a deeper than normal breath. "This is a very deadly plant," he said, referring to a purple plant that mushroomed from the ground. "Keep away from it."

The effort each comment required forced him to stay silent and build up for the next sentence, as if what he was about to say was holy. "That tree," he remarked, followed by a weighty pause, "must be a thousand years old." We stared at the huge trunk and the bulging roots sunk into the ground as if now exacting words were heavy for us. Time and age and nature seized my thoughts. A powerful force surrounded me, while the realization that life had existed long before I was born and would continue to do so after I'd died made family squabbles seem mere hindrances to the full experience of life.

No doubt the fifteen-year-olds enjoyed making me look like a wimp. It didn't matter that I was more experienced and far better educated. They were more primal and instinctive, qualities which out here, right now, counted more heavily. Little Kanakis was a worker, but silly and lighthearted at the same time, someone who would suddenly stop and start stabbing a stick into the ground for no reason except that he was bored and tired and a kid. He liked to correct me on my Greek. He called me out when I used the wrong article for gender specific nouns. He kept asking me how to say "sack" in Greek or how to say the correct plural form of "olives", carefully and clearly, enunciating the words because of my apparent stupidity. He'd asked me as he held the sack, "Panagiotis, what do you call this?" I had forgotten. "*Tsou-vaaali.*"

George never complained but toiled all day striking the branches, conscientious about knocking every olive from the trees. He was several inches shorter than his brother but he was more nimble and firmer in structure. He possessed a stillness that I knew would stand him in good stead as he grew older. He was a boy with unwavering ambition, I felt. Inside his head, even as he thrashed at the trees, he was constantly imagining a better life. Dad appreciated the way George worked and rarely yelled at him. Whenever he slowed down, Dad would ask him if he was alright. Both brothers respected Dad very much.

When the time came to have lunch, Dad served us each a plate of chicken and rice from a tin pot he took from the front seat of his Chevy. I used the jug of water to wash my hands before I ate, then before I sat down on a rock I had to brush away a fleet of ants. Dad and Kanakis ate at the front of the truck, while George sat alone in the front seat and Little Kanakis perched, swinging his legs, on the edge of the truck bed. We were tattered and tired, very few words were said. I ate an apple and snacked on walnuts to finish off my appetite.

By the end of the first day we had filled seven sacks of olives. I carried each thirty-kilo sack over my shoulder back to the truck. There were still a couple of dozen trees with olives we had to harvest the following day. Kanakis returned to his village, Arolithi, up in the mountains, while his kids stayed with us in the house in Patsianos. They shared one of the beds while I slept in the other; Dad slept on the couch. We woke at six-thirty in the morning and I was upset to find that my neck itched, as well as the top of my feet. But I did not mind that my shoulders ached and my hands were callused and blistered. Nor did I mind pulling on the same dirty jeans.

We were able to gather double the number of bags from the previous day. I was tired, but I stopped thinking about it. I hacked away at the branches and poured the olives from the fishing nets into the sacks. We worked fast and efficiently, but it was obvious we weren't going to be finished in two days. When Dad realized this, he said, "You're not leaving today."

"I have school tomorrow evening," I told him.

"You can't leave until we finish," he said.

"Fuck off!" I snapped back. "The plan was for me to help for the weekend."

"What do you have to do?"

"I have school! Fuck—I have work to do!"

"What work?"

"Don't piss me off right now."

It was past five and the sun was setting. We gathered the equipment and the olive sacks and loaded them into the back of the truck. I counted fifteen bags. Dad stopped in front of the olive sacks bunched in the bed of the truck and, nodding his head, said, "I hope you didn't fill the bags with leaves and branches."

We hid the equipment under the Chevy and climbed up the mountain to the Suzuki. We drove along the mountain on the dark and desolate road and to my left the bright white light from the moon opened up the countryside.

"What do you say," Dad said, "you can take the car tomorrow afternoon so you can make class? We can finish tomorrow."

I stayed focused on the glimmer coming off the sea and did not answer him immediately, but when I did it was easier for me to agree because he had asked me.

Dad stopped abruptly when we neared a food truck just off the road that had a string of white lights stretched from the trailer to the tables around it. He knew the owner.

"*Yeia!* You have food?"

"Yes! Yes!"

"What do you have?"

"E… souvlakia… salad."

"For sure?"

"For sure! Come."

Dad parked the car and got out. We lingered behind him.

"Come on!" Dad shouted.

We sat with two local farmers, Dimitris and Andreas, who were drinking *tsikoudia*. The brothers and I quietly watched Dad drink *tsikoudia* with his friends and talk about their olives.

"How many sacks did you fill?" asked Dimitris.

"Twenty-five and we still haven't finished," Dad said.

The owner looked at the kids and asked, "Do you want Coca-Cola?"

"*Oei*, we don't want it," Dad said. "Quickly, make the food. We're running late."

"Bring a Coca-Cola for the kids," said Dimitris. "And bring me a Coca-Cola Light."

As we filled our bellies with *souvlakia,* Dimitris treated us to a carafe of wine, then the proprietor treated us to *tsikoudia*, then Dad paid for Dimitris' and Andreas' drinks. It was difficult for me to understand them with their heavy accents. But they were talking about thieves stealing the equipment from the back of trucks. We had been there for an hour.

"Uncle, we have to leave," said Little Kanakis, "we have school tomorrow."

"We're leaving, right now," said Dad, as he filled his shot glass, and mine, one last time.

Dad raised a shot of *tsikoudia* to the proprietor and wished them all goodbye before we left. He drove fast on the way back to Patsianos because Kanakis was waiting for his kids in Kallikratis; his wife, a plump lady from Russia, was demanding them home. Now Dad insisted I leave on Tuesday and I complained.

"We're not going to finish tomorrow," he said.

I tried to speak in Greek to express my discontent, but my mind was tired and the words left my mouth poorly and Dad couldn't follow.

He said, "Learn Greek before you try to talk."

"Shut up," I said. "You lived in the US for thirty-five years and you don't know a lick of English. I've lived in Greece for three months. I don't want to hear shit!"

Dad gripped the steering wheel tighter, shaking his head.

"What can I say? If you talk that way. What can I say?"

"How much olive oil do you need? What are you going to do with it. You're not going to distribute it? You don't need me. I'm only staying until the afternoon. That was the deal."

Then George interjected, "You need to understand how much olive oil one family needs for the year…"

I left the car without saying goodbye and went straight to the bathroom, stripped naked and climbed into a hot shower that was a great luxury that evening. Never before had I appreciated pressurized water beating off my skin as I did then. The steam eased my tenseness and my ribcage expanded to the point where I felt the stretch in the back of my spine.

As I readied myself for bed, I randomly muttered, *He's so stupid… he just doesn't get it… what world does he live in… we're such different people.*

My muttering was sufficiently crude and amateurish for me to quickly dismiss it, although my discomfort about my relationship with Dad continued to peck at my mind. I walked up the two steps to the bedroom, turned off the lights, and lay on the bed. Through the window I could see the stars in the sky and it was strange for me because I noticed that the front of the bed was turned away from the window.

* * *

Dad arrived at the house around the time I woke up. I ate a *paximathi* with cheese and honey for breakfast. He made me a spicy mountain tea to drink but I refused it. Then he put a glass of milk in front of me.

"It's good. It's from the goat. Drink it!"

We sat across from each other, quietly. Now and then Dad's eyes would sink and he'd start to worry. We were about an hour later than we had been the past two days. The first thing we did when we reached the grove was unload the compressor and carry it over the rocky embankment. The cool metal handle soothed my sore hands. Dad stopped and stared at an olive tree.

"You see that tree?" Dad said. "That tree is sixty years old. I planted that tree when I was ten years old."

We stared at the tree together.

"Cool," I said, plainly.

I walked back to the truck for the other stuff. What Dad said about the tree didn't leave my mind. The problem was I didn't know how to respond at times like this when he veered towards the sentimental. The little details Dad occasionally shared about his life made me think he did want to communicate with me. But somehow, we didn't connect. The impediment was more than just the fact that I didn't speak Greek and he didn't speak English. I wondered if he was scared. Just as I was. But I was his son.

The beating began as soon as I had spread the fishing nets under the tree. One olive branch at a time. I was in my own little imaginative world. Dad was high up the tree sawing off branches. My forearms bulged and my hands were swollen; a sensation of fulfillment infused my body. My boots were satisfied that finally they were on a man's feet.

I had filled a bag with olives by noon and I carried through, with a few breaks to gulp down water. My body operated like a machine, but my mind remained human. Dad walked around the tree and picked up the leftovers that had missed the net.

"This is how I did it when I was a kid—I filled up a bag a day just with my hands."

"That's nice," I said.

After I had filled another bag it was about time for me to leave, but before I did, I spread one last fishing net around another tree and carried the two bags I'd filled to the truck. I considered skipping my class to stay another day. I looked over and saw Dad leaning against a rock, snoring, and the thought came to my mind—What if he died, right here? On the side of a cliff with his olive trees, here with nature? What if I left and this was the last time I saw him?

"Do you need me to help you carry anything else back to the truck?" I shouted.

He got up from the rock and took a moment to scan his olive trees, as if he had just discovered them, and then he said, "How many did you fill up?"

"Two sacks."

"Bravo."

"I'm going to leave now."

I saw him remove his wallet from his pocket and take out a few paper bills.

"Here. You worked hard today."

I waited for him to walk over and hand the money to me. He gave me one hundred and fifty euros and he didn't say thank you and neither did I. I climbed up the mountain and Dad yelled out, "Make sure you leave the keys to the house under the tablecloth. And don't forget to leave the wagon in the front. Be careful!"

I knew he cared for me a lot, because he worried for me a lot. He thought there was a lot I didn't know. Sometimes I wondered if he treated me like a kid because he wanted to start over as a father and the only way he knew how was to go back to the beginning. But having him talk to me like I was ten was too unbearable for me to handle, as I was stubborn for wisdom appropriate for my age. But Dad didn't have the vocabulary for that or, quite possibly, the sensitivity. All that a boy needed was his father and to appreciate his father was a very hard walk if he had never been there for him—in the way the son was conditioned by societal norms to expect—during his young days.

CHAPTER TWENTY

Karina was always eager to impress us during class and I challenged her answers on some occasions and she took offense to it; she believed it meant I didn't like her. We bickered often, mostly over trivial matters regarding translations, and I sneered whenever she answered a question I'd asked for Angela. One time, I had asked Angela a question about the word diaphanous.

"That means clear, correct?" I said.

"No," Karina interjected.

"Because you know Greek so well," I retorted.

Angela pressed on her temples with the points of her fingers.

"It can mean that, yes. Continue reading the text, Panagiotis," Angela said.

We were reading a text about the Greek landscape, weather, and culture. The text said Greece was made up of nine regions (they would be called states in the US). Crete was the most southern state and the Greek word for south was *notia*. I told Angela that the Greeks had it backwards and she told me that *we* had it backwards. I realized she was right when I thought about it, but then I started wondering why the English language had it backwards.

After we'd finished reading the text, we asked questions about various words and Angela explained to us the meaning in Greek. I learned that Greeks like to spend most of their time outdoors at cafés with their *parea*, that they are loud and impatient but they are also known for their *philoxenia* and *philotimo*.

"What does *philotimo* mean?" I asked.

"It means honor," said Karina.

"I like this class, because we have two teachers," I said.

Hanna and Lila burst out laughing.

"I can't. Please, Karina…" Angela pressed on her temples again. Karina glared at me, then tilted her head down toward her notebook.

"*Philotimo*. It is… it is… how can I explain to you…"

"An honest person?" I said.

"No. It's not that. It doesn't translate exactly."

"Certainly there has to be a word that's closely related to it. Like a moral person?"

"No…"

"A loyal person."

"It's someone who does the right thing," said Angela. "Do you understand it now?"

"Yeah. I think so. Thank you."

I was still perplexed by the definition, *the right thing*. I considered the way I handled the situation with Lucky as a good example. The way I had treated Viktoria, on the other hand, leaving her naked in bed, was a good example of *not the right thing*.

Karina left class quickly that evening. Afterwards, I walked down to the harbor. There were only two restaurants open at the harbor in late November and one of them was Italian. It was packed with Americans drinking. They were all soldiers who were stationed at the American Navy base here. I saw a little white-haired dog shivering under a vacant table and nobody bothered about it. I veered away from the harbor, through a narrow alley, to Fagotto. It was packed inside and I squeezed onto a stool at the bar. The bartender handed me a glass of water. I ordered a *mastika* with ice.

There were two pretty Greek girls sitting at the bar. They looked young enough to be college students. Greek women took great care in their appearance. They carried around them a majestic aura that struck me as lofty and dignified. However, I found it virtually impossible to engage Greek women in any sort of conversation that might, with luck, lead to *next steps*. Most wouldn't even look at me. And I was handsome, or so I kept telling myself. Almost without exception they kept to their own company, which included the odd male friend who invariably stood to one side looking bored while rolling a cigarette. *Krima*, I thought. What a shame.

I finished my drink too quickly, so I ordered another. Greeks were smoking all around me. I was the only person drinking alone. I withdrew my pen and scribbled.

I'm a lonely soul at Fagotto.
My drink ordered was Mastika.
My surroundings leave me feeling unwelcome.
But the drink keeps me safe and warm.
Each sip is meant to be explored,
With each new thought I let carry me for more.
To rush will only leave me sore.
And if I start to flail, just take another sip
And trust my mind will fix.
At some point my glass will empty—
mine just did.
So I do my mind a mighty favor and mine up another
Mastika.
Keep it plenty.

I was on my third drink and the alcohol was flowing through my bloodstream. My emotions and thoughts teetered, finally tipping me off the deck. She returned with force, when I thought I'd finished with her. How I wished she was here, if only for conversation. I brooded. Everyone at this bar bothered me. The cigarette smoke strangled me. Slightly befuddled by *mastika*, I couldn't write anything more in my notebook. All around me people were speaking Greek. The music was jazz, but it jangled my nerves. America was a distant place to me now. Moment by moment I felt myself slipping slowly off the face of the earth. The experience was all the more disturbing in that I could not reconcile my fragile state now with my peaceful frame of mind just this morning.

I returned home. I read back over our message history, lying in bed. She had never responded to the message I had sent her after her Thailand trip. I sulked at every picture of herself she had sent me. She was devouring my thoughts more intensely than ever. I knew that if I was to get any sleep I needed to write something. I carefully constructed a message to her.

"I've been trying to reconcile what it is about you that makes me crumble every time I think of you and you're not next to me and every time I try I'm left feeling more confused. I feel like I'm a stranger to you now, so I'm scared to contact you anymore without appearing obsessed, but I do really miss you Francesca. Goodnight."

My hand shook as soon as I pressed the send button. Immediately, I tossed my phone to one side and hid under the blanket. The morning arrived frigid. I pulled the fleece blanket tightly against me. I took a composed breath before I checked my phone. I dropped it onto my bed before I could read a word of what she had sent. I tried to keep my heart full of hope for as long as I could. It was a fast response, I thought. She must miss me dearly. I delayed the moment until it was unbearable. I reached out from under the covers into the crisp cold air for my phone, covering myself back up, with my phone between my hands, shaking.

"You're not a stranger, Peter! I miss you too but we need to move forward. It's not going to help to dwell on everything. I appreciate the time we were able to spend together and certainly think of you often."

My body tightened. I had known this was going to be her response! I jumped off my bed and dressed myself. Nobody was here to calm me down and shove reason at me. I became hysterical, which was odd, if I'd thought I was done with her. I rushed out of my apartment to the only place I knew that might set me at ease. I paced down the beach. The sea, calm and wave-less, hummed to me. I talked to myself aloud in order to rationally come to terms with things. She was finished with me, right? Analyzing her message word by word, line by line, I could come to no other conclusion. When she wrote, *I miss you too but we need to move forward*, I tried to reason that it meant she missed me and was waiting for me to return to LA, to marry her, so we could move forward together. But I knew it wasn't true. *Oh! You can't be losing your mind and know you're losing your mind at the same time, can you? This is just unrequited love! Lost love...?*

I thought I'd experienced all this before but now it felt worse. All I could do was speak to myself aloud. I must deserve this suffering, I told myself. For wasn't my past filled with an unhealthy lack of self-awareness and chronic insensitivity to others, women especially? This was payback for all the committed and tender women I had treated cruelly. I burst into tears. All I wanted and needed now, at this very moment, was love, but I had no one to give it to me. I was alone on a beach in Crete. Pitifully I disintegrated into a pile of dirt. My only option was to ask God for help. I looked up to the sky, because I guessed that's where he had to be, and I begged. I asked him for forgiveness. I expressed contrition for the sins of my past. For cursing at my parents. For my conquer-the-world-at-all-costs attitude, to my profit and at everyone else's expense.

Forgive me, God, for sleeping with dozens of women in my twenties. Forgive me for not using condoms. You do know I was a virgin until a month before my twenty-first birthday. I couldn't help it that afterwards all hell broke loose. Please, God, forgive me. If you sent Francesca into my life as retribution, it worked; you've broken me. I feel the earth now. Please now turn this pile of dirt into something worthwhile. Give me a life of love and joy and meaning, so someone may come and give comfort. I surrender.

I wanted to regret having seen Francesca that one last time. But how could I have resisted her? She was tender, but it was the edge of naughtiness she exuded that made me crazy for her. She was careful about what she wore, making sure that it was always fashionable. To match her taste in fashion she needed to dine and drink cocktails at higher-end establishments. She was a girl who had been in a long-term relationship that had ended when she discovered her partner's infidelity. She was the perfect type of girl any decent man would want to make his wife, so you knew she was never going to stay single for long. And when I was given the chance of a relationship with her, I was already set on Greece.

She was easy to be with and talk with. We were together long enough to experience what we loved of each other and briefly enough to hide what we hated about each other. This was my cruel reality. She didn't care that I suffered. I believed that she'd found another man, and I could only imagine that this other man had money. He worked at a fancy company where he'd spend most of his hours, but when he left he'd be with Francesca, taking her to the fancy restaurants in Los Angeles, taking her on trips to Mexico and Asia, to the all-inclusive resorts. She'd tell him the same things she told me. *You make me so happy*, she'd say, and during the middle of the day she'd send him messages saying, *I'm so excited for tonight. I miss you.* The type of message that tells a man he's doing something right.

I had no status to impress her with. My career and life were all over the place. I felt as if I was only the handsome man she used as an escape for adventure and sex. We made such great love that the sun sweat. But the idea of being with a *past* investment banker—and now a struggling writer—was too scary for her to want to come along for the ride. She wasn't a risk-taker. She was from meager means. And I could feel she was terrified of losing the security she'd built up over the ten years since she'd first arrived in LA from humble Portland by taking a chance with me. She was living the life that had enervated Lucky after a single day. Everything had to be ready and planned before she could settle and I had nothing ready and no plan for her except my physical self and my words of love and passion.

One morning, after sex, I had asked her to come with me to Greece. She had hesitated, as if it might be possible, then she had said, "I have to support myself… who's going to support me? I'm not high maintenance, but I'm *medium* maintenance."

She looked at me then as if waiting for me to reveal a vast fortune that would compel her to come. I said nothing. I couldn't. I couldn't lie to her like I had in the beginning. I had wooed her under a pretense, deliberately exuding a sense of security, so she would believe I was a person of importance who was wealthy enough to take care of her. We never would have gotten to this point if I'd told her I was a taxi driver who lived in Little Armenia. She wouldn't have been able to comprehend my ambition to be a writer. But maybe I should have said that, then we never would have made it past the first drink. But I fabricated a magical story that proved the perfect formula to set her mind spinning with curiosity. She had been very interested in me then. It was so easy that way.

I sat down on a bench. A Rottweiler and a mutt were playing joyfully, running and jumping on each other. Oh, how I wished to be able to play like that again. I hadn't felt that pure and uncomplicated since elementary school during recess on the playground with a nerf football. I looked at my hands; blood traveled around islands of pale blotches scattered all over. From my agony I harvested one acceptable, positive thought: you can't change your experiences but you can think about them and use them as accomplishments, if you want.

CHAPTER TWENTY-ONE

I chopped a clove of garlic very fine, tossed it into the pan and let it fry with the red, yellow, and orange peppers. I doused the pan with egg batter and sprinkled it with red pepper flakes. I topped it off with shredded *graviera* cheese. A pot of *malotira,* mountain tea, was boiling. I'd been living in Crete for nearly four months. It was the start of winter. "Happy Winter!" they said, the same as the Greeks wished each other a happy month or a happy week. It was a spiritual expression that lightened up the day. Every day throughout autumn the weather had been sunny and warm. The benevolent conditions continued on the first day of winter.

From my veranda the sea captivated me. Sounds spoke to me. An invitation to walk closer and spread myself over the top of it enticed me. What was this feeling? It was the same sensation I'd had in Sfakia on the cliff, where we harvested olives, which was when it had first struck me. What was it…? A few days before, whirling inside my head, was a tornado. But now I felt an extraordinary calmness… *ataraxia!* I surprised myself by knowing this word, thinking how I'd had it resting in my subconscious until this moment. It was a wonderful word that I discovered to best represent the current state of the atmosphere.

Ataraxia was palpable during my walk through the old town. The tourists were gone. The locals were taking their naps, the shops were closed. As I was walking through the Jewish quarter, the faint purring of a cat was loud enough to mute the whistling of a gypsy around the corner. A spirit permeated the land. I felt it when I stared out toward the sea, when I looked up to the snow-covered mountains that loomed in the distance beyond Chania.

As I walked along, I stopped at a bookstore to look for another Greek fairytale, but instead I caught sight of a shelf with English books. I found George Orwell's *1984*. I read the back cover and was intrigued so I bought it. Then I went to *Kipos* café, the Garden café, which was a good place to be in the winter. It was named after the park of the same name in which it was located. The café was a popular spot frequented entirely by locals. I found a table next to the fireplace, sharing it with an older man with unkempt hair and brown, thick-rimmed glasses who stared at the other patrons strangely. He held a newspaper, which I never saw him read, and a cup of Greek coffee that he sipped very slowly. He stared at everyone with more intensity than I did. I wondered if he was a writer.

The tables were marble-topped and they never stayed vacant for long. But the waiters, who wore white vests with black pants, never made me feel as if I had overstayed my welcome. I sat with a glass of red wine watching the wood burn in the fireplace. Finally I started reading Orwell. I had to stop intermittently and think about what he was saying. In one of my pauses, I happened to notice there were attractive women scattered all around the café. The smoke from their cigarettes rose into the air, lingering in a delicate blue haze below the chandeliers. Needless to say they were all in company. Not once did I catch a stare, while the aura they generated fumigated any chance of me developing an amorous sensation. It kept me controlled.

I stopped reading. I took a big gulp of wine. I wrote a poem.
Fly, fly away little bird.
Don't come back here.
This land is morose.
It sets you up to fling you
back out into the abyss.

Don't let the tease tell you
it's anything else.
It's only a tease.
I promise. I know this.
I've been knocked around too many times.
I get up because I continue to hope.
Leave your nest.

You little bird are something more,
you're special because it's not hope for you.
You fly for the thrill!
But here the thrill has run its course.
From here going forward is only anguish.
So this time, I tell you little bird, don't come back.
Fly, fly away little bird.

I set my pen down and closed my notebook. What wretchedness, I thought. But it was how I felt at that moment. I didn't force or manipulate it. It came out of me unfiltered and honest. After a couple hours and two glasses of wine I waved for the waiter. As I paid, I wondered if the older man with the brown, thick-rimmed glasses was not arranged quite properly in the head. But then again, who was? For all I knew, he might have been the only sane person left in the world. Maybe he was a remarkable meditator. Or, as I first suspected, a writer with something large and all-consuming on his mind.

I sauntered through the old town on my way back. In front of the Catholic church, close to the harbor, a young Greek musician was thrumming his guitar rolling lyrics off his tongue. What was his story, I wondered? Whenever I encountered an artist in the old town I invariably found them fascinating. Whereas I struggled madly to reach a global audience with my work and reap huge monetary gains, these artists apparently wanted nothing more than what was in front of them. I had passed this same guitarist many times and every time I noticed a generous number of coins filled his hat. I dropped whatever coins I had in there too.

Next morning I went for a jog. The beach was vacant, and the sand saturated from an early rain. The hotel resorts along the shore were closed. I ran as close as I could to the tip of the drift. The salt bubbled and hissed at my feet before retreating back into the sea.

Just then, *ataraxia* was at its strongest and, as water sprayed from the sky, I paused. My eyes witnessed a new phenomenon. Fairies were shooting from the sea to meet God's humming, leaving behind an arched trail of colorful pixie dust. The arch stretched high over the sea, the colors fusing one into another. My jaw loosened and my shoulders dropped. It was a warm morning for December and sunlight picked selectively through the dark weaving of clouds. When I looked down, the drift splashed foaming over my shoes.

Why do I write? I asked myself. *Certainly, it can't be for the money. A working screenwriter can make a decent yearly income. But at the pace I'd been going as an investment banker, I'd be quintupling the earnings of those guys at my age now. Why do I write then? It's cathartic. I hope I'm not doing it for the adulation. I don't write for me. It would be foolish to write for me. If I wanted to write for me, a journal would be sufficient. Why do I write? Maybe in time someone will read this. Some poor soul, who needs to be lifted out of the mud, will latch onto my words. Why do I write? I feel good when I write and I feel better when what I write makes our grossly contradictory society manageable for someone as confused as I am. Why do I write? It's empowering to think that a boy from peasant stock can succeed with words and share his perspective on a life very different from that experienced by a writer with an intellectual pedigree. Why do I write? Because I'm not saddled with degrees and distinctions to prove I can write, or rather, more pathetically, that I'm qualified to write. So when I write here in Crete, now, I write with less of a concern for a final climax than for the journey that appears to me as a perceptible phenomenon the loss of which, should I decide not to continue, could very well devastate people who have hope in me.*

Why do I write? I write because I'm selfish. And nobody else has the ideas and thoughts that I have. Only I have these ideas. Many are unconvincing, I admit. I guess I share the idea of a God. I'm more sure of this idea than all the others. In fact, denying it would be like denying the universal fact that water is a necessary element of human survival. This pixie dust isn't a coincidence. It's colorful. It could be an ugly set of colors but it's not. It's the most beautiful array of colors I can image. Why do I write? I write because living with dreams, with ambitions to find the pot of gold, is an exciting way to reject life as it is.

CHAPTER TWENTY-TWO

To celebrate the end of our autumn term and the upcoming holidays, my Greek school hosted a Christmas party and the students from the other classes were there. There were about a dozen students with the other classes included. Everyone was told to bring a small hors d'oeuvre or dessert plate, but everyone brought two or three items and we had to stack the food.

Karina surprised our class with little gifts. She gave me a tiny ornamental birdhouse. It glittered with gray sparkles and she had taped a large decorated card to it. I did not like the gift but I did like that she wore a tight red skirt with stockings and a Santa hat. I had never seen her more exuberant. She approached me as I was pouring another glass of wine. We spoke in Greek.

"Do you like the gift I got you?" she asked, smiling.

"Yes. Thank you. It is very nice of you."

"I'm the type of person who likes to open my heart during this time of year. And give people gifts."

"Everyone was happy you did."

"I'm not bad like you think."

"I never said that."

"I know you don't like me."

"What makes you think that?"

"You like to make fun of me."

"If I didn't like you, I wouldn't make fun of you as much as I do."

"Are you going to Sfakia for Christmas?"

"Yeah. When are you leaving for Spain?"

"Next week. I want to show you a picture of my sister's dog. He's so beautiful." She handed me her phone.

"Is your sister married?"

"Why do you ask?"

"I was just wondering…"

"Do you like my sister?"

"I don't know your sister."

"But do you think she's pretty?"

"You are both very beautiful."

At that moment Angela handed me a bottle of wine to open. I walked around and poured wine into everyone's cup. I shifted from Greek to English and back to Greek. The crowd was friendly and talkative. They were from all over Europe. There was an older Italian gentleman and a French couple in their thirties. And a hulking Norwegian man named Ketel. I'd seen Ketel at a bar before. He was a quintessential Viking. His Greek was terrible. In fact, none of the students from the other classes could hold a conversation in Greek.

Hanna and I only talked briefly because she had to leave. She was always leaving early, always catching the bus back to Kissamos. She didn't mean much to me now. The desire I'd had for her was gone. Lila wasn't at the party either. She had left a few weeks earlier for Poland. She was a pleasant person to be around. She was easy going and rational and smart.

Our class was good because we were around the same age and we knew about the same amount of Greek. I was the only Greek student in the school. To learn and to be in a situation where I might learn always comforted me. I did wonder what would have happened if I had a romance going on with one of the other students. It would be wonderful to speak Greek to her every day as we spent time at the harbor and sipped Greek coffee together without a care of what we were going to do next. Although the thought of having her meet Dad in Sfakia frightened me.

Karina rubbed next to me as I was replenishing my plate.

"It's not nice to joke with me," she said.

"How was I joking?"

"You say nice things but I know you don't mean it."

"Cause you're a psychologist now?"

"I know you like Hanna. And you're unhappy she has a boyfriend."

"You're very wrong."

"That's what I believe."

"I am only unhappy when I don't have someone to kiss and fall in love with. To find someone who loves you as much as you love them is a very hard thing to do."

We were off in a corner away from everyone else and, as I was inclined to elevate the mood, I switched to speaking in English and said, "I like to make love. To peel off a woman's clothes one by one and to lift her onto my bed. I'd like a woman I could hold and cherish and make love to for the rest of my life."

"You're full of yourself. You're good with words but I'm a bit hard to impress with words. I prefer facts. So maybe in the future if we have the opportunity again you will impress me by taking action."

She made it seem as if I had missed my opportunity, but the real truth was if I wanted Karina I could have her. Sometimes I thought I'd fuck her. But why though?

When the party ended, Angela insisted we take food home with us. I didn't want to take the sweets, but in her courtyard were tangerine trees loaded with ripe fruit that I wanted. I liked to eat tangerines when I walked or rested on a bench. I threw the rinds into the sea or next to tree trunks. I asked if I could take a couple. Angela gave me two full bags.

I decided it was too early to return home so I stopped to have a drink by the harbor. I spotted Ketel sitting alone and when he saw me I went over and sat next to him. He knew the bartender, Sophocles, who had a belly and black straight hair with a little gray that was slicked back, and whenever he pivoted quickly his bangs dropped over his forehead and he would run his hand through his hair. He served me a Greek beer called FIX. Ketel was drinking an old-fashioned. I listened to Ketel reveal his life to me. He was divorced and had a little girl back in Norway. He said he hated his ex-wife because she was always demanding more money.

"Why did you come to Crete?" I asked.

"I used to come here every summer with my family," he said.

He said he'd been living in Crete for over a year and half. He liked Crete a lot, he said. He was a businessman, although I had no idea of his business undertakings nor did I care to ask.

"Where are you from in America?" Sophocles asked me.

"I grew up in Ohio. But I was living in Los Angeles before I came here."

"Los Angeles!"

"Have you been?"

"No. Only New York and Cuba. I like Cuba."

"For sure Cuba is better than Los Angeles. And New York is better than Los Angeles, only New York is more expensive. And if you aren't rich, then New York is probably the worst place to live in the world."

"Anywhere is good, my friend, if you have good *parea,*" he said. I went silent. "What are you doing here?"

"I have family here. My parents are from here. My dad lives in Sfakia."

"You work here?"

"I write and I go to school to learn Greek."

"What do you write?"

"Screenplays."

He made no reaction to it, except he asked, "How long have you lived here?"

"Since August."

"You speak good for just a few months."

"Thank you. I'm trying."

"Do you hunt?" Ketel said.

"No. My dad does, though. He hunts rabbits up in the mountains."

"I like Sfakia."

"I'll be there in a few days."

"I like to hunt," he said.

"In Sfakia you can do whatever you like," I said.

Sophocles served us another round. Ketel's English was not good and I was too tired to talk to him anymore. There was nothing exciting to expect at the bar. No lady who would look at me so that I would look back. Sophocles served us shots of rum. I didn't want one, but I couldn't refuse. My anxiety returned. The alcohol only made it worse. I went to pay and Ketel stopped me.

"I got this," he said.

More Greeks arrived with their *parea*. They all seemed happy. Comfortable. It was past midnight. Ketel offered to give me a ride home. I walked instead. I thought about Cuba and if it was better than Los Angeles. Probably it wouldn't be for me. Los Angeles wasn't home for me either. I thought about Crete and the other people at the bar and Sophocles who was greeting the patrons he knew and appeared content. And I thought about what he said. For me to think one city better than another was foolish. Shit! To some folks Cleveland was just as good a place as Los Angeles or Cuba. And New York City was a wretched place compared to Canton, Ohio, for others. How cynical must I be to have made that judgement. How misanthropic, as the Greeks would say. It was clear to me now what Sophocles, whose name was aptly bestowed, meant when he said any place was a good place if you had good *parea*. And, it occurred to me, if you couldn't find good *parea* anywhere maybe you needed to fix your attitude.

CHAPTER TWENTY-THREE

I had an hour before the bus departed for Sfakia. I was in the corner of a café drinking a cappuccino with my notebook and pen next to a large window, watching people pass along the street. I watched children sing the *Kalenda* and people handing them money so the children were happy. Even the stray dogs were zigzagging along the streets with vigor.

Christmas was one day away. The spirit of Agios Vasilis, Santa Claus, was ever-present. It was sunny and the locals frolicked in the cafés and the shops and the restaurants. On my way to the bus station, I passed swarthy gypsies gathered for conversation in the main square. I wondered what they would be grateful for on this day. Was it their children and health? I felt slightly grateful that I did not have their life. I was no longer so sure I was grateful for leaving my finance job; in fact, I wondered whether I was the world's biggest moron to have left so much money behind. The feeling of not being able to buy gifts during this time of the year was as bad as it gets. It made me think that maybe all you needed in life was money. *I should be grateful*, I thought, *that I can at least purchase a bus ticket to go and see Dad and be with family for Christmas*. But the reality was, I wasn't grateful. I felt pretty much indifferent about the upcoming occasion.

"It's an amazing day today," I said to Dad when I arrived at Patsianos.

He was impressed by my new word, *καταπληκτική*, and he repeated it as he was watering the garden. Nowadays I was trying to speak more in Greek, practicing with banal, everyday stuff. To hear myself talk and to exercise my mouth muscles with multisyllabic words felt good. I ranted on about the Greeks.

"Everything is tomorrow!" I said. "I'm trying to reach the Greek consulate about the army and they're on vacation for all of December… Every café you go to they're smoking inside."

Dad didn't answer me, until I told him not to water the garden too much because he'd ruin the peppers.

"*Με φώτησες*," he said, humorously, meaning, "You enlightened me". It was a word of great power that I hadn't known he possessed. On other occasions Dad used words in Greek that, when I translated them, proved to be good words in English but he never knew the equivalent. *Watch out for the ladies, some can be conniving,* he'd said once before.

He had two small fields close to the house, on both sides of the road, where we were going to plant olive trees. I dug the holes and Dad cut down sturdy branches to tie against the baby olive trees. The ground was tough, the soil filled with rocks. I used a pickaxe to break it up, tossing the dislodged earth and rocks to the side. As soon as a tree was in place, Dad would hold the supporting branch steady while I refilled the hole with dirt. Then I tamped the loose dirt with the shovel. As we worked, farmer friends of Dad's would drive by and honk. Their trucks were black and battered. They wore black shirts and their beefy forearms hung over the doors of their cars and they were unshaven with wild hair. After about an hour of digging holes I could feel my forearms swelling up and my hands hardening. I'd stop to take a break and when I did I looked out at the countryside and toward the sea for a few moments before I started back up again.

"I can't understand why they don't build anything here," I said.

"You build something," Dad encouraged me.

"If I had a couple million dollars, I would build an agora. A beautiful agora two stories high. All the farmers could sell their products there. I'd sell it online, too."

"Add more," Dad said. "Good."

"This landscape exists in few parts of the world."

"This is the best place in the world," he said. "People from all over the world come here. Look at the nature!"

"You want to know the smartest thing you ever did," I said. "It was having the courage to leave behind this land for America."

"Why? If I stayed here, I would have a lot more. Look what they have here. Restaurants. Wonderful homes."

"And what would your kids have done? I know I wouldn't have been able to live in New York City. I wouldn't have been able to make the money I did."

"And where is your money?"

"Where's the money here?"

"What are you saying?"

"A family with a restaurant and a small vineyard and olive trees will make what?"

Dad shook his head. "Don't tell me."

"You have the opportunity to make money in America. I worked for people who made ten million dollars in one year. And they never even broke a sweat." I raised my index finger in front of my face. "In one year!"

I lifted my hat and swiped my forehead with the front of my forearm; three hours of digging holes was exhausting. Another farmer passed by and honked his horn. Dad and I waved.

"You can't go back to your job?"

"I don't want to go back," I told him. "I'm doing what I want to do."

"We'll see the results," he said, stoically.

We planted a dozen olive trees that afternoon. It was Christmas eve. I stared at the last tree we planted and, at that moment, I thought of how when we were harvesting olives Dad remembered a tree he had planted when he was a kid. The year was 2015. In a week it was going to be 2016. If the elements worked in our favor and rain nourished the roots, the trees would grow and in three to four years olives would hang from the branches. The trees would grow a little bigger each year. Maybe these trees would live a thousand years and somebody far in the future would regard them with wonder and think: *those trees must be at least a thousand years old.* I liked how I would have this with me, no matter what happened, for the rest of my life. There would be no regret and no disappointment regarding the olive trees. This was a remarkable thought and I was grateful for it.

CHAPTER TWENTY-FOUR

We returned to the house at twilight. Dad groaned wearily as he stepped from the car. The neighbor's dog barked until we walked through the gate and climbed up to the front door.

"Gather your things, so we can leave," Dad said. "We'll eat up there."

I didn't want to shower in Kallikratis because the water wasn't pressurized, so I showered before we left. I had forgotten to bring soap and shampoo but I noticed, for the first time, there was a bottle of J&J baby shampoo in the shower. I was a kid the last time I used that kind of shampoo. I knew Dad used it because he thought it was the most natural kind there was. After I dressed, I went to sit out on the veranda with Dad. He was sipping a *tsikoudia*.

"The shampoo you have is for babies," I said.

"Does it bother you?"

"I'm only telling you."

It was already dark even though it was only six o'clock in the evening. The air cooled and I felt comfortable in a sweater and jeans. It was peaceful looking across the landscape toward the sea. Except for the few lights flickering from the hotels on the shore and the occasional dog chasing a car down the street, we might have been the only people left on earth.

"We'll be the only house in Kallikratis with Christmas lights," I said, as I looked at the Christmas lights on the table.

Dad didn't answer. I could see something was festering inside him. He rose from his chair and said, "Let's go."

The temperature had dropped a few degrees by the time we arrived. I wrapped the lights on the clothing line that stretched across the courtyard. Next to me, Spirto wagged her tail. Her tail was always wagging which made me think she was a happy dog. Dad walked outside to take a look at the lights. "*Bravo*," he said. "Come inside. The food is ready."

We ate goat with *stamnagathi* for dinner. I wasn't so hungry. I was watching the TV as I ate. I craned my neck toward the ceiling.

"What time are we going tomorrow?" I asked.

"In the afternoon."

"Your ceiling is filled with bugs and spiders."

The ceiling was high, and you'd need a ladder to clean it. I thought about doing it right then, but changed my mind.

"We have to clean it tomorrow," he said, "with the vacuum."

"Kallikratis!" I said. "The whole world comes here."

Dad moved to the armchair in front of the TV and bellowed with exhaustion.

"Did you buy anything for the kids?" he asked.

"I'll give them money."

"How much?"

"Twenty euros a piece."

"There's a lot of kids."

"How much should I give?

He mulled it over as he took a sip of *tsikoudia*.

"Mom said I should give at least twenty euros."

Dad was picking at the gaps between his teeth with a toothpick. He was probably thinking about money. I was thinking about it. Maybe twenty was too much, although ten felt like too little, so maybe in that case it would be best to give them nothing. Dad opened his wallet and reached for some cash. "Merry Christmas!" he said, in English. I didn't check to see how much it was but there were at least two fifty-euro bills. "Keep your head on straight," he said.

I did not feel it appropriate to retire to my room so I lingered with Dad. I looked over at him and felt that watching him was like watching a stranger. What could he be thinking about so deeply now? His goats? His kids? His properties? His money or money in general? It would have been a supernatural moment if Dad had said something like: *You know, son. Life as it is now. Was life as it was when I was little. The only difference is that I have a lot less time.* He did open his mouth, though. But what came out was not what I wanted to hear.

"What happened to your cross?" he asked me. "You used to wear your cross."

"I lost it," I told him.

"You lost it?" He shook his head. "When you played football you wore your cross—it helped you."

"It wasn't the cross that helped me."

"Don't say such foolish things now."

"Jesus. The cross isn't what helps you. You help yourself by being a decent person."

"*Skase!* You're not okay."

We were silent for a few moments until he said, "New York changed you for the worse."

He went to the drawer by the TV stand and pulled out a *komboskini,* a braided amulet.

"Wear it," he said.

"No."

"What are you saying now? It's a *komboskini.*"

"That does nothing. I don't need a cross—I don't need a *komboskini.* Leave me alone with your Jesus crap, right now."

"*Alimono,* seriously, you need to go to the doctor. I'm speaking serious now."

Suddenly, unhinged, I pushed out of my mouth, "You're an idiot!"

As soon as I said it, a heavy silence filled the room. The look on Dad's face was powerful enough to light the wood stove with the bristles on his cheeks. It was an expression of intense rage I'd never seen before. Never with other people, never with his family. I was startled. One more step, I thought, and he was ready to lift off the ground and tomahawk me down to oblivion.

"I'll kill you," he said. "You are an antichrist."

In an effort to calm him, I began to explain my point in a clumsy mix of Greek and English. "You can't do bad things all the time—you can't lie, cheat and steal and think that just because you wear a cross, or a *komboskini,* or you go to church, that you are saved. It doesn't work that way. You just need to live your life every day as a moral and compassionate human being. Stealing from someone, then asking God or Jesus to protect you, is as idiotic as not believing in God. It lacks a fundamental understanding."

"You think those who wear a cross do bad things?"

"Wearing a cross doesn't make you a good person."

"If you were smart, like you say, you wouldn't talk like that. To your father! You wouldn't talk like that. You read all the time and what do you learn?"

"I learn not to let myself be consumed with pettiness and not to lead a life of blindness. You don't even have a single στίλο here."

"Στιλό! Dad repeated, correcting the accent. "Pen! Still you don't know Greek. You're here for six months and you still don't know Greek."

I stormed outside, walking far from the house into complete darkness, kicking at rocks. A light flared from the herbal café; it appeared they had *parea.* Dad and I were only good together for a short time. Any more than a day and we were sure to find some way to antagonize each other. He was exceptionally good at angering me. It was not only the stuff he said. It was also everything he didn't say or do that affected me deeply. Resentment festered inside me; so when he judged me openly I was incapable of restraining myself. Even the petty stuff he did like fart in front of me or swish *tsikoudia* in his mouth or shout at me if I touched the dogs only added fuel to our powder keg of a relationship. I admit that I was often no better; there were times I was abrupt and rude when he asked me basic questions or wanted help with simple tasks. The things I said made me feel awful. I tried to stay patient and I tried to behave decently but it only took a minor scrape to pierce the veneer of our relationship. Every time it happened it was heartbreaking and it had happened tonight. There was nothing to do but try and heal and start again.

CHAPTER TWENTY-FIVE

We were spending Christmas in Rethymno with Dad's first cousins.
Dad's mother's brother who died several years ago had six children.
We were going to the house of one of his daughters. Her name was
Yiamonda. Her husband, Manolis, saw us from the balcony when we
arrived.

Everyone was happy to see us. The kids shouted and screamed,
chasing each other under the tables and up the stairs. We sat down at
the large table that occupied the entire room. Manolis, who had a few
strands of hairs left at the top of his head and a firm build, poured us
glasses of wine, but Dad refused his.

"This is from Bordeaux. Try it."

"I don't like wine with drugs in it."

"Try it!" Manolis forced the glass into his hand.

"The wine from Kallikratis is the best."

"Of course. But it's good, isn't it?"

"It went down. We'll see if it stays there."

Eleftheria was the wife of Dimitris, another of the six siblings. She
approached me with a warm congeniality. She had dark hair and light
skin and the body of a woman who has had many kids and works a
regular job with little time to take care of herself. She liked to practice
her English with me.

"Panagiotis, why haven't you visited?"

"I'm sorry. I had school. I didn't have time."

"Come next week and stay with us. The kids don't have school. They will like it."

"Yeah. I'll come one day."

"No! You can stay at our place all week. We have an extra room."

"I *could* stay for a couple of days…"

"Think about it. You're here for six months and you still haven't come to our house. That's not proper."

Dimitris' brother George was here from Athens. He was a finance professor at the University of Athens. He liked to talk to me about finance. He introduced me to his sister's fiancé, Wilfred, who was French.

"Peter worked at Bear Stearns in New York City—on Wall Street!" George paused and waited and then said as an afterthought. "Now he lives here and writes screenplays."

"How many years did you work at Bear Stearns?"

"Only a year. When it collapsed I went to a boutique firm."

"Wilfred has an MBA from Cornell. *Ivy league*," George said.

"Peter, what kind of stories do you write?" Wilfred asked.

"Romance… drama… coming-of-age. The kind of stories no one wants to buy."

"They're that expensive?" he said with a sarcastic smile.

"People don't go to movies to watch reality; that's the reality."

When the food came, there was so much that they had to leave some of the plates on the kitchen counter, bringing them over one at a time as other plates emptied. There was lamb and goat and smoked pork and sirloin. The *tsigariasto* was finger-licking good. There were plates of stuffed mushrooms and eggplants. There were large bowls of arugula and lettuce salad with raisins and fruit and lemon dressing. There was, of course, a Greek village salad. I had learned to pace myself during Greek feasts and never leave my plate empty, for as soon as it emptied more food appeared. At the same time, however, if you ate too slowly your hosts would ask you why you weren't eating or they'd look at you with a sad face and say, "You didn't like the food?" Sometimes it could be tricky.

My glass was nearly empty again and Manolis filled it up.

"Don't drink a lot now," Dad said. He was sitting at the end of the table next to Manolis and George. Wilfred sat across from them and, I saw, was concentrating carefully in order to try and understand Dad and Manolis. Litsa, the youngest of the siblings, who was engaged to Wilfred, translated for them. The women sat at the end half of the table with the kids, cutting their food into pieces and having a lively conversation of their own. Manolis' sister, Maria, turned to me.

"Panagiotis, where do you like it better, America or Greece?"

"It depends. If you want to make money, America is great. If you want to live, Greece is better."

"Are you going to stay permanently?"

"I don't know. We'll see."

"Did you know Greek before you came here?"

"Not so good. I went to school and I read every day—books for kids."

"That's wonderful. Those books are great. Do you work here?"

"I go to school and I write."

"Did you go to school to learn how to write?"

"No. I studied finance and I worked at a bank."

"Panagiotis worked at a large bank in New York," George interjected.

"And you made enough money to do what you do now?"

"I made enough to support myself on simple means."

"And how do you do it? You write it and you send it to America?"

"Exactly. I write and I write more and I share it and I have to write again."

"Bravo. I'm jealous. What you are doing is very wonderful."

"Thank you."

"I wish you all the best… you need patience and persistence to write."

Yiamonda laid a huge piece of *tsigariasto* on my plate.

"No, thank you, *thea!* I'm full."

"You didn't eat anything, Panagiotis!"

I inhaled and exhaled, deeply. My stomach was stretched so tightly it strained my muscles. I felt as if I was going through labor, or something like that, if eating too much is what going through labor feels like. I must have been on my fifth glass of wine but I was still sober.

"I want to go to Las Vegas," said Manolis. "How is it?"

"If you like to lose your money and meet a whore, it's good."

He laughed at my remark. Dad winced, shaking his head in dissatisfaction.

"Don't drink anymore," Dad said. "Your mind is mixed up now."

"My mind works like a smooth-running machine!"

Dad looked down at his *komboloi*, like he always did, and said nothing.

My plate was still half full when the women cleared the table for dessert. The men kept talking. It was fine for me to say nothing and listen. Most of it I understood. They talked about the landscape, the property, the olive trees… how much olive oil they made this year… the infrastructure…

"We don't have lights in Kallikratis!" Dad said. "The mayor of Sfakia thinks we're still in the first century."

They discussed the Greek economy, the severely reduced pensions. They talked about how one day Greece will be strong again. I heard the kids upstairs playing in the bedrooms. Eleftheria shouted at her son, Stelios, because he had made his little sister, Stella, cry. I ate a creamy chocolate cake George's wife served me.

The women worked seamlessly together in the kitchen to clean all the dishes and store the food away. Eventually they sat down and relaxed at the table with the men, sipping espressos and eating dessert. I was enamored with the scene. The unity at dinner was a phenomenon I hadn't felt in a long time. The modish type might have thought the environment too outdated and masculine. But when I looked at it I saw all six siblings married. The wives understood their role and the husbands understood theirs. Between them was a bond and a commitment to family. The women were strong and resilient—

Litsa was a successful banker working in London. They had been raised in a small village, in a small house, with very little money. This across the board success didn't happen by pure luck. They were so conventional and proper it astounded me. They displayed such great discipline and a willingness to compromise. I respected it wholeheartedly.

Before we left, I handed envelopes with money to the kids. I wrote a message in Greek, but they were too excited about the money, running to their parents to show them.

Manolis tried to give Dad a few bottles of wine but Dad forcefully objected. He yanked the bottles away from Manolis before he could fill them.

"I have wine. I just want the bottles. The Coca-Cola bottles are good quality."

"Come on now! Let me give you some wine."

"I'm serious! I don't want wine."

While Dad and Manolis continued tugging at the Coca-Cola bottle, the kids hugged and thanked me.

"The important thing is the card. It's not the money," said Manolis' sister.

I snapped a group picture with my iPhone to share with the family back in America.

"We'll see you next week, Panagiotis," Eleftheria said, reaffirming her invitation.

As we left, Manolis waved to us from the balcony just as he had when we arrived. Dad grasped a plastic bag full of empty Coca-Cola bottles. He honked as we drove off.

"What do you think? We had a good time."

"It was nice."

There was a long moment of silence, then Dad said, "You could have worn a better sweater. That's a sweater you wear at home, not to someone else's home for Christmas."

"This is a fine sweater. Leave it."

After a shorter moment of silence, he continued, "You wore the worst sweater. *Αλήτης.* Only *αλήτηδες* dress like you did."

"Are you serious now? Serious?" I squeezed the door handle and tightened my jaw. "Don't worry about what I wear, okay? If I want to wear this sweater, I will wear it. I won't ask for your permission. I'm thirty-one-years-old. You think I have no idea, but I know quite clearly what I'm doing with my life."

"What do you know?"

"You really want to piss me off right now!"

"Because you don't know how to dress."

"You are an intolerable person."

I knew how to say intolerable in Greek because I'd looked it up after a past shouting match. Maybe this was something useful about our quarrels: learning new words and putting them into practice. To have said intolerable in English would have meant nothing. The word surprised him. It was a fitting word to describe Dad. When we raged at each other, it was pure frustration. When we had good moments, we understood each other, we had patience for each other; they reminded us of what should be and what could be, only we were still far from reaching an understanding with each other that could lessen our mutual frustration. The dinner certainly set Dad off, as I should have guessed it would. He wanted it to be our family together.

He wanted to bring me down in the hope that maybe I'd follow his lead and instructions better, yet it only made me angrier. Each time he accused me of something, I hated him even more. Even the thought of hashing out our father-son issues was as unrealistic as the goats grazing in the mountains suddenly deciding not to return to their shepherd on the day they were to be slaughtered.

"Stop the car," I said, "Let me out!"

Dad stopped on the side of the national highway at the Episkopi bus stop. As I waited for the bus back to Chania, I google translated the word *αλήτης.* Google told me it meant *bum.*

CHAPTER TWENTY-SIX

The day after Christmas dawned cold. The sharp chill from my tiled floor numbed my toes. I kept the air conditioner turned off to keep my utility bill low. From my kitchen door, I spotted a cat with irreparable battle marks sleeping on the table on my veranda. The cat was missing an eye and most of his nose and had scars running down his front legs. He awoke as soon as I walked onto the veranda and lethargically scampered down the tiled roof above my neighbor's front door.

Thick clouds blocked the sun and the sea lay dark. The alley below my apartment was quiet; the old ladies who habitually sat there, resting in their lawn chairs, had failed to appear. Another cat slept on the hood of a tiny black car, yet another on a plastic chair, while a third feline occupied my neighbor's doormat. The cats were the only sign of life and they looked miserable.

I felt uneasy and so after I'd finished a cup of orange juice with a piece of cheese, I walked to the old town and sat down at a café I'd never been to before. I ordered a chocolate croissant with a cup of *malotira*, the mountain tea I had grown increasingly fond of. I watched a middle-aged couple drag their suitcases over the cobblestones to a hotel across the street. Sitting next to me was another older couple drinking tea. I overheard them say they were on their way to Heraklion, in different English accents. The woman expressed concern that the boat from Heraklion wasn't going to depart today because of the weather. I thought it was strange to visit Chania during this time of year as it was desolate and cold and most stores were closed. They might have been archeologists, I thought.

After they left, I was all by myself at the café. In a few days it was going to be New Year's. I had no energy for learning Greek. All I could think about was how much I needed a companion. There was nothing else I wanted. The realization that this was not going to happen left me feeling restless and dissatisfied.

I decided to visit Eleftheria and the family in Rethymno. Dimitris picked me up on his vespa from the bus station. He took me to his home and then returned to work. Eleftheria was in the kitchen cooking. I kissed her on both cheeks. Her four children came to greet me, one by one. Stelios ran toward me, shouting, "Panagiotis!" as he wrapped his tiny arms around my waist. Erini, thirteen, and Stella, who was seven, greeted me before returning to the living room where an American animation movie with penguins, dubbed in Greek, was on the TV.

"Do you want to play soccer?" asked Nikos.

"Yeah. Let's play soccer!" said Stelios.

"Panagiotis, do you want anything to drink or eat?" asked Eleftheria.

"No, thank you."

"Nikos, go show Panagiotis to his room."

My room was in the basement. It was a pleasant room with two single beds and my own bathroom. I left my bag on the bed and went outside to play soccer. Erini joined us. Stelios and I played against Nikos and Erini. Nikos was a tremendous athlete for a ten-year-old. He wore glasses and looked like Harry Potter.

When the game ended, the kids wanted to play more but I was too tired and they kept begging me and I told them later. I sat down on the porch, where Eleftheria had left a large plate of fruit and a jug of water, and plucked at a few grapes. I watched Stelios bounce the ball off Stella's head and she cried. Then Nikos kicked the ball and it struck a plant vase which shattered when it fell and hit the cement. Eleftheria walked outside with her hands coated with a paste.

"Children, what are you doing now? Nikos! Stop it. I'm so sorry, Panagiotis. Stelios don't touch Stella again, *alimono!*"

In the evening, we hung out in front of the fireplace next to the TV. I looked after the fire. As soon as it looked close to flaming out I'd add another piece of wood. We watched TV and I asked the kids what the new words I heard in Greek meant. They were eager to explain and, as they only knew Greek, it was endearing to hear them doing so with other Greek words in their kid vocabulary. Reindeer was a new word I learned—τάρανδος in Greek, a masculine noun. But deer was ελάφι, a neuter noun. I had my work cut out for me.

Eleftheria shouted from the kitchen when dinner was ready. We all gathered around the table. Dimitris was still in Myriokefalo helping out his mom. Eleftheria had made *moussaka*: a classic Greek pie with minced beef, onions, potatoes, and zucchini with a béchamel paste over the top. She knew it was my favorite.

"Do you like it?" she asked in English.

"It's perfect," I responded in Greek.

"I need to call your mother to thank her for the clothes she sent us."

"She calls me every day. When she calls I'll give you the phone."

I thanked her plenty for the dinner, then I retired early to my bedroom. I wrote a few thoughts in my journal before I fell asleep.

* * *

Eleftheria was always busy. She made me food throughout the day. She cleaned the dishes. I offered my assistance, but she would never let me help. Her mind always seemed to be occupied, which I noticed by the way her eyes bounced off objects as her hands moved in the sink. She was always shouting at her kids to *Relax, please.* They never settled down and when Stelios made Stella cry, she strengthened her tone, and when it was Nikos and Stelios causing the chaos she always yelled at Nikos. She was an elementary school teacher, too, and I only wondered how she ever had time for herself.

I liked that she took an interest in my creative pursuits. She was aware of my fascination with Crete and she showed me a book about its entire history, but it was in Greek and I wasn't skilled enough to read it usefully. I was impressed by her and by her unceasing sacrifice for her children and family. Watching her made me realize that I was an overwhelmingly selfish man, in many ways.

For no precise reason I could determine, I felt the urge to leave after two days and so I said, impulsively, "I'm going to leave tomorrow."

"It's New Year's Eve tomorrow," Eleftheria said. "We're going to Myriokefalo."

"I know, but I'm going to Chania, to hang out with a friend."

"Your Dad will be there."

"I'll probably go to Chania."

She turned her head in a disapproving manner, as if she thought my behavior was very strange.

"Think about it," she said. "The whole family will be there."

During the evening, I was on the couch with the kids, the fire keeping us warm, when Eleftheria handed me the phone. It was Dimitris who was in Myriokefalo.

"How are you, Panagiotis? Tomorrow we'll celebrate New Year's Eve in Myriokefalo. I spoke to your Dad."

"He's coming?"

"Yes! He's coming."

"I think I'm going to Chania"

"What are you saying now? You're not going to Chania. We will all be together."

"I don't know about that."

"What are you going to do in Chania?"

"My friend is there."

"Everyone spends time with their family at home for New Year's Eve."

"We'll see."

"No *we'll see*. I'll see you tomorrow. You better not leave, *alimono*."

Eleftheria re-entered the living room.

"Panagiotis, it'd be nice for you to be there."

On the television was Snow White. Erini, who was double the size of Stella, snuggled next to her under a blanket on the other side of the couch. Nikos was on the floor with his notebook full of football cards. Stelios squeezed my arm.

"Come on, Panagiotis, you're coming—you're coming!"

Eleftheria brought us a large plate with toasted ham and cheese sandwiches.

"Your mother said she will call you tomorrow," she said.

I gazed at the fireplace. The wood burned strongly and the light from the fire reflected off the silver-plated panel guarding it. Stelios grabbed my sweater and rested his head on my arm. Eleftheria was in the kitchen cooking food for tomorrow. All the energy from the day's chaos had been consumed. This was easy. The storyline played out how one hopes it should and life was good this way.

CHAPTER TWENTY-SEVEN

Myriokefalo was the next village down the mountain from Kallikratis on the north side of Crete. It was dark and cold outside when we squeezed into Dimitris' truck. Eleftheria was in the backseat with her kids and I sat in the front with a large bag of food on my lap.

The kids were extra excited because *yiayia* phoned and said there was snow. Stella flung up her arms and Erini wrapped her arms around her. Stelios tried to tickle her and she made a sharp whimper.

Her enthusiasm reminded me of the magic of a child's imagination. The excitement and preciousness you see in their eyes at such times makes you want to nurture the moment as long as possible. Right now I felt very satisfied to be spending New Year's with them. I could not recall the last time I had celebrated New Year's with family.

Aunt Erini saw us from the kitchen window and came to the door to greet us. Yiamonda, who had light brown hair and an affable smile, wore an apron with rolled up sleeves. She came toward me and kissed me with her soiled hands held away saying, "*Xronia Polla,* Panagiotis!"

Stelios zoomed past my hip and chased George's Nikos up the stairs and across the hallway to see the new pellet gun he was playing with. The floor was a large open space divided into four: kitchen, living room, family room, and dining room. Dad was in the family room, next to the fireplace, talking to a neighbor who'd stopped by to make well wishes.

"*Kalosorises*," Dad said. "*Xronia Polla!*"

I strolled over to the couch and rubbed my hands in front of the fireplace.

"*Xronia Polla*," Dad said to me.

"*Xronia Polla*." I said to him in a deep quiet tone.

George handed me a shot of *tsikoudia*. Aunt Erini brought us a platter with cheeses and *dolmathes* and *keftethes*. On the television was a *bouzouki* show in Athens. Famous Greek people dressed in fancy clothes sat at tables groaning with food and drinks listening to live music. Some people danced, but mostly they stayed where they were while a grinning host walked around asking them questions. The women were all pretty and heavily made up, their outfits shiny and colorful.

Everyone who had been at Christmas dinner was here except for Litsa and Wilfred and Manolis' sister. Dad sat at the opposite end of the table from me with Dimitris, George, and Manolis. He wanted me to eat the goat intestines, called *endera*, but I pushed the plate away. I filled my plate with a lot of meat and grabbed a couple of *kalistounia*, little pies, soft and moist, some filled with spinach and others with *mizithra*. I ate wet rice at the end to help with my buzz. Within a short amount of time I again managed to overeat to the point where my stomach ached but this was okay because I would not eat like this again for a while.

For dessert, there was a large saucer of bad sweets: *kourabiethes* and *melomakarona* and *koulourakia*. And there was another saucer with the good sweets: grapes and apples and pears. Dad filled a plate with the good sweets. Yiamonda cut the *Vasilopita*, the New Year's sweet bread, and everyone was anxious to get the piece with the silver coin in it. When Aunt Erini found the coin we congratulated her and she turned pale. Dad told her to go to the casino. I looked over and saw George with a look of deep concern on his face. He was like Dad in never expressing his concerns, but you knew he was an anxious man.

After dinner we moved to different parts of the house. I sat on the leather couch in the living room. Aunt Erini warmed her hands at the fireplace. Dad remained at the table with Manolis, George, and Dimitris drinking wine. It was still thirty minutes before midnight when Dimitris' Nikos walked into the room dressed as Santa Claus, toting a large, red cotton bag over his shoulder. The kids screamed. Stelios tried to tug at his beard. He shouted names as he pulled out each gift. I got a green sweater and a coffee mug with Santa and his reindeers painted on it. Dad received a pack of cards and a pair of socks. Watching him open his gifts was like watching a child who'd never received gifts before and now, experiencing it for the first time, was slow to tear open the package.

On the television the fancy people stopped dancing as they watched for the final seconds to count down. I looked at my watch, then used my iPhone for the precise time. "*Xronia Polla!*" everyone shouted. "Many Years!" "*Kali Xronia!*" they shouted, too. "Good Year!" We all kissed and hugged. It was a lot of closeness and it was an alright feeling; it was entirely family.

Family, yes. You go back because you feel guilty if you don't. Hoping this time will be different. And it can be different, if only we release ourselves from past grudges to embrace the moment for what it is. I felt like a better person to let pass the grudge I had with Dad after our Christmas dinner. I lifted up Stella and raised her over my head. I swung her around like she could fly and she squealed and Stelios wanted me to lift him up too. On this night there were no fights. There were discussions and disagreements, of course, but underlying everything was a fundamental understanding and it was connected with the idea of family. The egotism, disapproval, and blame that occasionally arose between individuals never arrived on this night. It was a late night, too. We played poker until past three. We used white beans as the poker chips. Dad won everyone's beans.

"Go to the casino, now," Manolis said.

"You'll go there now, and you'll lose all your money," Dimitris said.

"Yes." Dad's head dropped. "That's how it is."

The game eventually dispersed, and people went upstairs one by one.

"You ready to leave now?" Dad asked me.

"You're not leaving!" Yiamonda said. "You're sleeping here tonight. My lord! There's so much snow outside. We have two couches. We'll all sleep here."

Yiamonda brought us blankets. Dad didn't resist. He slept on the couch next to the fireplace. I slept on the leather couch. Nikos slept in the armchair. When Yiamonda turned off the lights and went upstairs and the fireplace was almost flamed out, all was very quiet and calm. I could smell the toasted cinnamon from the *melomakarona* cooling on the stovetop.

In the early morning, Yiamonda and Aunt Erini were in the kitchen baking more *melomakarona*. I lay on my side looking out the window. Thick snow covered the street and the light made the valley sparkle. One by one the kids woke up and as they looked outside at the fluffy blanket of snow they shouted with excitement. Dad sat at the table drinking a Greek coffee.

Eleftheria grabbed Stelios before he went outside without a snow cap. Then she zipped up Stella's coat and covered her ears with a pink striped cap.

"Did you sleep good, Panagiotis?" George asked.

"Very good."

Out of the corner of my eye I saw a snowball smack the kitchen window. Aunt Erini, who was standing at the sink, didn't flinch. Eleftheria opened the door.

"Kids, play friendly. Stelios, don't you think about it!"

Dad passed by Eleftheria and, stopping on the porch, greeted the crisp cold day with great calmness. At that moment a snowball exploded off his chest.

"Kids, don't throw snow! I told you," Eleftheria shouted. Dad smiled. He grabbed a chunk of snow piled on the ledge of the porch, balled it with his bare hands and pegged Stelios square in the back. Then Nikos pelted Dad on the shoulder. Erini's snowball limped at

Dad's feet. He whipped several more back at them. He smiled and grunted and laughed. Stella squealed. Dad pelted Nikos in the face and knocked off his glasses. He was tossing snowballs as fast as he could make them. Yiamonda laughed from the kitchen window. I stood at the doorway. The kids heaved a flurry of snowballs and Dad rushed back into the house. At that moment, Dimitris walked down the steps.

"*Kalimera!* The *mayor* just woke up now?" Dad said.

"This is very nice, Peter." George said in English. "For us all to be here together." He stood up and pulled another chair from the dining table for Dad to sit down.

"We're going to leave now," Dad said.

"We're going to have lunch here today," George said.

"Panagiotis has to take the bus back."

"You stay here, Panagiotis. I will drive you down to Episkopi to take the bus."

"I'm going to take him!" Dad said.

The entire drive down to the bottom of the mountain was quiet. I waited in the car until the bus arrived. Dad insisted I take the socks he got. I told him, no. But he still insisted.

CHAPTER TWENTY-EIGHT

After the holidays had passed and I was back in my usual routine, I experienced another bout of anxiety about the army. In America, I had been excited about the idea of serving in the Greek army. Now, though, the thought frightened me. What if there was a war once I joined? The relationship between Turks and Greeks appeared tenuous. A mass influx of refugees was entering the country by way of Turkey. Rumor in Crete was that Turkey's autocratic government believed that the islands along the coast of Turkey belonged to them. It would be just my luck, I thought, if all hell broke loose the moment I was in uniform.

I had been living in Greece for nearly six months. Since the Greeks recognized me as a citizen, I was able to stay as long as I wished but I had to finish my military duty. Normally native-born Greeks served for at least nine months, but as I was born and raised in America the term could be shorter for me. However, I needed to prove I had lived in America all my life in order to serve the minimum of three months. This was the big snag, especially as I'd lived in various parts of the country—I had to deal with the consulates in New York, Chicago, and Los Angeles and they were all cumbersome. Over the holidays I had been unable to get hold of any of the consulates. The few emails I had exchanged with people in charge of issuing permanent resident certificates led nowhere, so I phoned the Greek Army office in Heraklion.

"It's mandatory for you," said a man in the office, "but you only do six months."

"Only six months and you don't need a certificate from the Greek consulate of my permanent residence abroad?"

"No. Only if you want to do three months do we need the permanent resident certificate from the consulate in America."

"They're giving me a hard time."

"If you want to go in March you don't have a lot of time. I can add your name and once the papers come, you'll do three months. Do you want that?"

I went silent, realizing the ramifications of this decision. Then I said, "Okay."

"You want me to enlist you for March?" he said.

"Yes. Enlist me for March."

"Okay. You're enlisted. Someone will call you with the exact date and location."

"That's it?"

"*Malista.*"

"So all I need is a certificate from the consulate showing I'm a permanent resident abroad and then I do only three months?"

"*Malista.*"

I jumped off my seat and hopped outside onto my veranda. Grabbing the railing I gazed out at the sea and then tilted my head down toward the alley where two old ladies rested in white plastic chairs.

"Good morning!" I said to them.

"Good morning!" they responded.

* * *

My Greek had improved significantly since my arrival, but I was eager to get better, especially now with my army obligation approaching, so I enrolled in a second Greek class located in the old town in Splantzia square.

On the first day of my new class I found myself in the company of five other students. There were Paul and David from Canada, Olga from Russia, Olivia from Sweden, and Gudrun from Iceland. They all knew each other from a previous class in the fall. Their Greek was terrible. Paul, a German who lived in Canada, was seventy-five-years-old with white hair and very pale skin. Gudrun was blond and thin and bohemian with unpronounced features. She looked a few years older than me. She watched me a lot in class. David was around sixty and nearly bald. He liked Gudrun and noticed how she looked at me and, no doubt because of this, was the least friendly of the other students. Our teacher's name was Maria. Hailing from Athens, she had dark, curly hair and fair skin with green eyes.

After the first day of class, I walked with Paul through the old town. He walked with ski poles because he had a bad ankle. He was intrigued by the fact that I wrote screenplays. He wanted to read one. I did not see any reason for him to read one of my screenplays, but as he didn't press me further about it, I became more eager for him to read one. So I offered to share one of my screenplays with him if he offered to proofread it. He agreed without hesitation.

I spent the entire next day reading over my script and making changes, then I went to a copy center and printed and bound a copy. I waited until the end of class before I handed Paul my script. He appeared more surprised to receive it than I was to give it to him. He invited me to join him for lunch across the street at a restaurant called, *Kouzina* EPE.

We shared plates of *moussaka* and *vlita*, which is an amaranth plant Greeks boil and eat with olive oil and lemon and salt. Paul spoke uninhibitedly to me. He was, I discovered, a well-educated and cultivated man. He had taught German to high school students. He lived in Crete from October until May. He didn't like it in the summer because there were too many tourists. He used to travel here with his wife, but she died a couple years ago. He had loved her dearly and was now struggling to manage life and find pleasure in it until his time came. He invited me to visit him in the summer in Winnipeg. This was only the second time I'd met him.

Our conversations were in English, except when we'd say Greek words. Paul liked to practice Greek words with me. We discussed how to properly order a beer and how to use the proper article to agree with the feminine noun.

"If you want another beer you say, *άλλη μια*. But if you want a different beer you have to say, *μια άλλη*," I told him.

"*Άλλη μια μπύρα, παρακαλό*," he said aloud to himself. "Another beer, please."

"Bravo!" I encouraged him.

He was a conscientious and equitable man in every sort of way. He always took the initiative in sharing the food. He was also considerate as to how I felt about the things we discussed. He became excited when the waiter brought a plate of panna cotta with dashes of caramel. He divided it perfectly down the middle with a knife. When the bill came we split it evenly and, after I had left a small tip, he gave me half the amount so it was equally shared by the both of us.

He moved very slowly, needing his ski poles to walk out of the restaurant. I offered my assistance down the two steps at the front door but he insisted he could do it on his own. We paused in front of the restaurant before he asked, "What are you doing on Friday night? I go to this restaurant on the other side of the old town where there are artists and musicians and they play music. It is very nice. Would you like to come?"

"This weekend I'm going to Sfakia—to help my father."

"Okay. Another time, then."

We said goodbye and he wobbled across Splantzia square while I turned down the alley toward the harbor. As I walked, I wondered if Paul thought that I didn't want to go with him to listen to live music and so he would not invite me next time.

The next day I was in Kallikratis. I felt bitter that I was here instead of in Chania. I wasn't exactly here to help Dad; it was more that I needed his passports to send over to the consulates. I was fine to leave immediately when I got them, but I agreed to stay for Saturday night in Chania.

The isolation of the village affected me worse than usual. It was sunny and cold when I got there. The moment Spirto saw me she padded toward me and rolled on her back, with her paws bent, squealing, but such was my mood I walked over her and went toward the house.

I slumped down in a plastic chair but had not rested for more than a few minutes before Dad hollered at me to remove the heavy bags of corn and sunflower seeds from the car and take them to the side of the house. Afterwards I helped him pour the corn into the barrel as he mixed in the sunflower seeds. When we had finished Dad climbed onto the edge of the wine tub and removed the large tarp and demanded I hand him the broom. I returned to the plastic chair and watched him gather up the dried twigs and leaves that bunched in the corners of the wine tub.

"Get up!" he shouted. "Why are you sitting down—we have work."

"What do you want me to do?"

"Hold the trash bag."

I stood at the edge of the wine tub and held the large black trash bag, and while I did this I stared at my surroundings. I noticed that the leaves from the mulberry trees were gone. I watched Spirto resting next to us on the ground. She regarded us closely with her chin on her paws. I liked to watch her because she set me at ease. She enjoyed being near us. She would watch the gate closely and if she heard a strange sound she'd stand up and pad toward the gate growling. Dad shook me out of my reverie when he said, as he tossed a dustpan full of leaves into the bag, "You're not leaving tomorrow because we're having *parea* on Sunday."

I straightened my frame and twitched my head with a look of bewilderment. "What *parea*? I said. "I have to be back tomorrow. I told you."

"You will leave on Sunday afternoon. Okay. Don't tell me no. We have work to do… Go fill the bucket up with water."

I did not have the energy to start a confrontation just then. I took a few deep, conscious breaths and rotated my neck in a slow, circular motion toward the mountain peaks above the village and, gasping, said to myself, *Relax, you know this is how your father operates. I'm here now and I will manage these next two days as patiently and calmly as I can. I will help Dad where he needs my help and I will not, under any circumstances, lose my cool and refuse his demands, no matter how crass or crude they may be. For he only yells for the good, as Little Kanakis said that day in the olive grove.*

I handed him a bucket of water and he splashed it around the tub. I filled up another bucket of water, then another, and another after that. I did this ten times until Dad finally said, "*Εντάξι.*" Okay.

I stood and watched as Dad mixed cement powder into a bucket with water and an oxidizing liquid. He stirred it until it turned into wet cement. He handed me half a broomstick saying, "Stir." He used a shovel to lift one glob of cement at a time and, bit by bit, covered the cracks in the tub while I kept stirring. "Bravo. That's how you do it," he said.

"How much longer should I stir?" I asked.

"Stir! Don't stop."

"I'm asking! How much longer does this need to be stirred?"

"It's cement!—you stop when we're done."

"You need to buy a machine for this," I said.

"You want everything to be easy for you."

Just in time I realized I had lost my composure. I stopped speaking at once and, after a few deep breaths, found myself in a calmer place. We finished the work by lunch time and Dad cooked a decent meal for us to eat. I filled my belly quickly, but my plate was still crowded with goat meat, so when Dad wasn't looking I wrapped the goat meat in a napkin and walked outside. I tossed a piece to Spirto and she devoured it. I threw another piece to the other dog who sniffed at it before gnawing it down.

I turned back toward the courtyard, intending to sit down, but I was conscious Dad may very well shout my name and have me do some more work so I went for a walk around the village. It was empty. There wasn't a human in sight. The herbal café was closed. I walked as far as a church that stood on a stony hilltop about a half-kilometer from Dad's house. The door was open. It was dark inside and there was a small, woven cane basket where you could leave money. There were a few euros in it and I added another. Then I watched the icons for a moment but failed to discover within myself any deep religious sensation. Only after I had retreated back outside was I hit with a sense of fear of the power of my imagination.

The isolation of Kallikratis was, I sensed, the bridge I needed to truly unleash my powers. However, in doing so, I felt I could well go crazy unless I had another being who understood me and was around for me to latch onto so I could stop and recalibrate. The irony was that I wished for this place when I didn't have it, only to recoil before the lonely and fragile state of creativity it inspired the moment I plunged into it. At the same time, I was still tethered to Chania which inundated me with constant stimulation.

Dad was resting in the courtyard when I returned. There was a pile of apple rinds on the table. I whistled and Spirto came toward me.

"The dog likes you," Dad said.

"Yes. Because I'm nice to her."

"You want to go and feed the goats?" he asked.

"Now?"

"In a little bit."

Dad filled a large bucket with corn and sunflower seeds and we drove around the tiny church on the hill toward a piece of land on the side of a mountain where his flock of goats roamed. Spirto followed us from behind. There wasn't a goat in sight.

Dad bellowed loudly and weirdly a few times. Spirto wagged her tail. Dad bellowed again. A goat appeared from a crevice in the mountain. Then, moments later, I heard a sharp metallic tinkling and a second goat, with a bell harnessed to his neck, appeared behind the first.

"Climb down and drop the food over there," Dad instructed.

I walked over the riverbed and climbed up a patch of rocks toward the feeding area. I dumped a large bucket full of food on the ground.

"Spread it around," Dad shouted. I refilled the bucket and dropped more food. Some of the goats advanced down the rocks and onto the road. Spirto barked at them but they ignored her. "Take a picture!" Dad said. I snapped a picture of Dad with a big smile grabbing the udders of one of his goats. I counted twenty goats; a couple of them were kids, cute little creatures, who stayed close to their mother. Each time I tried to approach them they'd hide behind her.

Dad brought a medium-sized buck back to the house and tied it to the tree. The goat bleated all night. The temperature dropped noticeably and I had to wrap myself in my clothes with the fleece blanket covering my head. I slept with an electric heater running next to me but at some point, after I had conked out, Dad turned it off.

I was not in the best of spirits next morning. Now that I had Dad's passports to send along to the consulates in the US, I only wished to be in Chania. I did not care to stay another day to spend time with his *parea*. I would not attempt to write today and would only be able to read for a short bit before Dad summoned me for another task. He always had me moving a thing here or a thing there and holding this and that. I almost lost my wits when we tried to move the wood stove from the living room to the kitchen and had to quit halfway because it was extremely heavy and Dad's back was in bad shape.

"We're going to freeze our asses again tonight," I said. "I hope you know this is the last time. I'm done with this shit."

Dad phoned one of the neighbors, Spiro. He was at the house in twenty minutes. He was a well-built man with meaty hands and thick wrists and bulging forearms. His pupils were small and his irises were green and, with his bristling black mustache, it made him look intense.

"It's not going to warm up the house from there," he said.

"It will warm up the house," Dad said.

"You'll need to put a bed in the kitchen."

"Put it there for now, I want to use it to cook."

Spiro and I moved the wood stove underneath a cement cover that protruded from the corner of the wall where the smoke could escape. Dad fed it firewood and it burned strongly and the heat crept across the kitchen. I huddled next to it to warm up my hands and body. Feeling warm for a change was a great joy. It was silly to think of it as a joy because it was a common comfort accessible to most people. But freezing your ass off all night and morning put things in a new perspective. To have this sensation was a fantastic luxury and I felt relaxed and calmed and I thought how, at this moment, reading a book would be the perfect pleasure. But then coming from outside I heard a loud, frantic shrilling that went on for a few seconds before suddenly going silent.

I walked toward the door, stopping at the threshold. The goat was hanging on hooks from the mulberry tree. His neck was half open. Spiro worked methodically and seamlessly, removing the skin as if he was peeling a potato. Within half an hour he had the animal in pieces. Dad thanked him, whereupon Spiro tossed back his hand saying, "*Tipota*," "Nothing," before nonchalantly lighting a cigarette and going on his way.

Dark crimson blood stained the cement and the broken-off hooves were on the ground. Dad mounted the goat's head on a stick and stuck it at the gate. Soon the insects would get to it and all that would be left to remember the goat by would be its skull.

That night the house was so cold we moved a bed next to the wood stove. Dad and I huddled by the fire, sipping tea. My hands clasped the cup for its warmth. I felt bothered, though I wasn't sure if this was because of the cold house or the fate of the poor goat or Dad's inconceivably stupid ideas.

"Bravo. Very smart idea," I said, referring to his decision to move the wood stove.

Dad was mute. He added more wood. We were warm when we were next to the wood stove, but the moment we moved away the chill off the cement floor and walls made it feel like we were in an icebox.

"Kallikratis!" I said. "The whole world wants to come here."

Everything around me was old and it irritated me. The wood stove was probably from the 1950s. Dad used a battered saucepan to heat up water on top of it. A large, thick, and exceedingly rough blanket, woven by my grandma, covered the bed, certainly had never been washed.

"Do you have a pillow?"

"What's wrong with the pillow?"

"This is a brick!"

"It's from your grandmother! Is something wrong with you…"

"With me? Are you serious? You're the one who can't change."

"Why should I?"

"Because we're not in the 1950s anymore. Since then they've created softer pillows."

Dad added more wood. I could see him stirring inside, staring at the fire.

"Kallikratis! The center of the world…" I said, grinning, my frustration spilling over. "You have the money. Here's a smart idea—add a thermostat! Good idea? Yes, it is a good idea if you have a brain."

"You don't have a brain."

"I'm not the smart one who moved the wood stove for all the hot air to disappear into the sky. Good job! You say there's something wrong with *me*? You can't change with anything! That's how life moves forward. Things change and you change with it."

"I see what you've done."

"I've done a lot."

"What have you done? You left your job because you couldn't do it anymore."

My eyebrows furrowed and I was stunned for a long few seconds.

"I left my job because I wanted to do something else. Something I liked, something more fulfilling."

"You left your job because they were going to fire you."

"I don't give a shit what you think. I've done everything on my own. You haven't done shit for me my entire life."

"What did you do for me!?"

"I'm your son! I shouldn't have to do a damn thing for you."

We huffed and puffed and the cold air seized the carbon dioxide from our mouths, making angry clouds before our eyes. The mood of tolerance and self-restraint in which I'd arrived at Kallikratis had evaporated in the face of Dad's stupidity.

"I paid for my school. I got my job on Wall Street. It wasn't you! You gambled all your money away. I made money!"

"God help you. Do your cross!"

"I'm not doing my cross!"

"Do your cross!"

I walked outside. It was freezing and starkly dark. A sliver of the moon hung over the black peaks of the mountains. I felt a sense of immense isolation, wishing I was back in Chania.

* * *

Dad spent all morning cooking. He had the pieces of goat boiling in a large pot next to the outhouse. I kept to myself, numb and silent, sure I'd never come to Kallikratis again.

We commenced lunch just before two. Dad's friends from Chania turned out to be very nice people. They were brother and sister. The sister had brought her son, who was Dad's accountant. Spiro was there too. Finally there was an old friend of Dad's from the army, with his wife, whom he hadn't seen in over fifty years until they bumped into each other at a dinner earlier in the week. The lunch had been organized, I realized, because Dad wanted to welcome his friend to his home and introduce him to his son.

It was a Cretan tradition for men to exchange pocket knives as a sign of remembrance and friendship. Dad had been dissatisfied with the pocket knife he'd given his friend so he gave him a better one today. I could see that Dad felt very good about it.

They shared stories from the army. The man told us that Dad was once hazed and they demanded he shave his mustache, but he refused. He said Dad was a strong and tough soldier. Dad remained silent and calm. He'd drop his head as a memory of his youth came to mind.

"Do you remember the snow, when we hiked the mountains?" Dad reminded him.

"I remember the snow. I remember the night without sleep…" said his friend. "We were in the special forces. The team all the other recruits were afraid of."

"Those were the old years. Today, it is different… It's like vacation."

Our argument from the previous night had passed in the good feeling inspired by the lunch. We buried it on top of all the other arguments we'd had, piled one on top of the other in a high mound awaiting the miraculous day we'd decide to set it in flames and accept things as they were. When I left, taking a ride back to Chania with his friends, Dad saw me off. The expression on his face betrayed great concern.

CHAPTER TWENTY-NINE

As I continued with my Greek lessons, I took a larger interest in my new classes that were on Tuesdays and Thursdays because the people were more enjoyable to be around. Except I was a bit relieved to notice that Karina had significantly calmed down. All I could suspect was that she was finally getting laid.

I always enjoyed sitting back and observing the other students struggle with pronunciation or with finding the meaning of words. Paul needed to know the direct translation in English of every Greek word and the teacher didn't like that. She usually gave a description in Greek which only confused him more.

I told him, "It's better if you search for the meaning of the word in Greek."

He retorted, "I'm seventy-five-years-old. I don't have time to waste."

When Paul struggled with the language he was hard on himself. And because he did not like to feel insecure when he spoke he usually abstained from speaking.

Of course, I experienced my own frustrations with the language, mostly due to my urgency to learn it quickly and correctly. However I had accepted the fact long before that speaking a new language was going to mean sounding like an idiot in the beginning. I made mistakes often. The Greek language is tough. First off, it consists of another alphabet. Then there are the genders and the cases, the long words, the distinctive meanings. Translating English into Greek always confused me. For instance, the word *password*, which I needed for the Wi-Fi, had several different meanings in Greek. Παρασύνθημα was the "secret word" you used to gain entrance into a restricted place. But Google translated it as "password." The password I needed for the Wi-Fi, however, was κωδικός. Google also translated it as "password." When you used the wrong word, the locals looked at you like you were silly and then spoke to you in English.

Many words I tried to use gracefully only made me appear foolish. Take the word *place*, for example. The verb form of the word was different to the noun. Greeks have a different word for *place* as in location. Another word I had to be careful with was *change*. There was change as in coins, ψιλά or ρέστα. Then there was the change in society or way of life, which was μετασχηματισμός, while a change of position or job was αλλαγή.

Most of the time I was genuinely proud to be learning Greek. I tried hard to discover new words that I could use in conversation. The children's books helped a lot, and I enjoyed the fairy tales. However, there were days when I was tired or simply not feeling up to it and I struggled to speak clearly. Other times I thought of it as a waste of effort. To convince myself of the fact I'd rationalize that I could better use the time to make money. But every day I learned a new word, it strengthened me in a way I was unaccustomed to, and my emotions and my spirit felt considerably healthier. As my vocabulary accumulated, I sensed the fabric of the culture seeping into me and the direct practical use of the language didn't seem so important by comparison. The sounds of a different language rolling off my tongue empowered me to continue going forward.

Yet even as I progressed, I continued to feel at odds sometimes. The reasons for this were elusive. But I'd experienced a similar thing in the US when I'd have to identify myself to a stranger and I'd tell them I was from Ohio, but only saying I was from Ohio and I was American left me feeling incomplete and I'd want to give them the entire picture, but then I'd think it wasn't worth it. Maybe I felt awkward living on the cusp of being Greek. Or rather, as a developing Greek returning to his homeland to reclaim his worth. I wasn't a foreigner whom Greeks would embrace as a guest as was the standard procedure with tourists. I felt compelled to identify somehow, yet I wasn't ready to make a claim.

The language helped me in my dealings with Dad. He criticized my Greek because he saw I was learning, and he did not want to soften me by applauding my improvements. His ways were old ways. He lived according to other rules of life that I found irritating and embarrassing and pathetic. I could see I was like my father, but only up to a point, as my education and travels had given me experiences he had never been able to have. Yet I was financially depressed and nearing middle age, so perhaps if I viewed my life from Dad's perspective, I might think that I hadn't done anything, either. Certainly, if Dad and Mom had sacrificed everything to provide me with the American Dream that was a tragedy and I felt guilty.

I wanted success. Only what was success? Moving to Greece to cultivate myself, learn the language, and connect with my ancestry. Society didn't value my decision, I felt. I sometimes suspected that people saw me as a lost and confused soul, an idiot—alternately, perhaps they were simply jealous or indifferent. Traditionally society measured success in terms of a big home, a prestigious job, a nice car, and a pretty wife. But I had been through that and seen the hollow nature of such things. In coming to Greece I was searching for a solid foundation from which I might follow an alternative path through contemporary society. Those status symbols may yet come, but to me the important thing was to cultivate myself as a dynamic person who was capable of many things. As Zorba says, "All Kinds. With feet, hands or head—all of them. It'd be the limit if we chose what we did!"

In terms of American ideology, living in Greece exacerbated my uncertainties of ever having a successful life. Yet I could not retreat from the course I had chosen for I strongly sensed that something life-changing was going to happen to me here and a different version of success could be attained.

CHAPTER THIRTY

A few weeks after I had arranged my documents for the consulate and mailed them, I received a call from the army office in Heraklion.

"Mr. Manouselis?"

"*Malista*," I answered.

"I'm George from the army office in Heraklion. You will be reporting to the army base in Rethymno on March 13."

"March 13. What time?"

"In the morning, anytime from eight to noon," he said. "You'll receive a letter in the mail. Is the correct address in Kallikratis?"

"Yeah. That's where my dad lives."

"Okay. *Kalos stratos*." The words meant something like, "Good Luck in the Army."

"Is that it?"

"What else do you want me to tell you? *Kalos stratos*."

"What about the papers for the three months? Did you receive them from the consulate in Los Angeles?"

"No."

"No?"

"Don't worry. If you sent them, we'll get them. Once we receive them you will do only three months."

"That's it?"

"*Malista. Kalos stratos*."

It was the ease by which the Greeks operated that frightened me. When the Greeks said don't worry, I worried. They liked to say, *don't worry*. For them, nothing in life was truly worth worrying about unless it was war and death and then they fought and mourned.

I called Mom to give her the big news.

"I'm going to the army!" I told her. "March 13 I have to report to the army base in Rethymno."

"Oh, God!"

"I'm going to be a soldier! A Greek solider. I'm going to serve my country."

"You're crazy."

"I'm going to ask them to ship me off to one of those islands that have all the refugees, like Mytilini."

"Oh, God—stay in Rethymno!"

"I want to go where the action is—"

"You're not alright. You're not a human of reason."

The news of my admission strengthened me. I had no idea what to expect once I was in the army. But in only three months, I reasoned, what could be the worst thing that might happen?

I phoned Dad and told him.

"I need to teach you how to shoot a gun, so they don't make fun of you," he said.

"That's what the army's for!"

"Call Dimitris and tell him you're going to be in Rethymno."

"I'll only be there for training, then I'm going to one of the islands with the refugees."

"I don't think they will let you go there."

"We'll see about that! I'm a soldier now."

I made the appropriate announcements to each of my Greek classes and in both situations Maria and Angela asked the same question.

"You have to go to the army?"

"I want to," I told them.

"*Bravo!* Everyone wants to avoid the army and you want to go… *Krima,* what a shame, you won't be able to stay longer… we have a lot to learn," Maria said.

I would have liked to have finished the entire term. I was finally grasping the grammar and this had helped me achieve a good learning rhythm. But as happens in life, my circumstances had changed, and I had to embrace the new undertaking.

Ironically, my imminent departure initiated an immediate effort by my classmates to cement a friendship with me. We snapped pictures together, exchanged emails, promised to go out for coffee. If I never saw any of them again, I felt the well-wishes and concern were appropriate and sufficient as a proper send-off.

Paul and I managed to have lunch before I left to discuss my script. We met at *Kouzina* EPE after my last day of class. I was eager to hear his feedback.

"Are you going to stay in Sfakia until you have to report?" he asked.

"For most of the time. I do want to see Faistos," I said, as I picked at the olives in the tiny bowl and left the pits on my plate. I kept the chatter snappy as I waited for him to tell me what he thought about my script. The carafe of white wine had arrived and he still hadn't said anything about my script so I asked him, "What did you think of the story?"

He tossed out some nonsensical verbiage first, then he said, "It was difficult for me to connect with… I didn't grow up in such a dysfunctional family. Was that your life growing up?"

"It's a fictional story. I didn't really blow up a police car."

"The kid's name was Peter, and he was Greek—although you said he was swarthy in appearance and I would never consider you swarthy in appearance."

"Would it be a movie you'd like to watch?"

"The way it's written makes me think it may be better on the screen. I've never read a screenplay before. It was interesting to read. Thank you for letting me read something you spent a lot of time on and is personal to you. I went through in pencil and marked grammatical issues I found. Do you want to go through the grammar together?"

Feedback, though sometimes demoralizing, was what you endured when you wrote your thoughts down on paper. Honesty never worried me, even if it was critical. Paul was honest during our times together. I liked this very much. As we were going through the grammar we rolled into a discussion of Greek grammar and then into a particularly interesting discussion about language and its evolution.

Paul said, "The more Greek words you learn the more you'll be able to use the words in English to communicate a meaning and no one will know the difference."

"Do you do that with German words?"

"Yes! I Canadianize my German."

"I guess English is an amalgamation of all the other languages?"

"The language found its form in the 1400s when the Germans were pushed north into Britain and they spoke their own language."

As Paul spoke, an insight appeared and I rattled off, "And language gets diluted and worse off year by year. The more English we speak the more vague and incoherent we become. One day we'll be no different to how chimpanzees communicate and then we'll have come full circle. It'll be a great thing, right?"

"Language has always been losing its luster. You're realizing this now because you know a second language. We continue to simplify. That's why English is a great universal language. It's simplified. All the words are inflected. You only need to understand the context."

"Yeah. And subtext. And if one interprets a different subtext that leads to war and murder—what a great fucking language."

"It is a business language… but very practical and all-encompassing which makes it nice."

The lunch lasted for several hours and we ate and drank plenty and when the bill arrived I could do nothing but chuckle. I handed Paul ten euros and said, "The way we ate today would have cost me over fifty dollars in Los Angeles. And the food here was healthier and tastier!"

"I liked the perch this time," he said. "Last time it was a bit dry."

CHAPTER THIRTY-ONE

On the day I moved out, Giorgia stopped by to inspect the apartment. She was satisfied with the cleaning job I had done. She appeared to have gotten over her frustration that I had to leave the apartment after only five months. When I handed her back the keys she wished me well and said, "*Kalos stratos.*" I loaded one last bag of my belongings into Dad's Suzuki and off I went to Patsianos.

I was more relaxed than usual on my way to Patsianos. Dad was back in the US for a few months and it was refreshing to think I would not have to worry about him shouting at me to work. He made sure to stop and see me in Chania on the day he was leaving. He asked me to drive him to the airport and to keep the car while he was away and to check-up on the dogs. Our last quarrel in Kallikratis nearly broke me, thinking I would never speak to him again. However, I could never hold a long grudge with him. Enough though he was crass at times, my instincts detected he had good-intentions.

By the time I had settled into the apartment, it was past seven in the evening. I sipped from a cold can of Mythos and watched the neighbor's dog bark incessantly. It was chained down next to half a telephone pole. After a while I tried to ignore the dog and focus instead on the sun falling over the edge of the mountain. The temperature was comfortable. I was isolated and alone but I did not feel lonely. *I have an entire week to myself,* I thought.

Just after nightfall, I prepared a simple dinner of goat and *vlita* Dad had left for me, which I ate out on the veranda. Stars pricked the sky and crickets chirped in the grass. Faintly scented with the herbs that grew roundabout, the night was utterly, gloriously peaceful. Toward bedtime, I did not have any of my usual anxiety attacks and I slept without worries.

Next morning, I went to Anopolis. I stopped at Chora Sfakion to visit the post office on the way. At first the clerk said there was no mail for Dad, but when I told him I was waiting on a letter from the army, he went to the back room to take another look. When he returned, he handed me an envelope from the army that was already opened. I shook my head as I returned to the car. The first page of the letter gave me the date and time I was to report to Rethymno and the second page was a list of items I was to complete before I reported. Unfortunately, I couldn't understand some of the items that were written in Greek.

From Chora Sfakion, the drive to Anopolis took about fifteen minutes. The road climbed steeply from the coast, ascending the stony flank of a mountain in torturous loops. The day was clear enough for me to see the island Gavdos far in the distance. At the top of the ascent, a road sign riddled with bullet holes informed you that you had reached the village of Anopolis. The shops I passed were all closed. The hotels with rooms for rent signs appeared abandoned. At the center of the village was a statue. I recognized it immediately. I circled around it before I parked my car off to the side.

Ioannis Vlachos was from Anopolis. They nicknamed him Daskalogiannis, John the Teacher, because he was well-informed and well-traveled and when he returned from his trips, throughout the Mediterranean, he'd enlighten the villagers with his wisdom. He was a successful businessman who owned four large ships with which he ran an import and export business. But then, at the height of his prosperity, he sacrificed his entire fortune and his life for Greece's freedom, dying in the most horrific way any man could die: flayed alive in front of his people. Legend has it he never uttered a sound throughout the ordeal.

I stared at his statue for a long time. He wore two Cretan knives tucked under his sash. Two doves were shown, one on either side of him. I read the engraving: *The first man in Crete to lead a rebellion against the Turks.* I found it heroic for one man, who had it all—wealth, knowledge, independence—to sacrifice his life for the sake of Crete and his country.

The prefecture of Sfakia, in which Anopolis lay, was the only region in Crete to maintain its independence from the Ottoman Empire. This is why my last name doesn't end in "akis" as most Cretan last names do. In other regions of Crete the Ottomans changed the last names by adding "akis" to the end of them. In the Greek language, the suffix "aki" at the end of words describes something little.

At the restaurant beside the square I ordered an omelet and a Greek coffee. I asked for a *ποτιράκι*, or small glass of water. Old, beefy men dressed in all-black watched me closely from another table. I ate quickly, then continued on my way, driving down the empty road toward the tiny village of Aradena. I coasted with my foot off the pedal and the clutch in neutral. The mountains overhead appeared to form a single continuous wall. Beneath the clear blue sky, they were large and grey and imposing. The combination was majestic and thrilling and, with the window down, I shouted in glee at the serenity. I was the only human in this setting of wild natural beauty.

I came to a road sign that said "Livania" and, for no reason except curiosity, I drove in that direction.

I arrived at the crest of the mountain within a few minutes. From up here the sea lay far below, opened up in front of me. I parked my car and walked to a large rock, my pen and notebook in my hand. I wrote.

The sun, the sky, the clouds!
The sea with its luscious palate of blue and green.
Turquoise is a real color, I see.

The breeze, the air, the hawks!
Gliding down below.
Africa far in the distance.
I've found earth at its most simple and primitive instance.
So many curious people who have crossed this sea.
The wars, and lives lost at the bottom of it.
Here I stand, at the top of the peak, enjoying
with pleasure what all those in the past have done
to bring me here.
I've neglected to appreciate all these luxuries.
I arrived without breaking a sweat,
so quickly with my modern utilities.
Going back will be too hard for me,
all I can show is my appreciation,
I thank you.
The deaths of the passionate who brought movement in life.
Let me never forget the past, nor shun the truth of it.
For that is the least I can contribute
to this spectacled creation by the supernatural we call God.

I closed my notebook and inhaled deeply several times. I remained motionless. Some people might think what I was doing and feeling was silly. Possibly it was. My delight in the view was genuine and all but overwhelming; yet I was proud of the calmness with which I enjoyed it. It was the kind of view which, by its sheer magnitude, made you a better person. And if you were able to remember what such a view once inspired in you, I believed, the chances were you would be a better and nobler person.

I was halfway through Anopolis when I realized I hadn't gone to Aradena. But I could not ruin the rhythm.

* * *

The rest of the week moved along smoothly. I spent my days writing and reading. I made a trip to Kallikratis to check up on Dad's dogs. Every day I enjoyed having the sea in front of me. With the sea in view I didn't feel alone or unhappy. I used my remaining few days before the army to take an excursion toward Heraklion. The morning of my departure I woke up very early. I laid a piece of *graviera* on a *paximathi* and drizzled it with honey for breakfast. I washed the dishes, scrubbed the bathroom, and swept the floor. It was unnecessary to water the garden for the time being so I left it.

It took me two hours to drive to Faistos, an ancient city on the south coast of the Heraklion prefecture. The road ebbed and curved and rose and fell as it traversed the wildly undulating landscape. You could very easily lose focus by staring out at promontories or mountains or at the effulgent sea.

It was drizzling when I arrived so I went to the café and ordered a Greek coffee. I watched the rain trickle off the olive trees near my table. I was the only tourist present. At another table were two locals who stared lingeringly at random objects.

I wrote a poem in Greek. It was my first Greek poem. I was proud of it. I wrote about the sounds I heard and about the large, open landscape, rich and verdant, and about the ancient stones softened by rainwater and withered by wind. I wrote about my great luck in finding myself here at Faistos on such a day. Right about the time I finished the poem the sun appeared.

Next I found myself in the middle of the ancient palace. Sunlight shining through the rainwater accentuated the colors of the stone. Halting me was a snail pushing hard across the sand-colored gravel to make it to cover. Its shell seemed ready to pop off it was exerting such great strength. I watched as it neared the precipice of a cinderblock. It had two tiny antennae that guided it. *Go my friend*, I whispered. *Don't worry. It's only me here now.*

I continued down the steps. My hands glided across the blocks of limestone. This was an ancient sanctuary over 5,000 years old, and *I* was the only tourist here. To see it as is was not spectacular to me, except when I linked it to man's journey to this moment, then my jaw dropped and I descended to another level of thought. The journey was Faistos' charm, I felt. The magnificence of Faistos was knowing through the knowledge of history and my imagination, that where I stood was a place that pioneered a way of human habitation that has been exponentially improved upon today.

When I exited the ruins, I saw a bus disgorging elderly tourists outside the gates. How unfortunate to have to wait until old age to make it here, I thought.

"Do you have a brochure?" I asked the lady at the gift store.

"*Malista,*" she answered.

There were two men at a table. They both had gray mustaches and wore jeans. The slender man wore a collared shirt while the stouter man wore a T-shirt. By the look of their swollen hands I took them for groundkeepers.

"Where are you from, my friend?" the slender man asked me.

"I'm a Greek-American, but I live here now."

"Yeah?"

"My parents are from Crete."

"*Yeah?* Where?"

"Sfakia."

"*Malista.* What's your last name?"

"Manouselis."

"*Manouselis?*"

"We're not all related…"

"Have a seat, my friend."

He poured me a *tsikoudia* and I told them my story. The lady working the gift store brought us a plate of fruit. Who did they think I was? I wondered. The rain started again and I could see from the window the elderly tourists rushing to the café.

"How did you like Faistos?"

"Delightful. It's unbelievable to think what they did here."

"It's a shame that it's raining today."

"It is perfect that it's raining today," I countered.

They offered me another *tsikoudia,* but I told them I was driving to Rethymno and should be on my way.

"Two *tsikoudias* won't ruin you," the slender man said.

I threw back another shot to repay their kind hospitality. The smooth burn of the alcohol opened up my chest. When I reached out my hand to wish them goodbye, their thick calluses imprinted themselves on my palm. "*Kalos stratos,*" they said. I knew they were proud I had made the trip and that made me proud.

CHAPTER THIRTY-TWO

Upon arriving in Rethymno, I looked forward to seeing Eleftheria and the family. She was cooking when I arrived. Every time I saw her, she seemed to be cooking. The kids shouted my name as I stepped through the door. Stelios rushed toward me and gave me a wild hug.

For lunch, Eleftheria cooked sea bass—*lavraki*. It was moist and succulent. Dimitris doused his fish with the juice of an entire lemon. Eleftheria filled everyone's glasses with water. Then we ran out of lemons, so she went to the kitchen to get more. When she returned she cut Stella's fish into small pieces.

"Eat, Stella," she said.

By the time she was able to eat and relax, Dimitris and I were nearly finished.

"Do you like the food, Panagiotis?" she asked.

"It's perfect! Thank you."

"How do you feel that you're going to be in the army tomorrow?"

"Good. I'm ready to go in and to finish."

"Three months—it will pass quickly. Anything you need just give us a call."

"Thank you."

"They're going to cut your hair for sure," Dimitris said.

"I know. Do you have clippers to buzz my head?"

"I have. You want me to cut it?"

"Sure. Buzz this mop off my head."

"Why does he have to go to the army?" asked Nikos.

"Because everyone has to go."

"But he's from America."

"He's Greek, too."

I helped Eleftheria carry plates into the kitchen. She insisted on cleaning them herself. Dimitris left to handle some work obligations. After he'd gone, I sat on the porch. Butterflies pranced about the front yard. The spring flowers were in bloom. *Tomorrow my situation will be completely unfamiliar to me*, I thought. This made me feel satisfied I was doing something outside of what I was comfortable with.

"*Petaloutha!*" Erini shouted.

"How did you call that?" I asked.

"A *petaloutha,*" she said.

It was the most delightful word I had yet heard in Greek. More delightful even than *thalassa*, the word for sea. I couldn't believe it was the first time I'd heard the name for a butterfly. Watching butterflies tranquilized me. A *petaloutha!* That was exactly what it was. In Greek it meant, literally, a flying flower. Butterflies were all over Crete. I saw them in white and multicolored—orange and black, yellow and green. The way they shuffled in the air as the sun shone on their wings was wonderful. The sweetness of Erini's voice was as innocent as the butterfly itself. It was a moment of great satisfaction.

* * *

We pulled up to the army base on Dimitris' moped. In front of the clearance gate were road barricades. They were meant to be filled with water or sand, but a soldier kicked them aside.

We proceeded through the gate. I had with me a duffle bag and backpack. I watched everything with intense curiosity. A nice breeze from the sea brushed my buzzed head. A young soldier with a smooth face, wearing a red beret and grasping a rifle, watched me closely. He looked restless, like he needed something to do. His eyes followed us as we moved to the inspection station that was in a small square building with a view of the sea. The men in charge wore red berets. First they searched my bags. They removed the scissors I used to trim my nasal hairs. They inspected my flip phone. At the next table, two soldiers younger-looking than me measured my weight and height in kilos and meters. They handed me a sheet of paper to carry to the next building. More recruits filed into the room as we left. Here, before Dimitris left, he hugged me and told me not to worry.

"Whatever you need—give me a call. Whatever you need," he said.

I followed some recruits up a small slope toward a barracks. Inside, I surrendered my Greek ID card. This meant I had surrendered my citizenship. It would only be reinstated after I had finished my duty. The soldier behind the desk asked me my profession. When I told him he raised his highbrows.

"Yeah?"

"That's correct."

He handed me a document to fill out and sign. I wrote my name in Greek. I wrote my real name as it should be written in the proper language. A big rush of authenticity passed through me. A fabulous aura straightened my lengthy frame. I nodded assuredly at the soldier as he grabbed my papers. He handed me a questionnaire to fill out. I scanned the questions in the room across the hall.

What is your relationship with your parents like?
Do you have siblings? What is your relationship with your siblings?
Are your parents divorced?
What is your family's economic situation? Good… Fair… Bad.
Have you ever wanted to inflict harm on someone?
Are you Christian Orthodox?
Do you think strange thoughts? Always… Sometimes… Never.

The questions made me chuckle. *Strange thoughts?* I was always having strange thoughts. Thoughts about death and humanity and eternity and why humans couldn't shit pellets like goats. To ask a Greek about strange thoughts, and to think of what Homer or Plato or Aeschylus wrote, was like asking a Nordic or Asian person, "Do you think with your emotions?" In Kallikratis or Patsianos, it was easy to let your mind wander. Strange thoughts were inevitable. For instance, one time I was certain the ants in Patsianos were the most intelligent organisms on earth. I watched them, fascinated, as they communicated and worked together to carry dead flies and minuscule flakes of brush down into their lair. They beamed in a straight, civilized line. Possibly they were the most powerful organism, too; I believed they used their antennae to communicate with other organisms in the universe and were responsible for earthquakes and tsunamis and tornados and all the other natural disasters that we blamed on mother nature, but which were really the ants sending a signal that triggered it all.

I checked "sometimes" for strange thoughts. A twinge of fear kept me from checking "yes". It wasn't an absolute "yes" or "no" for me with some of the questions. No, my parents weren't divorced, but they damn sure weren't in love, either. *Are your parents in love?* would have been a better question to have asked me. I watched the other recruits whip through the questionnaire, while I tilted my head up in contemplation over each question. There were a few questions I had no idea of the meaning of so I marked "no" to be safe.

The next station was in a cavernous room. A psychologist was sitting alone at a table. He reviewed my answers. When he looked up at me, I noticed his piercing blue eyes. He was a young boy, younger than me. Slightly heavy, with hair the color of wet sand.

"What kind of strange thoughts do you think?"

"*Me?* Only sometimes I think strange things…"

He stared at me. A touch of regret struck me.

"All normal things—nothing harmful. To tell you the truth, I didn't understand the question… my Greek is not so good."

He was silent for a couple of seconds. Then…

"Good. Thank you," he said as he stacked my papers on top with the others.

Next I left for the equipment room. It too was cavernous and it was filled with shelves of army clothes and gear. An officer handed me three pairs of military sweats.

"He's only three months, he doesn't get three pairs," said another officer as he reviewed my papers.

I grabbed my gear and, with my new boots untied, wobbled across the hallway to a bench. The recruit who was behind me in line sat down next to me.

"You're only doing three months?"

"It's because I'm a Greek-American," I said.

"America?"

"You're from America?" said another kid.

"Yeah," I said.

"He's only doing three months."

"You had to join the army?"

"So I can come and go as I please... I had to."

I was now in my uniform. Stitched on the front of my camo hat was an embroidered white cross encircled with a yellow wreath; they call it a *tsoker* in Greek. The final station was medical examination. They had to inoculate me. I resisted. The doctor jabbed the syringe into the vial, then he turned to me and said, "It's nothing, don't worry." After he injected me I stepped around a partition where another doctor, also younger than me, examined my teeth. My teeth were healthy. My body X-ray passed. My blood type was A positive. I was healthy enough to die fighting.

We marched to our barracks, a large rectangular block of cement, with rows of windows along the sides, on a bare patch of ground sloping down to the sea. Across the road stood a line of palm trees and another barracks. We lined up in front of our barracks. As we stood there, I scanned the unit. My fellow recruits were a mixed lot: many were flabby with hanging bellies, while others were so thin you wanted to feed them. Several wore glasses. Some had faces covered with red craters. Here and there was a genuine warrior, but these individuals were severely outnumbered by lambs. Everyone looked strange. They spoke quickly, in a mix of vernaculars from across the country, which I struggled to understand. The officers counted seventy-five of us; then we left our military bags (which recruits called "sausage bags") at the barracks and headed to the cafeteria. The city of Rethymno appeared, sprawled around the shores of its large bay, as we marched down the road toward the sea.

A small black and white kitten passed in front of me at the entrance to the cafeteria. One of the recruits reached down and patted it. The kitten closed its eyes and lifted its head and leaned into his knuckles. We entered the cafeteria in a single line, grabbing a metal tray, a tin cup, and utensils from a large metal shelf. Soldiers stationed at the base served us roast chicken, along with a side of vegetables and an apple. In the center of the room, in front of the tables, stood a large metal bin full of bread you were able to take as you liked. The tables were long and rectangular, arranged in rows, with a patterned yellow tablecloth overlaid with clear plastic sheeting. Greek pop music blared from the speakers. I spotted the recruit from the equipment room and moved toward him.

"Hello, my friend, sit down," he said. "How's it look to you?"

"Good, so far."

He turned to the boy next to him, saying, "He's from America."

"How did you join the military?"

"I'm a Greek-American."

"And you had to join the Greek army?"

"Not exactly, but to come and go as I please I needed to. I'm a volunteer, I guess."

"You volunteered!" His eyes widened. "My friend, what's your name?"

"Panagiotis."

"Marcos. *Xarika*. It's nice to meet you."

"And your name again?"

"Yiannis."

"You know what the Greek Army is about—*malakíes*! Only *malakíes*," said Marcos. He had a pale face with a pronounced narrow nose and green eyes.

The room where we slept was called a *thalamos*. Bunk beds lined the walls on both sides. I dropped my bags onto one of the bottom bunks and dust lifted off the blanket. I wasn't assigned a bunk mate. I introduced myself to the recruit in the next bunk. His name was Christian. He was blond-haired and of medium build, and he had an accent I didn't recognize. I unloaded my bags and organized my gear. As luck would have it, Yiannis and Marcos were in the same *thalamos*. Yiannis was tall, with a thin mustache, soft cheeks, and a stunted jawline. He waved his sandals in the air, shouting, "Damn faggots! They gave me two left-foot sandals."

A young man named Xaris was our *thalamarxis*, leader of the *thalamos*. He'd been serving for five months already and because of his performance they'd asked him if he'd like to be a *thalamarxis*. When he heard I was from America, he walked over to introduce himself. He was blond-haired, with light skin and a fresh face. He was only twenty-five-years-old and came from Heraklion. He had trained as an engineer and was quite charismatic.

On the first day, everyone in my *thalamos* discovered I was American. "*O Americanos,*" they called me. My bunk mates were pleasant to be around. There was a lot of humor, coupled with foolery, but anchored by the respect we had for each other. We each knew how to strike the right chord for our own comfort and enjoyment, although comfort is a relative term when you sleep on a bunk surrounded by fourteen other men. At ten-thirty there was rollcall. We stood in front of our bunks in our sweats. At eleven it was lights out.

CHAPTER THIRTY-THREE

We woke up at six in the morning. I struggled to leave my bed. I went to the toilet and there was no toilet nor any toilet paper. There was only a hole in the ground and two pads you fit your boots onto. Another recruit had finished using the stall next to mine.

"Excuse me, my friend, do you have any toilet paper?"

"Of course! Here."

I shut the curtain, squatted and the poop slid out of me. I shaved in slow motion and poorly made my bed. It was past seven by the time we lined up outside the barracks. There was a soldier missing. Sergeant Elias stood at the top of the steps. He looked very boyish with thick brown hair.

"This will not happen again!" he shouted. "We should have finished breakfast by now."

The missing recruit appeared from the side of the barracks. Sergeant Elias spotted him immediately. "Where were you?" he demanded.

"The toilet."

"And you didn't think to take a shit earlier?"

The recruit was silent. Elias turned to the rest of us.

"Tomorrow, if you need to take a shit, if you need to play with your testicles, you will do it before you have to report at seven. Everyone will be prepared and lined up at seven for breakfast. Understood?"

"*Malista.* Yes."

"I didn't hear you?"

"*MALISTA!* YES!"

We had only bread and butter and jam, with lukewarm coffee, for breakfast. I had no appetite for it, so I waited outside until everyone was finished and they called us into three lines.

In good order, we marched back to the barracks. There we lined up out front and an officer addressed us. He introduced himself as Captain Koutoudis. He wore a patch with three stars on his lapel. His gray hair was short and neatly groomed. He had smooth tanned skin. He wasn't a big man, but he carried himself with good posture. When he spoke, the words rolled smoothly and crisply off his tongue.

"Good morning," he said.

"Good morning," we responded.

"I didn't hear you."

"Good morning!"

"Welcome. I hope you all had a good first day. From here on— until you finish—you are all soldiers. Everything we do, we do together. The time we have together is short and there is a lot to learn. Soon you will all learn the military way of life. Every day you will be shaven and your bed will be made properly and the barracks will be clean. You are all expected to take care of yourselves in here. I know it is difficult to leave your families and be here now, but we will take care of everyone. We are one family. Wherever one spits the other licks it up. Does anyone have any problems or concerns so far? *Ela,* come on, what *aporias* do you have?"

A recruit raised his hand.

"My boots are too small."

"You didn't try them on?"

"They hurt my feet."

"You will change boots this afternoon. Anybody else?"

Now, several hands went up in the air.

"My beret is too small—"

"My pants don't fit—"

"Why didn't you try on your pants to see that they fit?"

The recruit said nothing. The Captain pointed to Yiannis.

"I have two left-foot sandals," Yiannis said. Captain Koutoudis shook his head.

"Everyone should try on their clothes and make sure they fit. If they don't you will go back and get the right-fitting clothes. Everyone will dress properly and wear the right-fitting clothes. You will not wear pants that are baggy." Captain Koutoudis looked at a soldier whose pant legs dropped over his boots like they were slacks. "Your pants will not hide your boots. Your shoestrings will not hang. If you lack discipline with simple dress and hygiene then how can you have discipline during a war?"

After the Captain had finished speaking to us, we returned to our *thalamos*.

"What are we going to do now?" I asked Christian.

"Make our bed," he said, "and clean."

Making your bed was important. The edges of the blanket were to be tucked under the bed so there were no loose ends. The bed sheet was to fold over the blanket to the proper length at the head of the bed. The pillow was placed inside a second blanket above this fold. The bed had to be in perfect condition without a single crease or sign of disorder. Yiannis sprayed his bed with a minty aromatic repellent, because he thought we had bedbugs.

We spent until lunchtime making our beds and cleaning the barracks. We had several breaks during which they served us a *koulouri* (bread shaped in a ring that you could almost fit your fist through) for a snack. During the breaks the recruits smoked and sipped frappés they purchased from the coffee machine inside the barracks.

On one of the breaks, I rested in the cement courtyard. It was a great fortune to have the army base next to the sea. The horizon was colored an orange hue. The sea beneath it was a deep, creamy blue. The elements made the city of Rethymno picturesque. A barb-wired fence outlined the perimeter of the army base. On the other side of the fence, where the land formed into a ridge, two goats rested next to each other in the long tough grass. I heard birds chirping. The air was crisp but not too cold. I removed my notebook from my breast pocket and I wrote, or rather I listened, and I dictated words that arrived seamlessly.

* * *

We reported for lunch at one-thirty. Nobody was allowed to leave the barracks without the entire group. Lunch was a half hour. I ate quickly, so I could relax next to the sea and enjoy the scenery. During this time the other recruits liked to lounge in the courtyard and smoke and laugh and screw around. Most napped when we returned to the barracks after lunch. I tried to read, but I lacked the vigor for it, so I roamed around the barracks. Word had spread to the other *thalamoi* that I was the American in the class and everyone wanted to greet me. I repeated the same story, with a smile, each time.

"My friend, come, sit with us," said a recruit. He and his companions were from another *thalamos*. "What is America like?"

"America… is like mosquitoes in humidity. Your only hope is to stay in motion."

"Why do you say that?"

"Because you asked me what America is like."

"Tell me something specific about the country."

"It's a country with much variety… food… culture. A good variety of beautiful women."

"I want to taste an Asian," said the recruit next to him.

"We got Asian… Hispanic, Black, whatever's got a heartbeat and walks on two legs."

They laughed. "I want to go to America. Once I finish here, I'm leaving. I want to go to Miami. I heard it's nice there."

"Miami is okay. If you like flashy people, it's nice. But you're not missing much not being in America. That's the honest truth."

"But you make money. You have the opportunity to make money. Yes?"

"Yes. You can make money."

"Here there exists no money. No jobs. And if there is work you make little."

"I believe the common man lives a better life here than the common man in America. That's the big difference." I said.

The recruit, who was short and stocky with dark hair, looked at me in perplexity; then he turned to his friend and whispered something to him and they chuckled. It struck me how difficult it was for people to see the good in their lives if one judged solely by the standard of having money. I could have told them that I was once a rich man and lived in the great New York City, in a nice apartment in the West Village, and I was dreadfully unhappy. But a person who was resolutely convinced that money equaled happiness might have thought I only said this to justify some kind of failure from my end. To show appreciation for the good, simple things Greece had to offer sounded foolish to them. Thus it was easier in these moments to say nothing.

At 1700 hours, or five o'clock in civilian time, we lined up in front of the barracks. The director of the Rethymno base addressed us. He was polite and a neat-looking man with a small belly. He smoked an e-cigarette, exhaling dense clouds of smoke that made his face disappear. After welcoming us, he encouraged us to come forward with any problems or concerns we might have. Then he departed and the sergeants hammered us on discipline.

Whenever any ranking officer addressed us, they said, we were supposed to snap our boots together and respond with our rank, name, and class number. We spent an hour working on this. The information was meant to be delivered quickly in a firm tone of voice. One by one, we were required to shout our rank, name, and class number. I murmured the words to myself before it was my turn to speak. Some of the recruits choked. It made me feel better to see native-born Greeks screw it up. When at last it was my turn I took a deep breath, straightened my posture, and, slowly and calmly, I delivered my best shot. "*Στρατιώτης Πεζικού* Μανουσέλης Παναγιώτης

2016 B *εζζό.*" I was neither intimidating nor loud, but I was clear and precise. The sergeants appeared satisfied.

After dinner, we were introduced to the building next to the cafeteria. It was called the *kapsimi* and was a place where you could buy snacks and toiletries. Next to it was a kitchen where you could order frappés, but no Greek coffee or espresso. We hung out at the picnic benches outside. The recruits ate candy bars and Fritos and Big ChoCos, a large chocolate croissant. They washed it all down with sodas. They rolled tobacco in paper and smoked one cigarette after another. I had to stand up frequently and move away, hovering on the edges of the groups, to avoid the smoke.

When we readied for bed, I removed the books from under my pillow and placed them on the window sill above the radiator next to my bunk. They had told us we couldn't have camera phones, but some of the recruits had smartphones. There was no Wi-Fi, though. With thirty minutes before "lights out" I scanned my lexicon for a few words I had written earlier. Then my phone rang. It was Mom.

"How are you? Is everything okay?"

"Yes. I'm fine."

"Everything's okay?

"You didn't hear me the first time?"

"I called you yesterday and you didn't respond."

"I was digging a trench."

"What!?"

"What's up?"

"Where are you now?"

"I'm in the barracks, going to bed."

"Oh, okay, so you're alright. How is it?"

"It's good. Everyone's nice. It's laid-back."

"What did you eat?"

"Chicken. *Fakés.*"

"Was it good?"

"Yes. It was roast chicken."

"Okay. Good. You're okay—Here, your father wants to speak to you…"

"Hello, Mr. Manouselis, how is it?"

"Good."

"What have you done?"

"Nothing. It's only been two days."

"How many people are you?"

"Seventy-five."

"That's it! Where are the kids from?"

"All from Crete—I met a kid from Sfakia."

"Yeah? What's his last name?"

"I forgot. He heard my last name and he introduced himself to me."

"For sure, they'll have kids from Sfakia. At the Megalo Pefko, where I was, we had one thousand in our class."

"Where's the Megalo Pefko?"

"In Athens! What did you eat?"

"Chicken."

"Was it good?"

"Everything is good. What can I tell you? We spent all day making our bed. We had lunch for a half hour, then a break for two hours. We organized our camo gear for an hour, then went for dinner for a half hour. Everyone is friendly."

Before the lights went out, we all stood in front of our bunks waiting for Second Lieutenant Staras. When he entered the room Xaris shouted, "Attention!" We raised our left foot and stomped it against the heel of our right foot, holding our arms straight and stiff on the sides.

Xaris gave him the report. Second Lieutenant Staras passed by each bunk bed watching us closely. On his lapel was a patch with one star. He was a mere kid, no older than twenty-five, I guessed. He had an abnormally large head, stocky build, with dark hair and light brown eyes. The brim of his *tsoker* was steeply tilted over his forehead. He moved back and forth across our floor two times before he said anything. He stopped in front of Yiannis.

"Στρατιώτης Πεζικού Σπιρωτάκις Γιάννης 2016 B εζζό," Yiannis shouted.

"Why is your towel hanging from your bed?" Staras asked.

Yiannis went mute.

Second lieutenant Staras continued to speak as he strode up and down the *thalamos.*

"Never will the *thalamos* be dirty. You will never have things lying around. The towels will not be hanging on the beds." He looked at a radiator. "Take that towel off it," he said. He walked to the head of the *thalamos,* stopped, and before he left he said, "We'll be better tomorrow."

We unhinged our heels as soon as he turned away.

* * *

The lights had been out for twenty minutes and I was still awake when Yiannis jumped off his bed and shined his flashlight on the wall. "Motherfuckers!" he shouted. "Bedbugs, I knew it!"

George from the bottom bunk stood up. Xaris turned on the lights. Adonis, in the bunk next to George and Yiannis, remained asleep, soundly snoring. Yiannis used his lighter and repellant spray to torch the bug. I spotted a bedbug skirting across the terrazzo floor and smashed it with my sandal.

"I told you—the *thalamos* is filled with bedbugs," Yiannis said. "They're going to fuck us all by the morning."

"Aman!" Marcos cried.

"Okay. Relax. Looks like they're hiding inside the bed springs and in the corners," said Xaris. "Use your spray now. We'll tell Captain Koutoudis in the morning."

By the morning, the bedbugs had cratered Yiannis' neck. George was bitten and so was Nikos in the next bunk. I was untouched. We left for breakfast right at seven. The black and white kitten stood at the entrance waiting for someone to feed her. Someone had named it Layla. I brushed my boot under her belly and she arched her back.

"Let's see what shit they'll have for us today," I said to myself, out loud, as we entered the cafeteria. At the food station there were cornflakes and milk.

"This is the best military base," said the recruit next to me. "To give us real milk, this is a luxury, my friend.

"They could have better coffee," I said.

"The coffee is shit," he said. "You need to go to the director's building. They make Greek coffee and espresso there."

"And how do you go there?" I asked.

"If you have *vizma*," he said.

"What's that mean?"

In English he said, "Coonneeections."

After breakfast we returned to the barracks and tidied up our *thalamos*. Nikos was at the bunk across from mine. He had finished college at sixteen. He was twenty-seven-years-old with a full head of grey hair. He was short, but firmly built. He straightened my blanket and brushed his hand over it to remove the wrinkles. When Second Lieutenant Staras entered we snapped to attention. We stood straight and stiff and had serious faces. Staras stopped at Nikos' bed and I saw that a sliver of blanket was spilling out from under the mattress in one corner.

"Whose bed is this?"

Nikos clapped one boot heel to the other. "Στρατιώτης Πεζικού Χαραλαμπάκης Νίκος 2016 Β *εζζό*. This is my bed, Sir, Second Lieutenant."

"This isn't ready."

"*Malista.*"

"Your pillow is upside down." He looked at Nikos, carefully. "How old are you?"

"Twenty-seven."

"Are you serious?"

"*Malista.*"

Then he turned to me. I clapped my heel to my boot, shouted my title and said my first name before my last name. He inspected my bed.

"Where are you from?"

"I'm a Greek-American."

"What are you doing here?"

"I'm not sure, exactly."

He looked down at my boots while his hands were cuffed behind his back.

"How is America?"

"A disaster."

"Where do you like better, here or America?"

"They are very different countries," I said. "Greece has the most beautiful landscape."

"But you make money in America."

"*Malista*."

"Why didn't you go to the army in America?"

"It's not mandatory. People join the army in America as a career."

"This bed is good. Bravo."

He moved away and I unhinged my heels, placing them parallel to each other.

We went outside to the front of the barracks. There were only seventy-four of us, after a recruit was dismissed for mental issues. We were ranked from one to four. If you had no health issues or physical impairments you ranked I-1. I was I-1. Those ranked I-1 faced no restrictions. They were expected to do everything that was asked of them. Only soldiers ranked I-1 and I-2 received rifles. If you had extenuating health or mental issues you were ranked I-3. If you were injured or seriously impaired you were I-4. Truly crazy recruits were I-5 and permanently discharged from the military. Captain Koutoudis appeared from his office and addressed the bedbug issue.

"We're going to burn the beds," he said.

We moved the metal beds outside in a disorderly fashion. We shook the dust from our sheets and blankets and beat the mattresses with sticks. The mattresses were old and marked with ink, except for a few new mattresses the occupants of which held onto carefully. To be sure we thoroughly wiped out the bedbugs hidden in the coils and the cracks at the corners of the beds, they used a stick wrapped in a towel and doused with some kind of flammable liquid, which was then lit. It took us until lunch to finish the task. I believed the bed bug issue was now fixed.

* * *

When we were free in the evening, I went and sat on a flight of stairs that wrapped around one end of the barracks. There were palm trees in front of me. Beyond the palm trees was a large cement-paved yard and beyond that were two more barracks, one next to the other, and beyond them was the sea. From the steps I could see the lights glowing on the Venetian fortress above the town. If I looked far to my right there was Psiloritis, the highest mountain on Crete, its peak coated in snow. The temperature was comfortable. The other recruits were scattered about the barracks. The sound of birds chirping mingled with their chatter. Together it created a harmonious environment. *Galini*, I thought, which meant "peacefulness" in Greek.

I was reading Kazantzakis, which made me think deeply about life. He wasn't only an intellect; he was a trenchant intellect who lifted me off the ground, each sentence carrying me to a new truth, high in the sky, where the discoveries seemed limitless. Kazantzakis wrote that Nietzsche had a powerful influence on him. According to Kazantzakis, Nietzsche wrote down feelings he was unable to put into words. Kazantzakis does a similar thing for me. He gave me something to latch onto and helped me stay strong and true to my life. I could relate to what he said. The tumultuous relationship he had with his father struck a chord with me. The fact that both of us were not only Greek, but Cretan, was another bond.

Often people asked me who my favorite writers were, and if I mentioned Kazantzakis and they said they had never heard of him, I immediately reacted with surprise. It was a shame that so many people had never read him or even heard of him. When you mentioned *Zorba the Greek,* people thought of Anthony Quinn. I never felt more alive than I did when I was reading a Kazantzakis novel. Reading people such as Agatha Christie, Jane Austen or Charles Dickens, on the other hand, left me feeling remote and displaced. Yet they were wildly more popular.

"What are you reading?" asked a recruit with bucked teeth set in acne-cratered cheeks.

"I'm reading Kazantzakis—*Report to Greco,*" I said. "Have you read it?"

"*Of course,*" he said.

"I like him a lot," I said.

"I read *Report to Greco* in school."

"He nourishes the… What is soul in Greek?"

"*Ψυχή*. Do you like to write?" he asked.

"Usually, yes. But I don't know if I'll ever make a penny doing it."

"Patience, my friend."

"Where are you from?" I asked.

"The far east."

"From China?"

"Sitia. It's a long journey from here."

"If we are all ever so lucky to be blessed with a long journey."

"You said it just right."

The recruit and I rested our eyes on the distance with our heads tilted up. My sight was caught by the lights from the Venetian fortress that appeared brighter as the day's sunlight tucked itself away. My thoughts were almost blank. I felt we had both found a shared moment nothing could jerk us away from.

CHAPTER THIRTY-FOUR

Every morning we hurried to make our beds, shave, and clean the barracks. We spent the rest of the day mostly idle. The recruits looked forward to the end of training, when we'd be given a ten-day break. I was surprised to hear that we'd have ten days off after only three weeks of training, but it didn't bother me because I'd have time to write.

I could see why the other recruits thought the military a waste of time. Nothing ever seemed to happen. We learned very little about fighting a war. But you could not be a renegade because we were one team. A team that was valuable if everyone showed equal commitment to, and respect for, the various procedures. As Captain Koutoudis had said, *we look out for each other.* It wasn't about besting the others to prove your worth. We learned discipline and we learned how to be prepared, which was the military credo. Someday there may be a war, and if we were to survive, it would hinge on performing small tasks well. Or so it was said.

I enjoyed two pleasures which eased the banality. The view of the sea provided me with constant solace and diversion. At every chance, I would stop and gaze at it, watching its color subtly change as the sun moved across the sky. My other pleasure was the Greek language. Hearing it continuously spoken kept my mind humming as I tried to discover the meaning of conversations I overheard.

On the day we learned the proper way to shift our position left and right and spin around, we separated into small groups. In my group was a young man named Stavros. He was nineteen-years-old and came from a village called Patsos, high in the Cretan mountains. He was short and had a similar shade of tan as me.

Entering the army was the biggest event in his life. The journey to the base had also been the longest distance he'd ever traveled. He was confused about rudimentary skills like forming a line. The group pivoted right and he pivoted left. He constantly struggled to properly fit his gear. He spoke with a thick, Cretan accent and smoked like a chimney. But he was the most interesting person I met during my time in the army.

Xaris noticed Stavros struggled to follow in tandem, so he took him aside and helped him. Yet Stavros still struggled. He gasped and raised his hand.

"I have a question?"

"What is it?"

"When are we going to have a cigarette break."

"You're asking for a cigarette break, now?"

"*Malista.*"

"What time is it?"

"Four-thirty."

"Okay. Let's take a break," said the *thalamos* leader in charge of the drill.

The recruits rolled their cigarettes. I bound onto an overhang in front of the barracks, lopping off my *tsoker*. From the corner of my eye, I saw another recruit tighten Stavros' wobbly suspenders and belt. Then he reset his *tsoker* so it lay properly on his head with the brim pointed down. Never at any point did it occur to me to offer him my help. This was when the meaning of *philotimo* became crystal clear to me.

In Stavros, I glimpsed flickers of what Dad might have been like when he was his age. Certainly, like Dad, he knew how to feed and herd the goats and sheep, how to trim their thick hair, how to care for olive trees and vineyards, how to squeeze milk out of the udder of a doe, how to kill a goat and a chicken and skin them. Like Dad, too, he was trained in the art of survival. In darker times this was a valuable skill. Nowadays, however, when people were surrounded with abundance, its importance had waned.

The one time we sat next to each other at the cafeteria, he looked at me with distrust, anxious to finish his food and get away from me. His behavior illustrated how someone from a small village with little interaction with the world might view outsiders with suspicion and distrust. Stavros couldn't comprehend what I, an American, was doing here in Crete. For all he knew I might have been a spy.

One night before bed I began to wonder what my life would have been like if my parents had never emigrated from Greece. Born and raised in the mountains of Kallikratis, I would probably have been just like Stavros. Certainly an intellectual endeavor such as writing may well have been beyond me. My grasp of the world at large would likely have been limited to a narrow black and white perspective. The rigid and inflexible nature of life in the mountains might have molded me into a person just like my father. A person whom I found intolerable at times. The idea startled me. The next time Mom called, I asked her about it.

"Forget about it," she said. "I never would have married your father if he wasn't going to America."

Mom so desperately wanted to leave for America that she was willing to sacrifice love? So it appeared. Mom's situation in Crete made a different life in a foreign country a necessity to her. The same could be said for Dad. Both needed to find a better life.

I hoped Stavros, if he decided he wanted a different life, would muster up the strength to do so also. The army was surely the perfect starting point for him. I noticed with Stavros' situation that the advantages of what one may have in life could not be directly attributed to one's greatness, rather circumstances made a person's life too, and the right thing to do was to not deride them and retard their development, but to guide them.

Though I initially failed to grasp that I could have helped Stavros, I was mildly satisfied with the leap I took in recognizing my behavior and determining to do better the next time I was put in such a situation.

CHAPTER THIRTY-FIVE

On Saturday morning, I woke up with a severely swollen neck. I killed two bedbugs on my pillow. They had sucked so much blood out of me that they overexcited themselves and left tracks across my sheets. Bloodthirsty dregs! My back and my shoulders were covered in puffy red blotches. When I looked into the mirror I wondered if I'd been part of an experiment. I showed Xaris my neck and asked to see the doctor.

I had to wait for the *thalamos* leader in charge that day to walk me to the infirmary. Another recruit with a bad foot joined us. It was a cold morning and the walk was a hike up a steep road. The building looked old and abandoned. The office was on the second floor. It smelled of cigarette smoke. I removed my shirt. The doctor, a young man, glanced at my body. I told him it was bedbugs and, in a single motion, he reached into a cabinet to hand me a cream.

"Is this what I need?" I asked, concerned. "What do you think it is?"

"Don't worry," he said, "everything will be alright."

He moved over to his desk and took a sip of his frappé. *Don't worry, everything will be alright...* Yeah. I never understood how people like the doctor settled on the idea that everything will be alright, when it was obvious to me that everything was not alright. Their home might be burning and they decide to shut the door and step outside for a frappé! I had no idea what was wrong with me or what the cream was I had to rub over my wounds. All I could do was hope it would pass.

For lunch, we had big white beans called *fasolia*. I finished my meal quickly, then I took my red apple outside and ate it in the courtyard. I was still sore from the doctor's visit and I didn't want to be around anyone. I was reminded of how much I valued my freedom. The city of Rethymno appeared teasingly in front of me. How I would have liked to spend the afternoon strolling through the old town and slumbering in a café with a book and my notebook and a beer. At that moment, it seemed like all one could ask for to make life good. Only companionship would make it perfect, as when your lover meets you after you've finished a good read and you share it with her. Not in a million years did I see myself as a soldier. I felt constricted in my chest. *Two more weeks till break*, I thought.

After a few days, my neck had grown redder and more puffy, so I tossed the cream in the trash bin and told Xaris I needed to see the doctor again. But Xaris replied that we were going to get our rifles, so I decided to let it pass.

The arsenal was a plain, windowless room set on a slope above our barracks, replete with rifles aligned in rows one above the other. The solider in charge, Sergeant Elias, had to use a step ladder to reach the rifles on the top rows. It was much heavier than I had expected. I read off the number of my rifle to Second Lieutenant Staras, who sat at a table with a young woman who also had a star stitched on her collar. "Don't forget your number," Staras said.

We waited outside the arsenal until every recruit had their rifle. I had never held a rifle before. I struggled to fit the strap properly over my shoulder. Engraved near the magazine slot was the number G3A3 and the year the rifle was manufactured, 1984. The year I was born. It was German made. A recruit next to me cocked his rifle and fired. It made a heavy clicking sound that echoed.

"*Malaka!*" shouted an officer, marching toward the recruit. "Who told you to cock it! Did anyone tell you to cock it?" The recruit froze.

"Nobody will cock their rifle. Understood? I'm talking to you! Understood?"

"Understood!" we shouted.

After everyone had been issued their rifle, we reported to Captain Koutoudis at the front of the barracks. He noticed that some of the recruits were handling their rifles as if they were made of porcelain.

"Don't be afraid of it, *palikaria*," he said, addressing us as warriors. "It's not going to break. It's okay to be rough with it… Hold it fearlessly. However, understand that you are holding a powerful weapon capable of blowing apart a man's limbs… This is now your best friend. You will clean it. You will be careful with it. *Never* leave your weapon alone. And *never* share your weapon with anyone… On Thursday we'll have night training with it and on Friday we'll go to the shooting range."

We separated into groups and bunched into a series of dusty rooms at the barracks across the street. In each room an officer explained the entire mechanics of the rifle. Second Lieutenant Staras was the instructor in my group. Next to him was a large poster showing all the parts labeled. He disassembled and reassembled a rifle for us a few times. He talked at length about stuff I couldn't understand.

After his lengthy lesson, we were allowed to disassemble our rifles and familiarize ourselves with its parts. The officers distributed cleaning kits and we learned to clean it. It was very important, Staras told us, that the barrel was pristine and there existed no specks of dirt when you looked inside it. It also must be oiled properly, he said. He warned us there'd be an inspection one day.

We were shown racks where we were to lock up our rifles at our barracks. The officers assigned us service duties as well. Now that there were rifles in our barracks, we needed barracks officers to keep an eye on things around the clock. Every two hours a new pair of recruits took over. Each day recruits were assigned a new duty. If you weren't a barracks officer, you were cleaning the cafeteria or the *kapsimi* or you had the day off. I had the day off, so I spent the time resting in my bunk reading *Report to Greco* and attending to the redness in my neck by adding more cream.

During the night, I worried about my neck. I had the sniffles and chills and I was sure it wasn't only because the temperature had dropped. My neck was awful in the morning. After breakfast, I skipped the training drills and went to the doctor. There were two doctors in the office, each with frappés.

"It's getting worse," I said.

"What did we give him last time?" asked one doctor of the other.

The first doctor looked into the book and read out the type of cream I'd been given. They exchanged a few words, then the second doctor walked toward the glass cabinet and took out a tube of gel which he handed to me. It was probably a sort of aloe vera. I tightened my jaw and shook my head.

"This is not going to help!" I shouted. "I have something serious."

"Use it three times a day and in two days, if it doesn't get better, come back here."

"What is my diagnosis? The other cream didn't help me. How is this one better?"

"Are you a doctor?" said the first doctor, sipping his frappé. "Did you study medicine?"

"No! That's why I'm here, to be treated by a doctor. The cream is not working. I'll take this, but I'll be back here tomorrow because I already know my neck is going to look like a grape. I have an allergy, probably. I don't think it's just bedbugs. It's been getting worse every day. I have a runny nose. I'm getting chills. This cream is shit! Is there a dermatologist around?"

"Go see one. Do you have your own insurance? Go to a private doctor."

"Do you have any allergy pills you might give me?"

He paused and inspected my back and neck again. "It's not bedbugs," he said to the second doctor as he moved to the medicine cabinet.

"Take these pills. Two times a day before you eat."

"Thank you!"

The recruits were on break when I returned to the *thalamos*. A soldier handed me a chocolate croissant for our mid-morning snack.

"What did the doctor say," Nikos asked.

"*Malakies*," I said.

"You have an allergy for sure. That's not bedbugs."

"He gave me some allergy pills."

George approached me and said, "I'm having an allergic reaction, too. I think it's from the pine trees outside. Your bed is next to the window. When it's open the pollen from the trees gets to you."

"That's probably it!" I said.

"Yeah," George said. "I'd shower with cold water. Ask Xaris if you can move to another bunk. You should have a sleeping bag, too. The blankets here haven't been washed in a long time—if ever."

"Thank you very much, George. The way you just explained it to me was all they had to say. You should be the doctor up there."

"This is the Greek Army," he said. "They're not doctors. They're studying to be doctors."

"Are you serious?"

"The doctor here is studying to be a dentist," he said.

I widened my eyes.

My chills intensified and so did my runny nose and the wicked cold front that arrived made it worse. I took the first pill with the *pastichio,* a beef pasta casserole, they served for lunch. The *pastichio* was good, but I only ate half of it. I ate the chocolate wafer bar that came with it, but I did not eat my vegetables. We had an hour break after lunch. I changed into my sweats, wrapped my pillow with a T-shirt and lay in bed under the light green sheets, making sure to keep the wool blanket away from my skin, but I don't think I slept. We soon had to report to the front of the barracks with all our gear, including our rifles. I felt very weak and was uncertain if I'd be able to make it through the rest of the day. I didn't want to go back to the infirmary. I gasped, grabbing my lower back, as I bent over into my sausage bag.

"Don't sit down on your bed with your uniform. That brings bedbugs," Nikos said.

"I know!" I told him.

I moved to the hallway to put on my boots. We wore our thick jackets. As we waited outside some of the other recruits approached me and asked how I felt. I told them I felt like shit. They told me to go to the doctor and I got upset. I didn't like the other recruits seeing me struggle. I hated them to think I wasn't strong. In the yard, we separated into groups of three, forming large circles. We learned how to salute with our rifle and how to turn right and left and spin with it. We were awful. The rifle weighed five kilos, heavy enough to knock us around. The air was cold and the rifle stung my hand when I caught the metal below the front sight. I lifted my rifle up innumerable times throughout the afternoon, slamming it against my left shoulder. My hands ached and, by the end of the exercise, my shoulder was painful.

Turning right and left with the rifle was a large undertaking for Stavros. I felt sorry for the poor guy and hoped he'd be able to get it right by the time of our oath of enlistment ceremony the following week. I was looking forward to the break.

To further worsen my mood, I was on cafeteria cleaning duty. This meant scrubbing the tables with vinegar, then sweeping and mopping the floor after dinner. It was late when I returned to the barracks, so I took a risk and shaved to give myself more time in the morning.

By then I could see that my puffiness had faded. My chills seemed to have receded and my runny nose had dried up. Word spread there was going to be an inspection. After breakfast, therefore, we disassembled our rifles and began to scrupulously clean them. Nikos grabbed my plastic butt stock and removed a lot of dirt from the rod inside the recoil spring.

When Second Lieutenant Staras entered the room, Yiannis delivered the report. Then, when Yiannis had finished, Staras walked to the middle of the *thalamos* and bent down to the floor, in a push-up position, looking under the bunks to make sure our gear was packed away in our sausage bags. As he returned to the front of the room he stopped suddenly in front of me. I shouted my title and name and class. He pulled a small, clean white cloth from his pocket and grabbed the barrel of my rifle. First, he scrubbed the rear-sight piece.

"What's going on with Trump?" he asked, scrubbing hard.

"He wants to be president."

"Is he going to win?"

"I don't think so."

He scrubbed the inside of the barrel and around the edges.

"How much money do they make in the army in America?"

"I have no idea."

"At the entry level?"

I really had no idea how much money American soldiers made, so I guessed.

"Thirty-five thousand a year, maybe."

He held the point of the barrel in front of his eye.

"Your rifle is clean, bravo," he said. "I know someone doesn't have a clean rifle."

He moved across to Nikos' rifle and grabbed the barrel.

"What did you do here?"

Staras blew inside the barrel.

"There are two or three large pieces in there," he said. "Did you run cloth through it?"

Nikos' face turned red. He looked constipated. "I don't know what to say, Sir. My sincere apologies."

Nikos laid down his barrel and scrubbed the trigger piece. As he did this, a fit of the giggles came over me and I bit down hard on the inside of my cheeks to keep from smiling. I looked away from Nikos and stared at the dark spots on the wall where Yannis had scorched the bedbugs and I thought of eating cream cheese with vinegar.

"Five days in the lock-up. That's what happens for a dirty rifle. You understand?"

"*Malista*."

"Reassemble your rifles and report at the front of the barracks."

I considered thanking Nikos for helping me clean my rifle, but then I thought it would be a crass thing to do, so I left the *thalamos* without saying anything.

CHAPTER THIRTY-SIX

We spent an idle day on Thursday preparing for night training. In the afternoon, we hung out at the *kapsimi*. Layla was with us. She enjoyed being around the soldiers, approaching anyone who was eating and meowing piteously, or creeping under the table and rolling her face and body against the soldiers' legs to notify them she was there. Usually she'd get their leftovers.

There was a really short recruit who was also named Nikos. He had a big head and a fantastic mustache, and was a great caretaker of Layla. He was the one who named her Layla.

"Why did you give her a girl's name?" I asked. "I see *arxithia,* testicles."

"No, my friend." He lifted her up and flipped her. Layla cried. "You see that? That's a pussy, my friend."

I cracked a smile and chuckled and so did a few of the other soldiers. There was good camaraderie when our group hung around the picnic tables smoking. To smoke a cigarette with another man was a ritual like drinking *tsikoudia*. The soldiers shared cigarettes and lighters and rolling papers. If a recruit ran out of tobacco, someone lent him some and he paid him back the next time. It was a way to pass time when nothing else was going on. We laughed and joked at the peccadillos one assumed in the army. I learned dirty words like *rothalaki*, which meant to masturbate, and how to use the word *arxithia* in the proper context. While they enjoyed their cigarettes, I enjoyed eating an Italian candy bar called a *Bueno* during these moments. A few times I almost lit up myself because I felt it would bring me closer to the others.

Lazy days made you lazy, though. It never occurred to me to stuff my pouches with cardboard even when I had all day to do it. I remembered it only when my bunkmate, Nikos, reminded me as were dressing for night training. The cardboard was to keep our pouches looking full because we didn't have ammo to fill them with. Nikos pulled some from his bag.

"Here."

"It looks fine to me."

"If an officer notices you'll be in trouble."

"They won't notice it in the dark."

"The captain will be there tonight. Just stuff them with the cardboard."

"Okay, give it to me." I slid my suspenders over my shoulders and buckled my belt. "Do we need our helmets?" I asked Christian.

"Yeah. Helmet and bayonet."

I unbuckled my belt and dug into my sausage bag for my bayonet. I unclipped my suspenders from my belt and passed the loop of my scabbard through so it laid on the left side of my waist. There were only sixty-nine of us now because five soldiers were at the infirmary. When Koutoudis appeared from his office a lieutenant shouted, "Soldiers, attention!" The captain's demeanor was more intense and focused than usual.

"Soldiers, turn right!" We turned right. "Soldiers, turn left!" We turned left. "Soldiers turn left!" We turned left again. "Soldiers turn left!" And again. "Soldiers, turn around!" We spun and faced him.

"We're getting better. But we still need work," Koutoudis said. "For tonight we have a lot to go through and we don't have much time. We will all have to pay attention and be careful. It will be dark and you will be carrying your rifle and it will be the first time you have ever done such a thing… Is there anybody with questions or concerns? Good. Soldiers, turn around! March!"

The woods existed on a declivity. The trees were pines and the ground was covered with their needles and there were many stones lying around among the needles and rooted in the dirt. We separated into three groups of around twenty soldiers each. My group started at the bottom of the woods and began climbing up through the trees. The goal was to make it up to the top of the slope without Second Lieutenant Staras spotting you with his flashlight. The more eager soldiers were easily spotted. I stayed low to the ground, crawling slowly. The only time I rose was to hide behind a tree. I'd slither around the trunk and find a large rock and bury myself in the ground, grasping my rifle. I imagined the drill was real, with live ammunition and a real enemy, and my adrenaline surged. I imagined a bullet would blow off my head if I was caught. I felt scared and timid. Most of the soldiers moved fast ahead of me. Staras was cutting them down one by one. Half our infantry was gone. By the time the exercise was over, I had only moved a few car lengths ahead. The strategy was to move together as one unit and we failed miserably.

At the next station, we learned how to camouflage ourselves with branches and straw grass and by smearing mud onto our faces and hands. Many faces were no longer recognizable. We broke off leafy branches and attached them to our helmets and placed them under our belts and suspenders. Some of the recruits went wild and decorated themselves really well. They looked like apes carrying large leafy branches on their backs.

There was a station where we practiced moving together as one unit toward the target and another station where we listened to Sergeant Elias and another sergeant talk at length about survival. I couldn't follow much of what they said. I was too cold by that point; the mud had crusted onto my face and hands, and my only thought was of returning to the barracks and being the first person in the showers to be sure I had hot water.

There was a liveliness back at the barracks that alleviated my discomfort. You could hear the recruits in the other *thalamoi*. I had wrapped my towel around my waist, ready to shower, when Adonis approached me and said, "Go to Stavros and ask him if he wants to play *rothalaki*."

"What are you teaching him?" said Yiannis. "Panagiotis, that's not a good word."

"He will laugh very much if you say it to him—come on," Adonis said.

Nikos whipped Adonis in the ass with his towel.

"*Θα σε κοπανήσω*," Adonis shouted, as he went after Nikos. I will thrash you.

"I'll do it," I said.

Just as I was about to go to Stavros' *thalamos* he appeared at the threshold of ours. He looked at me and said, "Manouselis, are you going to play *rothalaki* in the shower?"

"*Malista*," I said. "I'm waiting for you to join me."

He cracked a smile for the first time.

CHAPTER THIRTY-SEVEN

The plan was to go to the shooting range on Friday, but for some inexplicable reason the exercise was moved to Monday. The shooting range lay on the other side of a shallow gorge beyond the barracks. The dirt path that led there passed an intersection where there was a Lidl supermarket on one side of the street and an emporium selling Chinese-made stuff on the other. Further down the street were warehouses selling industrial products. Beyond them at the end of the street was the gate to the shooting range. A large sign read: DO NOT ENTER.

We passed an area with an obstacle course and walked down a hill and into a field. Across the field, behind a high mound of earth, was the sea. To the right of it we had an unobstructed view of Rethymno. Together we brought out tables and flags and shooting targets from a warehouse. We lined up ten targets horizontally in front of the high mound of earth. My hands were moist and I felt my stomach churning as I moved about with the other recruits performing each task automatically. Behind our shooting post and in front of the safety zone Captain Koutoudis stood on a large platform, accessed by a ladder, directing us with a megaphone.

I was in the second group. Christian stood to my right. His rifle wobbled in his hands. I ate sunflower seeds to help me relax. I couldn't crack open the shells as I was used to doing, so I sucked off the salt and spat the seeds out. I wore my ear plugs squeezed deep into my ears, but even so the noise from first group's shots sounded alarmingly distinct and my nervousness intensified.

Captain Koutoudis instructed my group to proceed to our shooting post. I could hardly hear him. At the shooting post lay a magazine loaded with ten bullets—half its capacity. I had been told the military, like nearly everyone else in the country, was on a budget. Second Lieutenant Staras stood over me as Captain Koutoudis shouted the procedure through his megaphone. I clicked the magazine into the slot. Then I hooked a bipod stand to the rifle and lay down on my stomach.

"Adjust your rotary sight," Staras said.

The target was one hundred meters away and the rotary sight had to be set at one.

"Wait until Captain Koutoudis tells you to cock it," Staras said.

"Soldiers, cock your rifles!"

I cocked it.

"Wait," cautioned Staras.

"Turn your safety off," Captain Koutoudis directed. Then, moments later, "FIRE!"

I pulled the trigger and with great precision and power the bullet zipped through the target and blasted off a large cloud of dust from the mound. I fired nine more times at my own pace. My adrenaline was high after the magazine clip emptied. We walked to our target. I had several hits, two bullseyes. An officer told us our score. We walked back to the safety zone and each of us shouted our score to Captain Koutoudis, while a man at a table marked it down in a large book. My score was low compared to some of the others. A perfect score was fifty. A couple of recruits scored in the high forties.

I found the experience of shooting the rifle exciting. But afterwards, when my adrenaline had waned, I considered the G3A3 rationally and found it a silly weapon. I knew no good would ever come of anyone who used it. It had been created out of fear and it would be used out of fear.

"How did you do, Manouselis?" Christian asked me.

"Not so good. I adjusted my aim after my first couple shots when I thought I was shooting over it. You?"

"*Arxithia.* I went for a second time and I still hit nothing."

"It's a silly game," I said. "Four days left, Christian."

We spent the final few days preparing for our oath of enlistment ceremony. During the ceremony, we would officially become soldiers. We would promise to protect the country and its citizens and to serve with dignity and honor and good faith. On the day before, we rehearsed the entire ceremony with the national anthem and the pledge streaming from the speakers. They ordered us in rows of three according to height; I was in the second row. There were two versions of the Στρατιωτικός Όρκος, or Military Pledge. I swore on the Greek flag, which displayed in the upper left hand corner a blue canton with a white cross. The Greeks formed this symbol to distinguish themselves from the Ottoman Empire, I learned. The other version of the pledge was tailored for the two soldiers who were not Christian Orthodox. This excluded mention of the allegiance to the Christian faith.

On the day of the ceremony, I put on my good uniform and my beret. Nikos helped me so my beret did not make me look like a chef. "You have to wet it," he said. The Gods were smiling: it was a calm, warm, sunny day. The ceremony was a spectacle. There was great camaraderie among the recruits that morning. We were like a football team on their photo day. Any way you looked at it, it was the end of a chapter.

A huge crowd of family and friends had turned up. We stood in ranks, all of us tall and proud in the sun. I felt nervous, afraid I was going to turn right when they shouted left or lag behind when we had to salute or perform some other task. I thought about Stavros, hoping he was going to be okay. He was toward the back. To my displeasure, I had failed, through sheer laziness, to learn the national anthem in time. But I did my best to swear the oath to Greece. I had written the entire passage down, Nikos helping me translate the ancient Greek words.

Dimitris and Yiamonda came to see me. She snapped a photo of me after the ceremony. It would have been good if Dad were there. He would have liked it. He'd find it easy to fall into company, proud to be able to share stories about the time he was in the special forces. It was unfortunate Dad was in America. He was the only one I really wanted there to see me. However, it was nice Dimitris insisted I come to his home later that afternoon because Eleftheria was preparing a feast for me.

When the ceremony was over, we changed into our civilian clothes and, with our sausage bags at our sides, lined up in front of the barracks one last time. Captain Koutoudis read out where we'd be stationed. It was a point of anxiety for many recruits. The soldiers looked very different in civilian clothes. One of the kids called me, "the Professor," because of my khaki pants and light blue collared shirt. I saw a lot of large brand labels printed across shirts and gold- and silver-colored decorations reflecting brightly in the sun. Some of the recruits' jeans were purposely ripped and tattered. Christian wore a black overcoat with the word "Gucci" in gold on the front right side. He was a Greek Albanian doing three months too.

Some of the soldiers were in tears after they'd learned where they would be stationed. Nikos was excited, though.

"I'm going to Cyprus and I'll get paid 500 euros a month!"

"That's great."

"Where are you going?"

"Chania."

"Very nice, my friend. Very nice!"

He bounced around making chit-chat and saying his farewells to the others. I said a few warm goodbyes to the recruits I'd developed a closer connection with. I made them write their contact information in my tiny notebook. For a large majority, I believed the experience was satisfying and they showed it.

I'd say the three-week training period ultimately proved a satisfying experience for me, too, as mundane and boring as it was at times, and even allowing for my terrible allergies and the student doctors. Freed from the pressure of having to make anything of my time, I found it a carefree period in which I was able to observe at my leisure the life around me. I had enjoyed dissecting and speculating upon the characters of my fellow recruits and the officers who trained us. We all came from different backgrounds and economic circumstances, each one of us with his own preferences, idiosyncrasies, opinions, passions, and desires. Unable to choose my surroundings, I had been forced to adapt to new people, different food, and a different social setting to the one I was used to. The other recruits and I had worn the same clothes, eaten the same food, and performed the same tasks together. How quickly one sees a country's true face in this light, I thought. Only once did I see a scuffle and it was quickly resolved, after which the recruits shook hands and apologized.

To me the importance of the military was not that it trained young men to fight a war, but rather that it taught them to live in a dignified manner. The overwhelming majority of recruits did not wish to be there. United by their innate unfitness to be soldiers, they respected and helped one another in every facet of training. If someone was hurt, there was always someone else nearby to offer their hand and unconditional support. The only connection the recruits had were that they were comrades and fellow Greeks. In my experience this is what it means to be a good citizen and a *πιστός φιλότιμος στρατιώτης*—a faithful and dignified soldier.

CHAPTER THIRTY-EIGHT

During my break, I appreciated the simple pleasures of life considerably more than I did before I entered the army. Things like relaxing on the toilet seat as I defecated with the door open; showering and walking naked to my bedroom, unconcerned about my scruff or whether my boots had been polished; fixing a Greek coffee in the morning; eating eggs; sleeping in; finishing *Report to Greco;* and, of course, writing.

Along with these good simple pleasures were less desirable ones too: jerking off, eating large buttery chocolate croissants from the bakery each morning, wasting time online reading incendiary gossip articles, and spending too much money on drinks at the local bars.

Nevertheless, a few days into my break, I felt recharged and in great spirits. Dad was still in the US and I hadn't had any phone calls with him. Mom provided me with frequent updates. Mostly she complained about why I booked Dad's stay in Ohio for over two months.

"It's too long!" She vented to me.

"What is he doing?" I asked.

"He can't settle down," she said. "He doesn't know how to settle his mind. He's always thinking something. Do you know what he did the other day?"

"What did he do?"

"He went and shot a squirrel and the neighbors called the police."

"Why did he do that?"

"Because they eat the pears in the backyard."

In the meantime, I'd communicated with Paul through email. We arranged to meet up and have lunch at our usual spot. From the language in his email, I got the impression he was eager to see me and hear more about my experiences in the army.

He was still using his ski poles to walk. His foot continued to give him pain, he told me, as we sat down at a table in the courtyard. Then he handed me a book in Greek.

"This is for you," he said.

"You didn't have to do this, Paul."

"I thought it would be of interest to you because it's about a Greek-American who returns to his family village in Crete and discovers an old vendetta."

I lifted my eyebrows, then looked down at the book. I read the first couple of sentences.

"You must think my Greek has gotten really good."

"You'll read it over time as your Greek improves."

"Thank you."

After we ordered, he asked me about the army.

"Everyone was nice and respectful," I told him. "Certainly there were moments when I didn't want to be there, but all round it was a good experience."

"And you were worried…"

"I've watched too many American war movies," I said. "I did see that I'm not meant to be a soldier. I'm no *palikari*, as they say."

"What does *palikari* mean?"

"A *palikari* is a warrior, someone who's brave and displays soldierly qualities."

"Why do you think that?"

"I'm a dreamer, someone who anguishes too much. Also I question everything. A good soldier does not ask questions. He simply does as he's told. What about you? How did the second half of the class go?"

"Everything has been fine. We only got through a couple more lessons after you left. I've spoken with Maria a few times. David and I went out one evening and I learned a lot more about him."

"Like what?"

"Well, I learned that he's a very wealthy man and that his wife left him and he has a son who won't talk to him anymore."

"How did he end up in Crete?"

"That I did not find out. Were you able to get some writing done there?"

"Not much. I wrote down some thoughts here and there. I read, mostly. Have you ever read *Report to Greco*, by Kazantzakis?"

"No."

"You should read it. It was the last book he wrote and it encompasses his entire life. I think it's his best work."

"I just finished a philosophical book where the writer has dogs think like humans."

"What's it called?"

"*Fifteen Dogs*. It all starts with a bet Apollo and Zeus make. About what would happen if dogs thought like humans."

"Sounds interesting."

"By the way, if you'd like to stay longer, to search for an apartment, you're welcome to stay at my place. I have an extra room."

"Thank you. But my dad wants me to check up on his dogs."

"Where does he live?"

"Kallikratis. It's a village at the top of the mountains in Sfakia. But he has a cottage in Patsianos where I'm staying now."

"Is that in Sfakia, too?"

"Yeah. It's the village just north of Fragokastello. I like it there. You have the sea. It's quiet and I can write well there. Now that my dad's not here to bother me, I'd like to get some writing done."

"Are you not close with your father?"

He noticed that I'd stiffened and leaned into the back of my chair.

"I apologize. You don't have to say any more if it makes you uncomfortable."

"My father and I are just different. He grew up in a village and wasn't educated. Then he immigrated to America. I will say, as my Greek has improved, I've been able to learn more things about him and it has helped our relationship."

"Like what?"

"For one, I learned that my dad could read. That the conversations he has in Greek with others are no different than the ones I have with Americans. And he has a vocabulary. And he has humor."

"He's not so much of a dummy as you thought, huh?"

"Did you have a good relationship with your father?"

"I wasn't close with my father."

"Your father wasn't in the German army then, was he?"

He nodded his head. "In fact, I never saw him again nor did I ever want to when I fled Germany. I didn't know it when I was young, but he was stationed in Crete. When he died I found his journal. In it he wrote about his time in Crete and how beautiful he thought it was. He wrote in pencil and a lot of it had been rubbed off... I think a part of me feels that was a reason I came to Crete and liked it so much."

"That's fascinating."

"So you know, I hadn't meant to upset you. I was just intrigued."

"How old were you when you left?"

"I fled when I was twenty-two to avoid the army."

"Jeez... the army stories of others make me feel silly to say I'm even in the army." I grabbed the carafe.

"No. I'm only going to have one glass," he said.

"As you like. I'm going to treat you to lunch this time. You bought me this book."

"It's a gift."

"I never thanked you for proofreading my script."

"Fine. I will not fight you." He took a sip of his wine and I took a sip of mine and we passed a moment in silence. Then Paul asked, "Have you ever been to Aradena?"

"I was in Anopolis and I forgot to go there..."

"I have always wanted to hike the Aradena gorge except I could never find anyone who wanted to do it with me."

"I hear it's a beautiful gorge. But it may be difficult."

"I'd like to go there and at least try and do half of it."

"This time of year would be wonderful to hike it."

"If you're free one day, I'd be happy to drive us."

"I go back to the army on Monday."

"I could do Sunday? On Friday my sister is coming from Germany and we're going to my cousin's in Heraklion, but I'm coming back on Saturday night. Then I could drive to Patsianos and pick you up on Sunday morning?"

"Umm…"

"I apologize if I've put you on the spot."

"No. I'd like to go there… Sunday, okay."

I enjoyed Paul's bluntness. We talked about all sorts of things that afternoon. He still couldn't speak Greek. We had a conversation about politics. I found it alarming because America from my viewpoint, after having lived in Greece for seven months, appeared set for political anarchy with Donald Trump making great progress and posed to win the Republican nomination. We cooled off when Paul switched the subject to painters. He liked to talk about art. I knew nearly nothing about the painters he mentioned, but I enjoyed listening to him talk about them. I told him I liked paintings of exotic, elegant women. The erotic kind. He spoke about Gustav Klimt, a great erotic painter, he said, whose paintings were predominantly found in his native Vienna. He recommended I go and see them some day.

At thirty-one years of age, I was at my peak physical potential as a human being. Paul, on the other hand, was in the autumn of his life at seventy-five. His mind was still lucid, and he was keen to share his experiences; while my ravenous mind needed constant feeding. Paul had a way of elevating and elucidating upon the ideas I shared with him. It was as if I was a chandelier hung with dusty crystals that he, with his wisdom, was able to polish until they sparkled and shone.

Nothing about our backgrounds was similar. The only things we had in common were our admiration of Crete and our mutual struggles with the Greek language. Paul had married at twenty-four and by the time he was my age had fathered four children. Being around him made me feel like an imposter at times, as if I wasn't worthy of his intelligence—I would suddenly remember that I was just a boy, from an uneducated working-class family, who not so long ago had cared and talked only about money. Conversely, it was money that had brought me to this point, where I at least had a chance to tame my stupid mind.

We lunched for several hours. Afterwards, when I said goodbye to Paul, I had the feeling that our relationship had suddenly fructified like vines which, absorbing the sun's rays, put out plump little buds.

CHAPTER THIRTY-NINE

I met Paul in the parking lot in Chora Sfakion. He was wearing blue jeans and a long-sleeved shirt rolled up to his elbows, a beige hat with the word "Crete" stitched upon it, and stout hiking boots.

"Would you like a croissant?" I asked.

"I'd better not. I brought a bag of fruit for us."

"Bring your stuff. I'll drive."

"Are you sure?"

"Yeah. You drove all the way out here. Save you a little money on gas."

I grabbed the bag of fruit and a large bottle of water from Paul's car. I tossed his ski poles into the back of my car and shut the hatchback. As we ascended up the mountain, we talked of ordinary things. Pale rocks, strewn with thorny scrub, piled up overhead. Below, cliffs fell sheer into the glittering blue sea. When we reached Anopolis and passed Daskalogiannis' statue, I asked, "Do you know him?"

"I know he wasn't really a teacher," Paul said.

"Not in the formal sense—"

"He was a very wealthy ship-owner."

"They nicknamed him Daskalogiannis because he enlightened the villagers with stories from his travels."

"I still wouldn't call him a teacher."

"I want to write a screenplay about Daskalogiannis," I said. "He was the first leader in Crete to start a revolt against the Turks. That was in 1770. There's a good story to tell about the Ottoman occupation that has yet to be told and, I think, using Daskalogiannis as the focal point could be powerful. He was rich and he sacrificed his life for Greece's freedom."

"The Romans and the Venetians ruled Crete, too," Paul said.

"I don't want to make a documentary," I said. "The snag is the language. It would be strange if I made the characters speak English, yet how do you make an epic film in Greek?"

"The films they make about Roman times don't have them speaking Latin."

"Yeah, but it's so far removed it's acceptable."

We'd hash out our thoughts, then segue into another stimulating historical debate, usually about American political history or ancient Greek history. At times like this, I didn't feel the age difference between us. This made me wonder if my mind had outstripped my body or if Paul was trying to relive his youth by stooping to my level.

When we reached Aradena, I stopped before the steel and wood bridge that spans the gorge, geared down to first and drove slowly across it, the wooden beams rumbling under the tires. On the other side, I parked the car and we walked back onto the bridge. It was higher than I'd thought. I shouted down into the gorge, which had an old paved *kalderimi*, or mule track, going down one side and up the other. Paul snapped a photo of me, and I snapped one of him. The bottom of the gorge, a dry riverbed, was full of smooth white boulders.

To enter the gorge you had to pass through the village. It was early spring and the landscape was lush and green. White clovers covered the grass. Goats grazed among them and bees sucked pollen from the flowers. We saw several cats that appeared to live uncomplicated lives, slouching along without a care in the world. I noticed a goat resting on his forelegs while his hindquarters were elevated, as if he was praying. We descended some stone steps and opened a gate in a welded mesh fence and walked along a footpath past old homes. The houses were built of stone and their walls remained intact, though there were no roofs. Despite their neglect, I didn't think of them as being dilapidated or rundown. The feeling of being inside them and walking by them was clean and soothing and ancient.

We passed more goats drinking water at a trough. Paul moved slowly on his ski poles, so I waited for him whenever I got too far ahead. Beyond another welded mesh fence, we descended into the gorge on the *kalderimi* that wound down the face of the cliff. As we went down, Paul suggested I write a story about two Greek gods sitting over a fire arguing about words. One, he said, would be a modern god, who'd argue that language has been improved by being streamlined. Opposed to him would be an ancient god who'd fight back vehemently, arguing that human emotions and feelings are too complicated for simple words.

"Tension would rise," Paul continued, "Zeus would have his thunder bolt and Poseidon his trident. The modern god would control the nuke. A dramatic climax would ensue."

It was a silly idea, but it made me hypothesize about how the ancient Greeks must have sat by a stream, with their goats and a view of the sea, sipping an elixir of sorts, or munching on lotus plants, and fighting over the precise meaning of things. From the beginning, each word had its own unique meaning. For instance, *balls* are not testicles, testicles are *testicles*, you can never call them balls—ever! Because they are testicles. It must have gone on and on like this, until an insanely comprehensive vocabulary of words was created that was able to describe every feeling and object and action in existence. My mind spun just thinking about it.

"Maybe the idea could be a parody," I said to Paul. "Certainly, not dramatic."

When we reached the bottom, we waited a minute while Paul caught his breath. We were the only hikers around. The red-ocher walls of the gorge soared above us. Hawks and crows flew above them. We passed scattered goat carcasses with cracked skulls. Halfway up the track that zig-zagged up the other side of the gorge a goat was bleating. It looked distressed, but I was unsure if it was stuck. I glanced over my shoulder and asked, "How are you doing over there?"

"Let's continue forward."

We reached a point under the bridge and sat on large stone slabs in the shade. We had only trekked half a kilometer. Paul handed me the bag of fruits. I bit into a big yellow apple. We must have been four hundred feet below the bridge.

"I had this dream," I said. "I was on a mountain peak, when some supernatural being—maybe God?—spoke to me. 'Yeah… I remember,' the supernatural being said, 'Don't worry, you are doing just fine. You must understand that you are not the only one. There is an entire universe of people like you that I must help. I will continue to provide water… just keep doing what you are doing.' Then the supernatural being was gone. I can't remember anything after that. Since then I've been mulling it over trying to find a reason why I should have had a dream like that. Strange, huh?"

"And to think that the New Testament was written one hundred years after Jesus' death," Paul said. "What stories and exaggerations they could have imagined as they were writing it. How many people of that time experienced the supernatural as you did in your dream."

"You have to read Kazantzakis," I said. "The mental leaps he takes to tackle the spiritual are mind-blowing."

"Have you ever read the Bible?"

"A few passages here and there, but that's the extent of it."

"You know I'm not a religious person, but I found it to be rich with thoughts and ideas… Only people misinterpret it."

"Yeah. Sort of like when you have a démagogue who convinces fanatical believers that Christians are the only good people and all others are evil."

"This doesn't only happen with Christians. You also have extremist Muslims. On the island of Lesbos there are currently three times the number of refugees compared to local inhabitants."

"I requested to go there, because of the refugees, but they put me in Chania. I'm kind of glad it worked out this way. I only wonder what's going to happen with all these people. If a war breaks out, I'll have to fight. Turkey is causing chaos. They're the ones bringing the refugees over here and taking all their money."

"This is how wars start."

"How do you mean?"

"History has shown that when inhabitants flee their territory to new land eventually war ensues. Resources dry up. The original inhabitants of the land fear the newcomers. It's either a case of the invaders killing the inhabitants and taking over or the inhabitants moving on. Rarely will they live and work together in harmony."

"People are more informed today. They are less likely to react impetuously. Fear and deceit is uncovered by the ease of communication. People just need to love each other."

"That's silly. Can you really love everyone in the world?"

"Of course! We have to."

"Every generation has the 'let's all just love each other' idea. Love is the answer. Look at the '70s. It was the period of love. The hippies. People started to believe it would change, that after Vietnam everyone would love each other. But you know what happened? The '80s arrived! You're not saying anything new to me."

"Hopefully this time it will be different. At least it has to be for the sake of humanity."

At least that's what I hoped. I wanted everyone to be as Kazantzakis says: *something spiritual*. Yet Paul possessed the advantage of experience. All I knew was what I wanted to know. What I wanted to hear. And, finally, what I hoped for.

"What anchors you?" I asked.

"What if respect was a far more accurate and useful notion than love?"

He was eating a large peach and the nectar from it, dribbling down his chin, made him look wild. Peeling an orange, I nodded and said,

"I saw that a lot in the army." I turned my head and caught sight of a butterfly which made me happy.

"*Τι ωραία πεταλούδα,*" I said.

"What did you say?"

"Did you know the Greek word for butterfly is *πεταλούδα*?"

"Pe-ta-loutha."

"How do you say 'butterfly' in German?"

"*Schmetterling.*"

"That sounds like the name of a chainsaw."

I tossed the orange rinds behind my back. I heard the goat crying again.

"To hike down to Marmara might be too difficult for me, as much as I want to do it," Paul said. "I wouldn't want to burden you in case something happens."

"You mean you don't want to leave me with your dead body?"

"Yes. And out here, by the time help arrives, the crows would have gotten me."

"Yeah… I'm not ready to be burdened with that just yet."

"Would you like me to take a picture of you before we head back up?"

"Sure."

He snapped a picture of me and I snapped a nice picture of him with his ski poles. He looked very white and old and it was certainly not unreasonable to think he could just keel over.

"Do you think that goat is stuck or is it just making routine?" I asked.

"I can't tell from here. It does sound like a distressed cry."

"Maybe's he's learning how to fly and he's scared…"

Paul moved better back up the mountain. He was glad to be in the car and have the window down. At that late hour of the day, as we returned down the mountain, the sea appeared like a sheet of glass. Paul didn't say much, but I knew he had enjoyed the hike and was disappointed he hadn't been able to make it all the way down to Marmara beach.

"We'll hike the entire gorge in the fall," I said.

"Yes. My foot will be better then."

"That will be our goal—to finish the Aradena gorge."

"There should be no reason not. I may opt for ankle replacement surgery in the summer if things don't improve. I have to do it. It was a goal my wife and I made for each other."

He still loved his wife dearly, I could tell, and as he talked about her a look of pain passed across his face. Yet from the easy way he spoke of her, I felt no sense of violating his privacy with my questions.

"Did you travel often to Crete together?"

"We came here, but not as often as I do now. We traveled to a lot of places. But as we got older traveling became more difficult. And we had to be more careful. One time we were in Barcelona and after we'd checked out of the hotel a gentleman whom we thought was with the hotel asked to carry our luggage to the taxi and so we handed him our luggage and once we were outside he disappeared. Luckily I carried our money and passports with me."

"When did your wife die?"

"In 2012."

"How old was she?"

"She was born in 1940… she'd be seventy-six today. So seventy-two. We missed our fiftieth anniversary by two years." He went silent, pondering the realization.

We had lunch in Chora Sfakion, at a restaurant located at the seafront. The temperature was pleasant and the breeze was soothing. We ordered a plate of octopus with a Cretan salad and a carafe of white wine. Paul made sure we split the bill. We hugged at the parking lot and he wished me good luck with my remaining time in the army. He reminded me about hiking down to Marmara beach in the fall. I was satisfied and happy that I'd spent the day with Paul. He balanced me out. I felt good that he felt happy we did it. And I was sure I'd miss him over the summer while he was back in Canada.

CHAPTER FORTY

The army base in Chania was about a quarter of the size of the base in Rethymno. On the other side of the barb-wired fence were apartment buildings that surrounded it. I arrived at the security gate, with my papers, at seven in the morning. A soldier escorted me to the barracks, where soldiers were outside smoking and chit-chatting among themselves. A sign read, "5th Battalion Support," above the entrance.

I walked across the lobby and up a small set of stairs to an office. A private with a blank face marked off my name from a list in a book. Another soldier led me to my *thalamos*. I dropped my bag next to a bunk halfway down a row. The bottom and top beds were both empty so I took the top. The soldier placed my notecard inside a plastic sleeve attached to the front bar of my bed. On it was my name and my father's name and my military specialty—*τυφεκιοφόρος*—which meant I was a front-line soldier. If there was a war, I'd be one of the first to die.

The officer in charge of the barracks wore the two stars of a lieutenant. He looked over my files. Then another officer entered and interrupted us.

"The director wants to see him, before he goes to SPEN."

"What's SPEN?" I asked.

"You're going to Rethymno for training," he said.

"Serious?"

"Yeah. The director wants to see you before you leave."

"So I'm not staying here?"

"You're going to SPEN for two weeks."

He escorted me to the director's building. The director was a captain named Gelptis. He was an affable man with a smooth face and gray hair and a sarcastic demeanor that I found attractive. Upon learning my profession, he insisted I have him in one of my movies.

"I'll make a movie about the Greek Army and you'll play the director."

"Aspasia!" Captain Gelptis shouted to his secretary in the next room. "Did you hear that, Aspasia? He's going to have me in one of his movies. You'll have Aspasia in it too?"

"Sure. I'll have all of you. But you'll all be famous then. Are you sure you want to be famous?"

"Of course! Then I can retire," the captain said. We shared a good laugh. "You're a good kid. Good luck with the SPEN. I'll see you when you return." I shook his hand. "Do you think I need to lose some weight?" he added.

"You're good the way you are."

"You're a good kid!"

I returned to the barracks where there were a handful of other soldiers waiting to leave for Rethymno. I recognized some of the faces from the LEN. When the army truck pulled up, we climbed into the back and off we sped, all of us grasping the tarp bars. We stopped at the army base in Souda Bay where we waited around for an hour.

I relaxed in the lounge and watched a morning talk show. The soldier with the remote kept changing the channel. Every Greek woman on TV had dyed-blond hair. I asked the soldier why that was and he said that it was because Greek men liked blond women. The soldier next to him noticed my accent and asked me where I was from. I told him my parents were from Sfakia. He was from Sfakia, he said, from a village called Askifou. He had only one more month left of service. I asked him what his plans were.

"Zimbabwe."

"*What?*"

"Africa. I'm going to Zimbabwe."

"And what are you going to do there?"

"They have Greeks there—in the fur business."

"There are Greeks in Zimbabwe? How old are you?"

"Twenty-two."

"You've been in Chania the entire time?"

"No. I was in Mytilini for six months."

"Mytilini? That's where I asked to go, but they brought me here. How was it?"

"*Tromero.* Unbelievable."

"Why?"

"A dead refugee washed up on the shore." He watched my jaw drop. "A kid. We barely slept—not one day off."

When they called us to return to the truck, I said goodbye to the soldier and wished him good luck in Zimbabwe, adding that I'd ask for him if I ever visited there.

"It shouldn't be a problem to find another Greek in Zimbabwe," I said.

"No," he agreed and laughed.

* * *

The new barracks at Rethymno lay on the other side of the base from the barracks we stayed in during LEN training. Now, to my delight, I was stationed right beside the sea. We settled immediately into our *thalamos.* I took the top bunk next to the window.

"What do we do next?" I asked the soldier next to me.

"We have to go to the barracks next door and get our gear," he said.

I returned with my helmet, belt and suspenders, ammunition pouches, backpack, bayonet, and plastic canteen. I left them on my bed and a small group of us then went to the arsenal for our rifles. After we locked them up at the barracks, we lined up outside for lunch. There were fifty-five of us, slightly less than we had for the LEN.

Our Captain appeared from the barracks. His last name, Patsis, was stitched above his left breast pocket. We waited while a subordinate provided him with the report. Then Captain Patsis turned to us and, in a deep and powerful voice, welcomed us to the base. He was a tall man with a solid frame and a narrow face. He was probably only a couple of years older than me, if that.

"We have a lot to get done and there are only two weeks," he said.

He warned us to check and make sure we had all our gear and, if we didn't, to have it taken care of by the end of the day.

On our first day they let us out at 1700 hours and I returned to Chania. I bought the day's paper, went to a café, and looked over the apartments listed. I got word from another soldier that we were allowed to leave the army base at night and sleep at home on the days we didn't have service duties, so it was an idea of mine to find an apartment in Chania a few months before the summer.

All the apartments I inquired about were unavailable. We didn't have to return to the base until 2200 hours. It was then only 1900 hours, so I pulled out my lesson book from Greek class and worked on a few exercises. After thirty minutes, I stopped working and worried about finding an apartment instead; then, when that passed, I began watching the many pretty girls around me. I knew it was impossible to go on a date with any of them, but I watched them avidly nonetheless. How much better life would be, I thought, if *just one* of these pretty girls was my girlfriend.

I worried some more, back at the barracks, about my future. Suddenly, life after the army appeared intolerably complex. I was concerned that I could never find peace with the simple things in life. Later, when I was having a hot shower, I worried less by concentrating hard on enjoying the moment. That was something.

Next morning, as I lethargically dressed in my uniform, I looked out my window toward the horizon beyond Rethymno. The sky was cloudless and the sea placid and creamy. As the sun rose, wonderful hues of orange and red and yellow spread across the sky. I watched, awestruck, as the colors deepened in shade and the sun bathed the earth in a powerful radiance and the sea grew clearer. All I could think was: *what a situation.*

This, I told myself, was going to be my view every morning for the next two weeks. Surely, if you had to serve in the army, and undertake bootcamp training, there was no more idyllic setting on earth in which to do it.

CHAPTER FORTY-ONE

One day, after breakfast and cleaning duties, Captain Patsis led us on a long hike. We wore full gear, which made our expedition feel authentic. Cars trundled overhead as we trudged through a passageway under the national road. Back in the sunlight, Captain Patsis marched us past car dealerships and residential homes, the ground rising as we left Rethymno behind and edged closer toward the mountains. Some five kilometers from the base we reached a plateau of dirt and rocks near a small village, the name of which nobody knew, where we paused momentarily.

Cicadas drilled in the hot still air. Gulping down water, the sweat dripping off me, I looked toward Mt Psiloritis which dominated the center of the island, its snowy peak gleaming in the sun. Behind me, the sea was clearly visible and I was struck by the legendary associations of Crete's highest mountain, which according to Greek mythology was the birthplace of Zeus. I had just begun to relax when Captain Patsis' voice boomed, ordering us to turn back.

We marched directly to the shooting range, where we broke into groups of two and commenced with training drills. At the first station, one of our training officers taught us how to properly align the rear sight with the target. My partner stood behind a tiny paper target, ten meters away, and marked the spot in pencil that I pointed out to him as I simulated a shot. Then I reset and realigned the rear sight with the target and he made another pencil mark. At the next station,

Second Lieutenant Sakalidi, a woman, taught us how to properly toss a grenade from the ground. It was an art which I'd never really thought about before. The trick was to hurl the grenade without being seen by the enemy and getting yourself shot or worse. At another station we familiarized ourselves with a MK 48 machine gun. We stood in a circle around the instructor, all of us a little awed, as he pointed out the gun's features and explained its workings. This was followed by a tactical foot march during which we learned how to proceed in formation toward a target and, on our troop leader's command, simultaneously drop to the ground and fire.

Next morning, we returned to the shooting range to put the drills into practice. We formed lines of six and moved in an orderly fashion on the large open field. We went as a group to a table, where they handed us blanks for our rifles. One soldier in each group was appointed to use the MK 48 machine gun. I was curious to fire the MK 48, but Master Sergeant Papadakis, a solid, no-nonsense sort of man with a harsh tongue, didn't pick me. He picked another guy instead, who looked more like the fire-eater type. Before we loaded our magazine with blanks, the master sergeant told us to cock our rifles and fire them in the sky. The soldier next to me didn't cock his rifle, and Papadakis took notice.

"Cock your rifle," said Papadakis.

The soldier stared at him.

"*Malaka!* Cock your rifle."

The soldier fidgeted with his rifle.

"*Malaka*, are you serious? You don't know how to cock your rifle?"

We all watched as Papadakis seized the rifle. "Serious, *malaka!* It's like you telling me you're going to fuck some girl and you don't know if you have to use your finger or your dick." Papadakis cocked the rifle, pointed it to the sky, and pulled the trigger. The rifle made a solid click. I turned my head away and lifted my lapel over my mouth.

They had given us ten blanks each for our rifles, while the soldier with the MK 48 got twenty. We lined up behind the group on the firing deck. There were no targets set up. I watched the groups ahead of me, listening to them shout and communicate. I kept repeating the words we were to shout. However, some of the words were unclear to me.

"How do you say…" It was the word for "Fire." I asked the soldier next to me.

"*Pier*," he said.

I whispered it a few more times. When the group in front of us finished, we moved to our position. I was on the far left. Alexandros, our troop leader, was in the middle. Suddenly, Alexandros shouted, "Proceed!" We ran forward and when he shouted, "Down!" we dropped as one to the ground. Alexandros then shouted, "*Pier!*" I shouted, "*Pier!*" after everyone else, pulling the trigger of my rifle. The blanks fired very quickly. I stood up after everyone else and we continued forward. Then, on Alexandros' command, we dropped to the ground again and Alexandros shouted, "*Pier!*" whereupon I shouted too and fired my rifle after everyone else.

"*Malaka, tauftoxrona!*" Papadakis shouted at me from the other end of the range. "You have to say, '*Pier, tauftoxrona!*'"

I didn't know what *tauftoxrona* meant nor did I think the middle of a training exercise was the right time to ask him. Captain Patsis stood off to the side, next to me, and Second Lieutenant Sakalidi followed behind us. We charged forward. "*Pier!*" shouted the others, then I shouted, "*Pier tauftoxrona!*"

Papadakis came at me hard. He didn't know I was the Americanos.

"*Malaka!* What the hell are you doing? Are you making fun of me?"

The other troops burst out laughing.

"I don't know what the hell *tauftoxrona* means," I shouted.

"*Tauftoxrona! Plaka mou kaneis?*"

"Leave him alone—*O Americanos*," Captain Patsis said. He and Lieutenant Sakalidi were trying to keep straight faces, but eventually their lips fell apart and they broke into smiles. I felt like a complete imbecile and I laughed, too, still unsure of what was going on.

"It means 'simultaneously,'" a soldier in my group said to me. "We have to say 'fire' all at once upon Alexandros' signal."

"Manouselis—*trela* you are!" said Yiakomakis. Crazy! He smiled and hugged me.

CHAPTER FORTY-TWO

As the end of SPEN training drew near, our daily activities intensified. We were introduced to the obstacle course. It was sort of like you see in the movies, where soldiers crawl under barbed wire, sprint along a balance beam, leap off tree-stumps, hurdle over and under logs, scale walls, and hop in and out of ditches, while the unperturbed and crisp-looking officers shouted at us that we weren't moving fast enough. The day was hot and, as we sprinted around the field, performing the necessary acrobatics at the various obstacles, we sweated like galley slaves. The only one who appeared to enjoy himself—apart from the officers—was a nineteen-year-old professional soccer player who was serving because he hadn't played in enough regular season games this year. He dominated the course, passing me easily despite me having had a fifteen-second head-start.

I was gasping and wheezing at the end. A cold chill broke out on my forehead. I needed a solid ten minutes before I returned to a stable condition. The other recruits were just as bad, or worse, everyone standing around, bent over with their hands on their knees, sucking in oxygen and broiling in the heat.

The officer read out our times. Mine was decent, but far from the best. After a morning of this, it was all we could do to march back to the barracks for lunch and a bit of rest before we headed to the shooting range.

Surprisingly, despite our weariness, there was plenty of banter at lunch. Over the *moussaka,* Yaikomakis taught me how to say "Go fuck yourself" in Greek. I repeated it after him, "*Na πας να γαμιθείς."* The other recruits giggled at my accent.

"How do you say it, Manouselis? Tell Nikos," said Yiakomakis.

"*Na πας να γαμιθείς,*" I repeated, and everyone laughed madly again.

The banter from lunch carried over to the barracks as we geared up for the afternoon drills. We were still laughing when our *thalamarxis* stomped in and told us to hurry up and line up outside. "*Na πας να γαμιθείς,*' I murmured to myself, glancing at Yakomakis, who winked in approval and rolled his eyes. At this stage the actual meaning of the phrase hadn't quite registered on me, so it was just a sound emerging from my mouth.

"Hurry up," repeated the *thalamarxis.*

"Go fuck yourself," I said.

The *thalamos* broke out in uproar and the *thalamarxis* appeared lost for words at the fluid way I hurled the expletive at him. He came unstuck, knowing the other soldiers had encouraged me, and let it pass.

"*Trela,* Manouselis," said Yiakomakis. "Let's go—don't forget your helmet."

"Are we shooting real bullets this time?"

"*Malista.*"

By the time we had trudged to the range, we were drenched with sweat all over again. The mindless repetition reminded me of high school two-a-day football practices which had always seemed like a never-ending drag. I had grown tired of wearing the same smelly uniform day in, day out, of strapping on my boots and making sure they were polished and checking that my laces were tucked away and my sleeves were folded correctly and my *exartisi,* belt and suspenders, fitted properly over my shoulders. *Na πας να γαμιθείς,* I said under my breath, in a half-joking manner, glad my vocabulary had improved with this new phrase and even more glad to unleash a round from my rifle.

Orange cones were arranged all down the shooting range. The targets were set up in front of the dirt mound at the end of the range. The instructors handed each of us a magazine clip loaded with ten bullets. On this occasion, I felt easier and more comfortable with my rifle. I stuck in my ear plugs and marched to the starting point. My magazine clip was in my pouch. At the pit of my belly the *moussaka* sat comfortably.

We started three hundred meters away from the target. Captain Patsis stood to one side of our group, calm and commanding as ever. On his command, I removed the magazine from my pouch and snapped it into position. He shouted at us to cock our rifles. With rifles cocked we moved forward under our group leader's command. After fifty meters, two-hundred-and-fifty meters from the target, we kneeled on one knee and fired a couple shots. Standing again, still in formation, we continued towards the target until we were about fifty meters away, whereupon we went back down on one knee and fired the remaining bullets in our magazines.

Upon returning to the start, I felt oddly elated. Throughout the exercise I had been unemotional and precise. So it didn't surprise me that, when the scores were read out, I registered my best total yet.

* * *

Next day, in the pine forest, my nose ran uncontrollably as I stood with my fellow recruits watching our master sergeant and sergeant build their tent. They spread the shelter piece over the ground. The letters "US" were painted, in black, on the canvas.

"Bring me the stuff from the sack," said the master sergeant. A soldier retrieved the sack and left it next to the two men.

"Come on, *malaka*! Take out the stuff from the sack. We're not at city hall, where one works and twelve others sit around and drink frappés."

In the sack were the stakes and metal poles and a hammer. The master sergeant lifted up the front end of the tent and placed the point of the pole through the grommet. They spread one flank of the tent and nailed stakes through the loop chords sowed to the end of it. Then they tightly stretched the other side of the flank and nailed stakes through the loop holes. Finally they erected the backend of the tent with another pole that was placed through a grommet.

The rest of us paired up and found spots in the woods to erect our tents. I was paired with a soldier called George. He was a large, slow-moving man cursed with the worst facial features of his parents and a quirky sense of humor. He and I found a good spot between two trees. We kicked away all the pine needles on the ground. We buttoned together the shelter pieces, forming the tent. George nailed the corners of the tent to the ground with the wooden stakes and, using my spade, I dug a trench around the perimeter of the tent as we'd been shown.

"It's not going down securely," George said. "It's like there is a mountain underneath."

I lifted out the dirt and there was a boulder.

"I just trenched the tent," I said.

"We'll pack it with dirt."

"I agree. It's only for one night."

After our tent was set up, we went for lunch. A long row of tables, spread with food, stood in the parking lot at the top of the woods. We filled our tray and returned to the woods where we ate sitting on slabs of stone. Our officers ate with us. The meal was spaghetti with minced beef and it wasn't too bad. We filled our canteens from a large container of water, right to the brim because it was another hot day.

After I'd finished eating, I walked back up the slope and stacked my tray on top of the others, then went back to our tent to lie down. On top of my camping mat I saw several large cellar spiders. I smashed one of them with my bayonet, then I removed all our equipment and used the shovel to clear the ground of any remaining brush. After, I replaced the camping mat inside the tent and lay down using my sweater as a pillow.

That night, when we went to the shooting range, I was eager to fire using a night-vision scope. The air had cooled slightly, but it was still quite mild. Above the tops of the pine trees the sky twinkled with stars. A couple of rifles, with night-vision scopes attached, waited for us at the shooting posts. The instructors reminded us of what we'd learned about using the scopes. They gave us four shots each at a target that was two hundred meters away. I lifted my rifle to my shoulder and, fitting my eye to the scope, saw that the target looked very close and clear, illuminated by a bright florescent green light. Despite telling myself to be calm, butterflies flitted about my stomach as my finger closed around the trigger. I fired off my four shots quickly, concentrating hard on the green-lit target. It was over in an instant and, when I had finished, I felt a rush of exhilaration sweep over me but was unsure if it was a good thing or not.

Afterwards we ate dinner at the cafeteria, then I went and got my pillow and sleeping bag from the barracks before returning to the woods and settling down to sleep. The wind shook our tent and cold air lingered inside. My throat worsened and I used my sweater and wrapped it around my mouth and nose. I turned over from one side to the other, then back again, on the camping mat on the hard ground.

At some point in the middle of the night George got up and went out on patrol. Then, at three in the morning, a strong gust of wind pulled a stake loose and the corner of the tent lifted up and dirt and pine needles covered the inside. I got up and replaced the stake, using my hand to pack dirt around it. As soon as I let go of the stake it came loose again. I knew another strong gust of wind would expose the inside of the tent. I paused to think. Loud snores came from the other tents and I could hear the whistle of the wind in the pine branches. I removed the spike and laid a large rock on top of the loop grommet. Then, climbing back inside the tent, I lay down with my face buried in the pillow and tucked my hands down my pants.

At four o'clock George returned. I heard him fumbling with his gear but my eyes stayed shut until we woke up at six. Both the air and the ground were moist. I felt horrible. My limbs ached and my nose ran like a tap. It was bitterly cold. We tore down our tents and packed them back into the bags and carried the bags to the parking lot where we stacked them together before returning to the barracks to shower and shave. I was very happy to find that the water was hot and poured from the head powerfully. Afterwards, dressed and clean, I skipped breakfast and went to the *kapsimi* to buy another pack of lemon drops. I returned just as the master sergeant called us into lines and marched us back to the barracks. We cleaned our gear and then we went to the training field. There most of us practiced the obstacle course for the following day's ceremony, while a separate group rehearsed a tactical exercise. Finally, we practiced marching in proper lines, forming groups and learning how we were to approach the director and receive our certificate.

On my last morning at the base, I watched from the window of the barracks as mother nature performed in a way I'd never seen before. It was something you could not describe and would never see in a picture. You had to be there, at the precise minute, for that was all the time you had to enjoy the exotic colors that irradiated the landscape.

"Can you believe this view," I said to my bunkmate, Manos.

"It is very beautiful," he said.

I stayed in front of the window as long as I could. *Bye, bye Rethymno army base*, I said to myself. *If I never see you again, I'll be happy.*

"Let's go, Manouselis, let's get our diploma," Manos said.

The ceremony took place at the training field. It was more personal than the ceremony for the LEN. We individually approached the director. I snapped to attention and saluted him.

I shouted, "*Στρατιώτης Πεζικού*, Μανουσέλης Παναγιώτης 2016 B *Εζζό*."

And he said, "I see you learned Greek."

I had never met him before and the fact that he knew of me, the soldier from America, made me feel valued and important.

PERSPECTIVE

After the ceremony we packed our bags and said our goodbyes to the officers. "*Xarika*," Captain Patsis said as he shook my hand. The Master Sergeant Papadakis, who yelled a lot wished me well, too. I boarded the tourist bus with all the soldiers who were returning to Chania. The bus took us, via the base in Souda and the NATO base in Akrotiri, to the 5th Battalion Support base. The base behind the courthouses in Chania. There I reported to an officer who handed me a sheet of paper and said, "I'll see you back in ten days."

CHAPTER FORTY-THREE

It was because of Easter that I was able to have another ten-day break. Greeks dropped everything for Easter. Shepherds sold off flocks of lamb. Bakers worked extra hours to make many loaves of *tsoureki*, the sweet holiday bread made at Easter and Christmas. People planned trips to visit family in faraway locations. City dwellers returned to their childhood villages in the country. Yet even allowing for this, I may not have got a ten-day break if I hadn't told my superior that this was my first Easter in Greece and I wanted to spend it with family. All it took was the word "family." In Greece, if you mention family and the need to be with them, it opens many doors.

I did not run off to Sfakia because I had found an apartment just outside the old town, near the *Kipos* Park. The apartment was tucked in at the back of an old building housing both residential and commercial tenants. It was small, a street-level unit with a covered parking spot out front that you could only get to if you drove through the narrow arcade that went through the building. The owner had recently remodeled it, installing cheap appliances; in the bedroom on the second floor were two single beds on uneven wooden frames. I argued with the owner, trying to convince him to install an air conditioner by summer, and when he agreed, I paid him the first month's rent with a security deposit and he handed me the keys.

The apartment was not ideal, but I liked that it was cheap and close to the harbor. The stadium was also very close and most afternoons I went there to work out. I did pull-ups on the bars, sprints on the track, and ran up and down the steps. Since entering the army, I noticed, I had lost a few pounds. In the mirror, the lines at my hips were sharp and defined. Slight shadows outlined the muscles in my stomach, which was something I hadn't seen since I was a kid. All the standing and hiking had tightened my ass so my pants fit better. When I took jaunts in the old town I seemed to move with a new fluidity and my converse sneakers felt weightless on my feet.

Most evenings, I went swimming in Nea Chora. The water was pleasant and at this time of the year, in the middle of spring, there were few tourists. I swam laps, enjoying the feeling of strength in my arms. Then, one evening, Dad phoned me. I hadn't seen him since he had returned from America, which no doubt bothered him. He called me when he arrived to arrange picking up the car from the army base. Then he called me again—the day after I finished boot camp—and we'd argued about me getting an apartment and I hung up on him. Now, typically, given his manner, his first words to me were hardly a surprise.

"*Yeia sou*," I said.

"The dog hung himself," he said.

"Which dog?" I asked.

"The brown dog. He tried to jump the fence and the chain was caught," Dad said.

"He goes on to a better life, I'm sure," I said.

"Listen. I'm coming to Chania—I'll pick you up. We have work to do."

"No way!" I said. "I'll be there for Easter, I told you."

"Come here first. For two, three days."

"I told you to hire someone if you think you're too old. You haven't understood yet that we can't be together? Every time we see each other we have a fight and I'm tired of it."

"Because of you."

"Of me?"

"You don't listen."

"I'm not here to argue. When are you coming tomorrow?"

"In the morning. In the evening we have to go to the lawyer."

"*You* have to go to the lawyer."

"We're going! Both of us."

"I don't have time. I have to get furniture."

"Why?"

"I need a dresser for my clothes."

"You said the apartment was furnished?"

"Not completely."

"What can I tell you. You shouldn't have gotten an apartment. You're in the army now. You don't need an apartment. You sleep there—you come here and stay now. You don't need an apartment now."

"I'm not going to argue with you."

"Do what you want."

"I always do."

"We can go together and buy the furniture, if you want."

"You're giving me a headache," I said.

Dad grunted and shrugged off my comment saying, "After you'll come a few days before Easter, please." And before I could answer he said, "Okay. Good. We'll talk, goodbye," as if we'd reached an agreement, and abruptly ended the call.

Next day I met him at his accountant's office and we went straight to Ikea. When we neared the Ikea sign I said, "Turn right—there at the blue building."

"There?"

"Yes!"

"The Chinese place?"

"Ikea is Swedish."

"That's Chinese."

"Just turn there and don't say anything, please."

Dad's eyes widened and he froze until he figured out what the place was. We walked in silence from the parking lot to the shop. A lady showed me the section with the dressers.

"It's cheap," Dad remarked as he scanned the floor.

After some thought, I decided on a stained white wooden dresser. I added two sofa pillows and a night stand.

There were times with Dad where I thought we were getting somewhere, that we were on a similar wavelength or at least understood each other's perspective. But just when I had begun thinking that, something would happen and it would all go wrong. Something like this happened after I had moved the furniture into my apartment and we put it all together and then ate lunch. Afterwards Dad went for a nap and, when he awoke, the trouble started.

"Let's go to Kallikratis now," he said.

I jerked my head toward my shoulder and gasped.

"Let's go," he repeated.

"I'll see you at Easter," I said.

"We have to go to the lawyer now," he said.

"No. I'm not going."

Dad stood up swiftly and left without saying anything. Was I a bad son? I wondered. Or was Dad just good at making me feel like a bad son? I wanted to help him and I felt shoddy after I'd rebuffed him; I knew the fault was not all his. I comforted myself with the reflection that our relationship was a work in progress. The only problem was, I remained uncertain as to whether we'd ever reach the point where we could have civil conversations.

Moments later I found myself thinking about Mom. I missed her. And I knew she worried for me and I didn't like that she worried. She was the kind of woman who would never stop worrying no matter the situation. She'd carried a bag of worries along with her for her entire life, it seemed. She worried a lot about money. A lot about her kids and their health. She would only be happy, I realized, if I got married, preferably to a Greek girl, and settled down close to her and raised a family.

One day, as I was writing, an idea came to me. I thought I'd do something special and surprise Mom. I had a picture of myself when I was in the LEN that I'd bought from the army photographer. My first thought was to send her the picture. Then I began writing a letter. I started in English, but after a couple of sentences, I decided to write the letter in Greek. It was the first time I'd ever done something like this and I felt amazed: thinking in Greek changed my thoughts and the way that I wrote. Suddenly my words and sentences accrued great passion; I spilled words of appreciation and love without restraint. I didn't manage to finish the letter on my first attempt. It was not till the following afternoon, at a café by the harbor, that I finally signed off.

I felt immensely proud of my letter and the things I had said in it. I told Mom she shouldn't worry for me. That I appreciated all she'd done for me in my life. I told her I had the best mother in the world, that she was kind and friendly and *philotimi*. I said I understood more clearly everything she had sacrificed for me now than I did when I was younger. I told her that I loved her.

The only card I could find was black and had a rose on the front with the word "Love" printed under it. I transcribed the letter from my computer onto a sheet of paper and taped it to the card. I then walked to the post office where the wait was very long. The Greek people who were waiting appeared rushed and agitated. There was no line. Rather, an unruly crowd of people filled up the room. I watched as a young woman walked in pushing a baby stroller. "Oh lord!" she said, gesturing theatrically, before pushing the stroller to the front of the crowd. Then, as soon as the man at the counter had finished, she went in front.

"Miss," said the man behind her. "We have a line. You have to take a number."

"But I have the baby with me!"

"You have a baby. Ouf! Go ahead of me," said the lady whose number was called next. The gentleman said nothing. And what could one do? A woman with a baby wielded great power in Crete.

CHAPTER FORTY-FOUR

On Easter day we stopped at Kanakis' house, before driving to Dimitris' in Rethymno. We entered his courtyard down concrete steps adorned with a flower pot on each step. The courtyard was ornately designed with plant pots and vines all around the sides. Around the edges of the concrete dark green moss crept out of the corners. Kanakis was tending a lamb roasting on a spit. As soon as he saw us his face lit up and he said, "*Xristos anesti*!" Christ has risen!

"*Alithos anesti*!" Dad and I responded. Truly he has risen!

"Kanakis! Bring some cups," Kanakis barked at his son. Then he turned to me saying, "Come here, Panagiotis, so I can see you." He embraced me, then he handed me his pocket knife and told me to cut off a piece of meat.

The metal rod passed through the body of the lamb emerging through the opened throat and out its mouth. The lamb's chest was wired shut and, as it rotated, grease dripped down off its skin and landed, hissing, on the coals. I trimmed off a small piece of the lamb's thigh.

"This is very tasty," I said.

"It needs a little more time," Dad said.

"It's ready now," Kanakis retorted.

"In ten minutes it will be good," Dad said.

Little Kanakis returned with some cups. We rested on old wooden chairs, under the grapevines, and sipped *tsikoudia*. We picked at a bowl of peanuts, leaving the shells on the table. For a while, Dad and Kanakis made small talk; then Kanakis expressed concern that I didn't have a woman in my life. He said time was running out for me and, if I waited too long, I wouldn't be able to get married. I replied that I was still young and had another five years before I needed to think of settling down.

"Panagiotis, listen to me. I'm telling you. I was the same as you. I laughed at everyone who was young and married. But years will pass and you will regret it. I'm telling you."

"*You* help me find a good Greek girl," I told him. "I try!"

"I will find you one."

When the time came to leave, Kanakis tried to make us stay, insisting that we eat here. Dad said we had to be leaving as we were already late. Before we departed Kanakis seized my hand and, squeezing it tightly, said, "Don't forget what I told you, Panagiotis. You'll regret it."

"Yes, yes. Thank you."

"I'm so happy to see you, you know I love you."

"Thank you."

"Come here and stay with us whenever you like."

"Thank you, Kanakis."

On the way down the mountain, Dad and I were quiet. I could feel that he was happy to have stopped at Kanakis' with me on Easter day. The tension stirred up from our squabble a few days before had eased and, as with previous squabbles, the fallout was largely forgotten.

"Mom said that Aunt Ann and Uncle Dee are here."

"Yes," Dad said. "That's what I heard."

I felt good about the rest of the day and was sure we'd have a good time together.

We arrived at Dimitris' to find a small festival in progress. Two lambs roasted on metal *souvlas* in the driveway. A large table stretched across the front yard. The kids were chasing each other. As usual, Stelios ran toward me and burled into my stomach. Then I said hello to Nikos but he replied somberly. His eyes were red, which made me think he'd been crying. I greeted my Aunt Ann and Uncle Dee with hugs and kisses.

"What's wrong with Nikos," I asked Aunt Ann.

"Dimitris killed the baby goats," she said.

"Aaaah… Happy Easter!" I said with a smile.

"He's been miserable all day, poor thing."

Dad and his brother, Uncle Dee, stared silently at each other. Dad held his *komboloi*. Dimitris greeted us from the driveway.

"And I thought we were late!" Dad shouted back.

"We're going to eat now," Dimitris said, raising a large platter of meat in his hand.

An absurd amount of food crowded the table: *kalistounia*; roast lamb; *moussaka*; *tzatziki*; a *marouli* salad; a huge Greek salad; two types of cheeses, soft, creamy white *mizithra* and the firmer, more salty *graviera*; fried potatoes; potatoes baked in the oven. The effort that had gone into the day astonished me. I still hadn't seen Eleftheria.

At the table I sat next to Uncle Dee and Aunt Ann. Aunt Ann asked me what I thought about Greece. "It's great," I said. "I'm a soldier." I enjoyed telling people that I was a soldier. It made me feel proud and confident, but I also knew I wouldn't be able to say it for much longer, so every opportunity I got I said, with a smile on my face, "I'm a soldier."

Aunt Ann looked at me with an expression of concern.

"Are you okay?" she asked.

"I couldn't be better," I said.

Uncle Dee flattened his mouth and asked, "Where are you living?"

"I'm in Chania. I'm on a ten-day break for Easter."

"Is that right?" He looked away after he said it, relaxed and contemplative. A moment later, his eyebrows raised, he asked in a whisper, "You've been to Kallikratis?"

"Too much."

"Were you living there?"

"No. I had an apartment in Chania before I left for the army."

"Is that right?"

"How are you doing, Uncle Dee?"

"We're good, Pete… everything's… What's your plan? You going to stay here permanently?"

"Uncle Dee, I see no further than a few days out," I said, adding, "I'll finish the army first… I'll stay for the summer… And then we'll see."

"Have you been to the house in Patsianos?"

"Of course. Many times."

"How is it?"

"It's nice. It has water and internet."

"That's great to hear, Pete. That's terrific."

"You look exactly like your father with that mustache," Aunt Ann said.

After we had finished eating, everyone split off into different groups spread across the yard. I saw Dad talking to Litsa in the corner by the rose bed. Stella and her cousin sat in the child-sized swing, twirling their arms and dropping their wrists and tilting their heads as they talked about whatever seven-year-old girls do.

Dad came and sat down next to me at the table. His face was animated. He gestured felicitously toward Wilfred's father, who was visiting from France and didn't know a word of English. Dad shouted something that sounded vaguely familiar and, although I failed to understand it, both he and Wilfred's father smiled and clinked their wine glasses together.

"Wow. Your English has improved," I said.

"And your Greek?" he retorted.

I ridiculed Dad and he ridiculed me. At times like this, when we acted like kids toward each other, our relationship found an odd connection. It was like we were equals, not father and son, but friends and partners in crime. Dad had a sense of humor and, even more, a sense of rebellion. He liked to stir the pot up and cause a bit of chaos to make life more interesting. I admit that on many occasions I enjoyed it, except when it was a judgmental attack on me.

I did not see the same humor or urge to rebel in Dad's brother. They didn't look much alike either, except for their glossy tan complexions and their medium-brown-colored eyes. Dad never talked about Uncle Dee to me, so I didn't know him very well, but he seemed a kind man burdened with heavy thoughts. I could never image how different one's perspective on life evolved when one was pulled from his mother and brother and put on a boat for fifteen days to America at ten-years-old, like he was.

I sensed that Dad and Uncle Dee had endured a tough upbringing in Kallikratis that, in the way of such things, had created a barrier between them.

CHAPTER FORTY-FIVE

On my first day back in the army, I was assigned guard duty. I showed up at the post five minutes early to exchange with Yiakomakis as he needed to go see the doctor. He handed me the satchel with two loaded magazine clips and I strapped it across my chest. The first two bullets I clicked into my rifle were blanks.

At moments like this I always felt a great responsibility to protect my surroundings. I watched the gate closely for any suspicious activity. I stood tall and straight which helped me remain vigilant. The only intruders I saw were the stray cats that squirmed under the fence or jumped over the wall from a nearby tree. A few times, at the approach of a vehicle, I had to remind the soldier who was controlling the gate to attend to it. Each time he laid down his smartphone and popped from his hut. I watched civilians on the balconies near the base smoking and sipping frappés. My rifle was attached to a strap I laid over my shoulder. I held the barrel pointed down at the ground. Our post was covered with a roof which kept us cool during the day. I stood like this for two hours, until my replacement arrived and I passed on the ammunition satchel.

It was halfway through my second interval of guard duty that my discipline crumbled. It was two in the morning and extremely cold. I envied the gate controller in the other hut, which had a bed. His door was closed and the blinds were shut and it was clear he was either sleeping or watching TV or on his smartphone. The security of the army base during the night depended on the soldier on guard duty and two soldiers on patrol. My legs grew tired. At times I sat on the steps of my post for a few minutes to relieve the stress on them. Or I leaned against the cement barrier that rose to my solar plexus, thinking how inconvenient it was not to be in bed. As I leaned against the concrete I jotted down some thoughts in my notebook. Then I wrote a poem. Finally the soldier who was to replace me arrived. I hurried back to the barracks where I quickly undressed and climbed into bed.

The routine remained the same for my final few weeks in the army. I spent my days sweeping pine needles from the parking lots and washing and folding uniforms in the laundry room. I made trips to nearby army bases and helped with the spadework. Some mornings we exercised. The food was terrible, so we circumvented the cafeteria and ordered food from outside each day. The officers knew we were doing it, but it was just another rule that was overlooked. We hung out in the lounge and watched TV and screwed around at dinner time. After dinner, I usually went back to my bunk to read or get in an hour of sleep before my next service duty.

One Saturday night we had a party in the lounge room. One of the more popular soldiers was leaving the following Monday. The others snuck in whiskey and vodka and the musicians brought their instruments. We ate gyros. I was impressed by how many soldiers knew how to play an instrument who weren't with the music group. Everyone who could play played their favorite tune. I rested on a torn-up black leather couch grasping a small plastic cup of whiskey. Each time my cup was empty, someone refilled it. We had the windows opened for the smoke to escape. Far off in the distance we could see the mountains glowing in the light of a full moon.

A soldier named Stasis thrummed on the bouzouki while another called Nikos simmered on the lyra. The melodies elicited great passion. We tipped back our heads and, closing our eyes, sung the words. A fellow named Rousis, from Chania, had his boots up on a chair, cusping his cigarette in the fold of his hand. I nestled deeper into the couch. At one point I accidentally tipped my cup off the armrest, splashing whiskey onto the floor, whereupon the soldier with the bottle rushed to refill my cup.

Throughout the evening there was an air of camaraderie that felt very special. It was this feeling that would give you the courage to sacrifice yourself for your brother in the heat of battle.

After the party, at 2230 hours, we stood in the lobby for our nightly report. There were giggles and heckles. The officer on duty must have known we were drunk. As I stood in line, trying not to sway, I felt incredibly happy. I cared for my comrades in a way that I had never cared for anyone before in my entire life.

I did feel my tenure was unfair compared to the normal nine-month term most of the others had to serve. I could have served another month, if I had to. However, I was happy to think I was soon going to complete this endeavor. I recalled when the idea of joining the Greek army first breached my consciousness. At the time, I didn't think I would act on it; I didn't think I would actually move to Greece and serve in the military. But I did. And I knew this was all made possible by Dad, who took care of all the paperwork to make me a Greek citizen.

I wondered how I would define my identity once I received my release papers and they returned my identification card and I'd have my US identification card to set beside it—two identification cards, in two different languages, under two different names. One thing was sure: I would not claim allegiance to one nation or the other if by decree I was forced to make a choice on such a matter. I knew my patronage would be both to the Greeks and Americans. And if a Greek citizen questioned my patriotism, I would tell them outright, *va πας να γαμιθείς.* And if an American citizen questioned my patriotism, I would tell them the same, go fuck yourself. Fully aware of the significance of what I said and what it meant.

However, I knew my nationality was only part of my identity. There was an elaborate string of DNA involved in being a human being. I was more than just a Greek or an American. I represented my creator and my creator said I could be anything I wanted to be so long as I had the courage to live truthfully. No more would I watch over my shoulder, in a stultifying way, or conform to outdated rituals created by the few for the many. This was my rebel nature speaking. It was the same nature as Dad's. Hopefully the summer would bring further evidence of my recent growth and development. I wouldn't search for it or even expect it, but it would come nonetheless and I knew it would be a wonderful feeling.

On my last day I returned all my equipment except my boots and *tsoker* and beret. I had an old uniform that I kept when I worked in the laundry room. I had a checklist of items for officers to sign off on. Before I completed the checklist, I had to go to the army base in Souda to get paid. Amazingly I was owed twenty-six euros for the three months I had served. I was happy about the twenty-six euros which I intended to spend, every penny of it, on a good dinner.

Back at the 5th Battalion Support, my last stop was the director's building where an officer returned my Greek ID. I received a document verifying that I had completed my army duty. I also got a one-way ticket to be used if I was called back to serve in the army. Everyone wished me goodbye. They used the phrase *kalos politis*, which means something like "good luck as a citizen." I snapped a few photos of the barracks and of myself standing in front. I waved to the soldier on guard duty. I shouted goodbye to the gate controller, intent on his smartphone, and I opened the gate myself. *Pikse*, I thought. It was a word the soldiers used often when they liked to joke with another. Then as at the end of any accomplishment, a sudden dip of nostalgia hit me.

CHAPTER FORTY-SIX

After leaving the army a great feeling of freedom overcame me. I strode to the harbor as if I had wings on my feet. People I recognized greeted me, smiling. I greeted them with an even bigger smile. For the first time in my life, I felt like a man. The raw toughness I had only feigned before genuinely seemed to be mine now. Pretensions no longer fooled me. I saw through people. I possessed a psychological power that made every aspect of life appear conquerable. My arms were swollen, my wrists thick and my hands calloused. My mind felt lucid. Nothing intimidated me. Everywhere I went I was resolute and fluid and calm. I understood the Greek vernacular and used it confidently.

To gain even more freedom, I went to the police station to get an EU passport. The lady there told me my photographs were not the right size and that I needed to visit the tax office and buy a voucher. *Fine*, I thought. So I entered the tax office and there was one man waiting in front and a large crowd stood bunched up behind him. I noticed the gentleman in front was a Greek-American with a US passport; he was short and flushed and looked very impatient. Another man, holding a motorbike helmet, passed me and approached the Greek-American waiting at the front of the line.

"Excuse me, sir. I just have a signature to get. I have my bike outside, please."

The Greek-American flung up his hands wildly and shouted, "What do you think I'm here for?! I'm not here to buy the building! I'm here for a signature too!"

I smiled. *I love the Greeks*, I thought. The man with the motorcycle helmet disappeared into the crowd behind the Greek American, while I waited at the very back, unruffled.

Even when Dad phoned me and said, "We have work to do," I remained calm and composed, even though it wasn't clear what work he needed my help with.

"*Ta horta*," he said. The grass. "We need to cut it. I'll come and get you. We're going to have a party. Kanakis will come."

"Bah!" I said.

"Why!?" he asked.

"*Plaka sou kano!*" I retorted. I'm joking with you.

Back in the calmness of Kallikratis, I missed the stimulation of Chania but I felt content. My first day and night went by peacefully and I looked forward to the small party Dad had organized for the following day to celebrate my accomplishment in completing my army service. All was peaceful between us, until the morning I awoke to Dad shouting, "Wake up! Wake up!"

The day, it seemed, had already begun. Little Kanakis was in the orchard with a man I didn't know, a friend of his father's, packing hay into the hand baler. Big Kanakis rested in the courtyard under the mulberry tree.

"Welcome! Welcome, the *palikari*!" Kanakis said, hanging out his hand. "*Kalos politis!*"

"Thank you."

He squeezed my hand, holding it firmly.

"Come inside and eat! I have oatmeal," Dad shouted from inside the house.

"You are a special person. You finished the army. Nobody can tell you that you're not a Greek."

"Come! Eat! We have work." Dad stood at the doorway holding a saucepan. The cats were scattered about in front of him, watching him closely. "Leave him alone, Kanakis. He has to finish the work before the sun is strong."

I felt ready to sweat it out in the field with my forearms swelling and small gashes forming on my hands and arms from the prickly weeds. I grabbed large armfuls of hay and pressed them into the crate. Labor of this kind made me feel decent; to work alongside Little Kanakis and their friend, Yiannis, was honest and natural, like the conversations we had as we toiled. We worked together, exerting ourselves, growing tired but determined to complete the job while the temperature steadily rose.

"Panagiotis, you missed a spot," Little Kanakis jabbed at me.

"I'm sorry, *master*," I said.

"Don't say that—nobody's a master."

"Only the sun," I retorted.

We completed the job just past noon. Dad told us to leave the stalks of hay scattered around the field. I brought out a pitcher of water and we all rested next to Kanakis around the white plastic table under the mulberry tree. My sweat glued flakes of hay to my arms. Kanakis looked immovable, resting on a white plastic chair, dropping back shots of *tsikoudia*.

"You are all one special group of people," Kanakis said. "I was in the military for twenty-four months. I was in the navy, and afterwards I worked with the merchant ships." He paused. "I was a captain," he said in English. "I go to America. Miami. New York." He repeated himself and his pace slowed. "Twenty-four months in the navy…" His eyeballs were glassy. He placed his hand on my arm. "I love you. I'm very proud of what you've done. Whatever you need, we're all family." Then he fell silent for a few moments before continuing. "I worked a lot. I had to. We were poor. Very poor. We didn't have money for bread. When I was young with my siblings and parents we all slept in one room…"

I looked over at Little Kanakis who was quietly listening. And while Kanakis was looking straight at me, it was apparent the message was intended for all of us. Like Dad would've done if I were in Little

Kanakis' place. As I listened, I wanted to pull out of him all the stories he had. It was my pleasure to listen to him reveal his past. I remembered walking along the harbor in Chania and seeing men, many decades older than me, sitting on benches staring at the sea. I always used to think that one day I would sit down next to one of them, look at him honestly and openly, and ask him to tell me of the world. Things I didn't know. What to expect as I grew older. How I might do things so as to avoid the regrets and pettiness that troubled so many people as they grew old. I thought the old man I spoke to might help me avoid turning into a spiritless zombie who lived only to prattle and consume, someone who could find nothing decent in the simple things in life. Maybe, I used to think, he could tell me something of the world that would help me use my judgement to crack the code which mystified me.

When Kanakis finished speaking we all fell quiet. I was deeply moved, thinking that, compared to this moment, everything I had read and all the places I had traveled to had taught me nothing.

"Pour me a glass of water, please," Kanakis asked me.

"Don't drink any more, Kanakis," Dad chimed in, with his usual assertiveness, as he passed by toward the gate.

I bit into a plum, then I plucked a berry from the mulberry tree. It was wet and soft and the purple color smeared my fingers.

"Panagiotis… Listen to me. To have a wife and to make a family is a very wonderful thing. Don't wait until it is too late. You are a *levendis*. You can gather all the women you want. But you have to settle and find the one who will love you."

"I need to find one whom *I* will love, too," I replied.

"Of course! You have to love her. I'm telling you don't wait. You will wait and it will be difficult to find one."

"I guess I just need to be rich and then it won't matter."

"You have to fix a good, strong family…"

Suddenly, beyond the gate, Spirto was barking, and Dad shouted, "Come here! Come here!"

Little Kanakis and Yiannis walked toward him. I stood up and saw that Dad had gathered up his flock of goats.

"Panagiotis—come here!" Dad shouted.

I had rested long enough to feel the aches in my knees and in the joints of my fingers. My lower back had tightened. Dad stood at the opening to the driveway herding the goats toward a narrow passageway enclosed by stone walls. Little Kanakis darted after a goat that separated from the flock. The goats moaned and oscillated chaotically. As we closed in on them, one would slip away and we were forced to widen our territory, until we could bunch them together again.

"Run! Panagiotis, Run!" Dad shouted.

We closed in again and a goat escaped. "Leave it!" Dad shouted. He barked with greater intensity until the goats had scooted across the dirt driveway and into the trap, and when the goats realized they were trapped they moaned louder. Dad moved through the goats looking at each one carefully. The goats' heads were turned, buried in the crevices of the stones or under the rear of another goat. Dad moved further through the flock. There were about twenty of them crammed in the narrow passageway.

"Come here—Come!"

Little Kanakis and Yiannis walked into the herd. I stayed near the entrance. The goats moaned with greater intensity. A goat that Dad tried to grab by the horns skirted along the stone wall and through the flock.

"Catch it! Catch it!"

The goat saw me and stopped.

"Grab it! God damn it! Grab it!"

I stepped toward it as it climbed onto a protruding stone and leaped into the air, charging straight at me and I caught it in a hug. I held its horns tightly. I felt an unfamiliar pandemonium come over me. Dad approached me, scanning the herd as he passed through it. The goat was shaking, its heart pounding. Turd pellets flowed like a waterfall from his hind. I could feel the life in him. His eyes were glossy. Dad tied one of his front legs to his back leg with a length of rope. Then he tied a noose over his neck and pinned him to the gate. "Hold it!" he said.

Then he went back into the herd with Yiannis and Little Kanakis. While I clasped the goat by the horn, I saw Dad stick a probe up the rear of a baby goat and then he snipped a piece of its ear and gulps of blood dropped onto the dirt; the ground was so dry that the blood turned black. At the same time the goat I was holding jerked aggressively, with so much force I was surprised he didn't snap his neck. His diaphragm continued to rapidly expand and contract as he took panicked breaths. He buried his head in the wall, trying to hide.

Dad barked at the rest of the goats and they scattered. Then he took the goat from my clasp, untied it, and pulled it into the courtyard.

"Hold!" he told Little Kanakis. "Where did my knife go?"

Big Kanakis pulled out his pocket knife. "I have a good one."

"No—That's not a good knife."

"It's good. It's sharp—Here…"

"That won't cut. Where did my knife go?"

I grabbed a knife on the cement enclosure around the mulberry tree, next to a meat hook.

"This you mean?"

"Speak! I'm looking for it and you're holding it."

Dad stepped toward the goat.

"Hold it. Come here, Panagiotis. Hold it."

I froze.

"Come here. Goddamn it! Hold."

They flipped the goat over on his back. The goat hurled, "Baaaaaah! Baaaaaah!" Big Kanakis stood over us. Little Kanakis held his horns. Yannis held his hind legs. Dad pinned his head to the ground. I stepped away. His mouth gaped and his tongue extended, surprisingly long, over his front teeth. Everything seemed to move in slow motion, unraveling in flashes. Dad handed me the knife.

"Cut it!"

My heart pounded against my ribs. The goat's dashed pupils narrowed.

"Cut it! Cut it!"

As I stood there, holding the knife, my mind went away from me. The only thing I was aware of was Dad repeatedly shouting.

"God damn it! Cut it! Cut it!

"Leave the kid alone," Big Kanakis said.

A flash of consciousness swept over me and I dropped the knife. Seizing it, Dad ran it in a swift and practiced arc across the goat's throat. A piteous wail came from him and hot, red blood gushed out as Dad drove the blade deeper, severing muscles and tendons until the animal's head dangled from its hideously gaping neck. The shrieking stopped suddenly as the goat's spirit departed and its body appeared to go rigid. Dad's hands were covered in thick red blood. The animal's facial features looked frozen in death, his mouth open and tongue hanging out. The dashed eyes looked empty and glassy like a doll's. The smell of his blood permeated the air. Spirto was nowhere to be found.

Dad rinsed his hands at the water container and came back scrubbing them with an old rag. The goat's hind leg twitched. Dad looked disgusted.

"A soldier! What soldier? Re, Panagiotis. You call yourself a soldier. You went to the army."

Dad snapped off the goat's front hooves as he yelled.

"A soldier!" he taunted. "How are you going to kill a Turk! How are you going to kill a Turk!"

Dad gasped as they lifted the goat onto the meat hook hanging from the tree.

"You went to the army!"

"It's alright, Panagiotis." Little Kanakis said to me.

I walked away, past the gate where Spirto was tucked under a cove of rocks. Her head was down. She watched me closely and I looked back at her, then I walked further away. *This was typical of Dad*, I thought. He was the kind of person who, if he could do something better than you, he made sure he showed you and he did it by humiliating you.

I had always been a meat lover, but later that day, when we gathered at the table for dinner and Dad brought out a large plate of goat meat, I couldn't swallow the plump piece I chewed on. My stomach squeezed. I felt unworthy to eat meat anymore. I hadn't been able to look my friend in the eye before I sent him away. I felt like a coward.

"Eat!" Dad said. "Why don't you eat?" It seemed he could only shout each time he addressed me.

"Leave me alone—I'll eat."

"Panagiotis, in the old years, we only ate meat for Christmas and Easter, if we were fortunate," Kanakis said. "To have meat all the time, you are lucky."

"I'm not that hungry right now."

Dad brought more wine from the cellar. Everyone else was satisfied, to feast on the abundant spread. But as I sunk further into myself, the food made me sick. Eventually I left the table and walked outside for some air. The sun had set. There were stars visible and the moon was a smokey fingernail high up over the dark rim of the mountains. Tears rolled down my cheeks.

"I'm sorry, my friend. I'm sorry I couldn't look you in the eye," I whispered.

CHAPTER FORTY-SEVEN

All my efforts during the last nine months to mount the flag at the top of the mountain seemed to have come to nothing. Now, in the blink of an eye, I was back at the bottom. I thought I had finally reached manhood, but then there was Dad to show me I was too modern to be a man in the traditional sense.

Then summer arrived and it was easy to forget about everything except enjoying yourself on the Greek isles. Swiftly, it felt, I abandoned my self-proclaimed manhood. This was going to be my first full Greek summer. The energy in the atmosphere elevated; Crete swelled in population as tourists spilled out onto the streets of Chania. The vendors were fully stocked and ready to reel you in with their offers. I knew the patter. *This is good price. It goes very well with you.* If I replied that the shirt seemed a little small they'd seamlessly retort, *I've never seen anyone look better than you, right now. I'll give you a good price.* In their genial spirit, set against the picturesque backdrop of the Venetian harbor, these encounters felt like a game.

Other changes took place. The benches that had been removed during the winter were bolted back in position along the edge of the harbor. Innumerable lights suddenly glittered on the rooftops. Every morning I listened to electronic dance music from Avicii or Kygo. I shaved off my mustache. My face was smooth and shiny. After the rigors of army life my spirit felt lightened. I felt an urge to indulge and act wild and meet interesting people from all over the world. I was living in a fantasy, indulging in a potentially endless bout of hedonism.

At an expensive store near the harbor, I bought a few cool, button-up floral shirts. I also bought a fancy pair of Persol sunglasses, which made me look fashionable and rich. All around me a spectacle was unfolding and I felt I had to be part of it. The foreigners who were arriving in Greece, more and more by the day, brought with them energy and excitement and extraordinary influences. Mingling with them around the harbor, or in the narrow backstreets, I greedily imbibed everything I could until I felt myself expanding. It was like I was living a great myth, free of the army at last and with no language courses to attend because I no longer felt any need to learn Greek formally. As the days passed by, my life assumed a whole new feeling. I looked forward to accruing indelible memories that I would be able to access at a later time when life had returned to normal.

The man who would jumpstart my summer of pleasure was Ricky Mazzo, my best friend, who visited in July. It was his first trip to Europe. Ricky was finally breaking from his shell, taking himself out of the Midwest to experience another culture and country where English wasn't the principal language. Before he finally took the plunge, I had to reinforce the nature of the trip to him many times. He had changed his mind on several occasions before saying *Fuck it!* and booking a ticket.

I was excited to see Ricky. He was the most entertaining kind of friend one could ask for. He was simple in the sense that he didn't entertain a single philosophical thought. He was a successful salesman who could make conversation with anybody. He was an extrovert, as he liked to continuously remind me. Before he flew out from the States, I told him about Mykonos and he was stoked. "You're an extrovert, Pete! That's what I love about you, dude!" I didn't understand why he thought *I* was an extrovert, but I loved it.

At the airport we embraced in a big hug. Ricky's light brown hair, which he monitored as if it were his baby, jutted from his black RVCA cap. His bulging biceps—buttered with coconut oil every morning—emerged from the sleeves of an immaculate cream-colored silk shirt. Ricky's eyes matched the color of the sea, owning an intensity that could be searing. He seemed pumped, excited, flaunting his good looks as he strode through the terminal, colorfully splattering his conversation with words like "Cool!" and "Dude!" and "Awesome!"

I could hardly contain myself with Ricky here. Clearly he was still the "Memorable Maz," as I had nicknamed him after he once told a girl he lived in hotels (and it had worked, by god!). In his ebullient company I could stop pondering in my perpetual puritanical ways and, for ten days of chaos and disorder, become an amoral socializer.

I had a rough and dirty itinerary planned for us. We had six nights in Crete and three nights in Mykonos. The first morning we hit up Agia Marina. I took him to a beach club. He was impressed at how clean and clear the water was. I told him to wait until we got to Elafonisi. After a few hours at the beach, we hung out poolside. Ricky chatted up our waitress and she was very friendly to him, although he was irked by one recurring trend.

"Dude! None of the chicks are checking us out. What the fuck?"

"There are a lot of local girls here today," I explained. "This is what I've been having to deal with all year. Chania's like a small town and girls feel that if they are caught talking to a foreign guy their friends will think they're a slut. The women of Crete are very self-conscious. They take the label of slut harder than penetration in the ass."

"Dude!" said Ricky, "We're good-looking guys."

I tried to remind him that it was only his second day and things would change fast. We got lucky, too, because on our way back we were stopped at a light when I spotted Karina walking down the sidewalk.

"Hello, beautiful!" I shouted at her in Greek. She did not turn her head immediately, but when she did, she cracked a smile as soon as she recognized me.

"Who was that?"

"Some chick I went to Greek class with."

"Dude! Call her up. She's hot."

I texted her when we returned to the apartment. I told her I missed her and that my buddy from the US was in town. I told her he was Polish to upgrade his image for her. "Let's all go out one night, bring a friend," I texted.

"Okay. When?" she texted back. Boom!

Karina and her friend met us outside a seafood restaurant in Platanias where Ricky and I had eaten dinner. Karina wore a summery white dress. Her face was lightly made up and she exuded a tantalizing aroma. Her friend's name was Ana. She was a blond and came from Norway. Freckles speckled her pale face. She wore a black and white skirt with a tank-top and sandals. She was quiet and timid and appeared taken aback by the big, boisterous hugs with which I greeted them both. From the start, Ricky was firing, chatting up Ana as if he were selling her rivets.

We went to a club and took a good spot at the bar. I pointed out the price of a bottle of Stolichnaya to Ricky. He snapped his head back in surprise, exclaiming, "Cheap as shit!" The waiter brought the bottle with a bucket of ice on a tray with juices and soda water. Ricky and I took our vodkas straight.

"I think your friend really likes Ana," Karina said, leaning across and speaking into my ear to make herself heard above the music.

"He's very excited to be here. Do you like him?"

"What do you mean?"

"What do you mean, what do I mean?"

"I don't understand."

"You should have invited Hanna, too."

"I asked Hanna, but she couldn't come because she has to work every day and the last bus to Kissamos is at ten-thirty."

"She's always worried about that damn bus! Why not just stay with you for the night."

"I told you she works every day."

"I know that. Can't she just stay the night and take the bus in the morning?"

"Why are you asking me that?"

"Never mind."

"Where did Ricky and Ana go?"

I scanned the floor and the tables but I couldn't see either of them. I recognized a guy I knew from Chania with a girl. I raised my glass to him, then introduced him to Karina and he introduced his girlfriend to us. She hailed from Canada and was very pretty, a half Greek mulatto. I made them each a glass of vodka with orange juice. Then I turned around and there were Ricky and Ana.

"We should order another bottle?"

"Dude, no. I'm not going to drink anymore."

"We only have a fifth of a pint left. I'm ordering another bottle."

"Dude! We don't need it."

"Yes, we do!"

The second bottle came and I found myself very buzzed. I pushed myself onto Ana and we chatted enthusiastically. Afterwards the details of the conversation remained vague, but I remembered that my arm was around her and she held me up and Ricky had his tongue down Karina's throat. Then my friend handed us shots and that finished me off. I remembered Ricky driving me home and me telling him that the car was manual. I remembered he said, "Dude, I was a valet at Ohio State! I know how to drive manual."

Then I said, "This isn't Columbus. The roads are wild and if you're not careful they'll turn you into a souvlaki!"

"You're so fucking drunk!"

"Did you fuck Karina?"

"Yeah!—I took her to the corner and rammed my cock up her ass!"

"That's my boy."

The next thing I remembered, my arm was wrapped around the toilet and I hurled out chunks of salmon while Ricky stood over me and said, "Man's lowest point."

I said, "Dude, we got to get back to Columbus and watch a game."

CHAPTER FORTY-EIGHT

After a few days in Chania, I thought it was important for Ricky to experience the countryside and get away from the tacky tourist havens and unrecognizable destinations, so we went to Sfakia.

He enjoyed the drive and snapped many photos on the way. We stopped the car at a viewing point where, looking out from the top of the mountain, virtually the entire south coast appeared in all its grandeur. Ricky was amazed, gushing expletives left and right as he drank in the vision. To see him like that, almost childlike, made me feel good. We went to Orthi Ammos beach and he enjoyed the swim, even though there were very few girls around in comparison with the beaches near Chania. We embraced the energy the isolation brought us, speaking less as we absorbed the austere magic of our surroundings.

Dad had come down from Kallikratis and was at the house in Patsianos watering the olive trees when we returned from the beach. He was wearing a pair of oversized trousers and tattered tennis shoes and a grey tank-top. I introduced Ricky to him and he said, "Hello, welcome. How do you like it here?" Then, straightaway, before Ricky had answered, he asked, "Are you hungry?"

"Yeah!" Ricky said.

"I make lamb stew."

"Heck, yeah!"

I was uncertain about how Dad would receive Ricky or how Ricky would react to Dad on their first encounter, but I was in no way nervous that Dad would embarrass me or Ricky would judge me. This was a great feeling to have with a friend and this was how you knew you had a really good friend.

Dad made sure Ricky knew everything we ate was from his garden and animals and olive trees. Ricky liked the food. I ate the lamb but I didn't feel good about it. I thought about the slaughtered goat and remembered I was a coward. We ate yogurt with honey for dessert, then we took in the sunset from the veranda. Dad introduced Ricky to *tsikoudia*.

"I make this *tsikoudia*," he said.

There was a long moment of silence while we were hooked on the landscape, the sun going down over the sea. Then Dad asked, "You find any girls to make sex with?"

Ricky almost fell back in his chair. He loved it. We took back another shot of *tsikoudia*.

"*Se-coo-dea*," Ricky said.

"You can also call it *rakí*," I said.

"*Rocky*," he said.

"What time are you coming tomorrow?" Dad asked.

"We'll come for lunch," I said.

"Don't forget to water the garden in the morning."

"*Malista*."

We watched Dad limp down the slope to the road carrying a large jug of water.

"Your Dad's a really cool dude, man."

"He's okay," I said.

Introducing Ricky to Kallikratis the next day was a moment, along with many others during this journey, that I'd remember and value for the rest of my life. I knew from the moment we arrived that the visit was going to be worth it. Dad was waiting on the doorstep, ready to greet Ricky with a shot of *rakomelo*, honey-flavored *tsikoudia*. Ricky threw it down and then eagerly followed as Dad showed him around, hanging on every detail of the house in the observant way a writer would. He questioned the pictures of our family. He was curious to know who was who. Dad stuck next to him like a guide, delighted to share with Ricky everything about his life, knowing that I, too, was imbibing the details.

"This was my father... This is Panagiotis when he was a boy..."

"This place is so awesome," Ricky blurted out. He asked Dad if he could take a photo of the photo of him in the army.

"This was me in the army, special forces," Dad said. Then he grabbed a bowl of apricots on the table and insisted Ricky have some. "These are from my orchard."

The lunch was the exact baked fish lunch I'd eaten before. Ricky stabbed the fish and Dad paused and watched as he opened up the fish and then Dad glanced over at me, to check on how I was doing with my fish, as I trickled sea salt over it.

"Do you like?" he asked Ricky.

"This is delicious."

We rested in the courtyard and ate more apricots in the lazy, unhurried way lambs graze in the fields before leaving for Heraklion to catch the ship for Mykonos. It was a moment of tranquility, free from worries and distractions, as Dad watered his garden and Ricky and I quietly chatted about random things as young men do. As we sat there I realized how much I appreciated the efforts made by Dad when Ricky arrived. He had lent me his car for the ten days that Ricky was here. He cooked us two very good meals. He was proud to welcome Ricky into his way of life.

CHAPTER FORTY-NINE

The cruise ship we boarded in Heraklion filled up at Santorini and from that moment onward anticipation was high within us. I knew precisely what the next three days were meant for. I knew exactly what was expected. I knew how Ricky was going to take on the experience. Yes… these next three days were meant for partying.

We disembarked from the ship at Mykonos into an environment loaded with visitors ready to do the same thing. People wore shiny glasses and hand-crafted watches. Many, both men and women, had well-toned physiques that were obviously scrupulously cared for. This was not only my first visit to Mykonos; it was the first time I had ever stepped foot on another Greek island. All I knew of it was its reputation for hedonism. My first glimpse of the crowd on the dock evoked a feeling of exhilaration.

"Savage!" Ricky said.

"This is what we've been waiting for."

Compared with Crete, this was like another planet. While the former was old, dignified, grandiose in the heroic fashion, Mykonos was the place where the foolish boy trades his family's livestock for a bucket of wine. From the port we strolled to Little Venice, one of the focal points of the action, a place of nightclubs and fancy international restaurants. All was calm, with few people about; the action here only begins in the evening, we heard. Navigating the maze of narrow passageways beyond, my eyes bounced off the

288

whitewashed buildings. Elegant store owners smiled our way, as if we were their next customers. Our hotel was tucked behind a gallery just off a busy walkway. The room was small and it was furnished with refurbished antiques. Immediately, we pushed the twin beds to opposite corners.

Because it was late afternoon we decided against the beach and strolled instead around Little Venice. Each turn brought a new surprise. The new territory, full of expensive and shiny things, gleamed before us.

Gradually the evening rolled into full swing. Well-placed lights shined on the fresh faces that filled the laneways. Being an extrovert never felt easier than it did on Mykonos. We passed exquisite galleries and I heard many different languages being spoken. Purple-flowering bougainvillea brimmed over whitewashed ledges and walls. We stepped into a gallery strewn with flowers. I greeted the gallery assistant in Greek. She was small and lithe, with a sculpted face framed by shoulder-length black hair, dressed in an all-white dress. When she heard Ricky's American accent she introduced herself to him. Ricky's eyes widened. He looked glad to finally meet an American girl.

"Where are you from?" she asked him.

"I'm from Ohio!"

"I'm from New York."

"AWESOME!"

I left them to it and observed the artwork. The paintings were oil-on-canvas and consisted mostly of fishing boats with fishermen out at sea. I tried to feel the artist's personality in each piece. If I couldn't sense some kind of struggle in a picture, it failed to interest me. I glanced over to the desk where Ricky was talking up a storm. I heard the woman say that her name was Sarah and that she had been hired to work in the gallery for the summer.

"We have three floors and a rooftop with artwork," she said.

"Hell, yeah!" Ricky said, almost jumping out of his skin.

We moved upstairs. The woman must have believed we were serious art collectors because she went to the trouble of providing details about every piece we showed interest in. I stopped before a painting that piqued my interest. I sensed the influence of Dali in the artist's work. I tried to connect the specificity of the individual aspects. There was, I sensed, a wonderful story in their oddity.

"I like this painting," I said. She edged forward, then sidestepped to the other side of me so she could take a closer look.

"This picture is only $5,500," she said.

I swallowed. "It is beautiful."

"We should hang out tonight," Ricky said.

"Sure!" she said.

"What's your number?"

I walked up to the rooftop. The view from up there, of the entire town, was heavenly. The sun fell away, but enough light remained for me to notice the sharp contours of the whitewashed buildings. I hung my eyes on a fancy villa an alleyway's width across from where I stood at the edge of the rooftop. A girl was lying on a lounge chair reading a book. She was wearing a long white dress with flowers on it. I was curious to know what she was reading. After a moment I shouted out, "What are you reading?"

She paused, unaware that I wanted her attention. I shouted out again, "What book?" and, when she held it up, added, "Noam Chomsky!"

"That's right!"

She went back to her book. I turned and walked to the other side of the roof. I stared out at the sea. *Noam Chomsky*, I thought. *She's reading Noam Chomsky in her palatial villa on the Greek island of Mykonos.* I found the idea attractive. There was something contradictory about it that pleased me. I wanted to know what sort of woman she was. What was wrong with reading Noam Chomsky in Mykonos? I thought about it.

From what I know, Chomsky's a socialist. And so, what would impel her to want to read the philosophies of a socialist if she enjoyed the finer things in life like a villa in Mykonos sipping from a bottle of Veuve Clicquot? Then at once a piercing idea came into my consciousness: the idea of an adaptable—a bendable and a mendable human being—was not so far-fetched as I thought. The idea this could be true was stimulating to conceive. This was the exact opposite mentality I stayed attached to that stirred up my depressed moods. My understanding of life was to define yourself, to narrow your focus, to specialize and pursue your specialty with great vigor, to avoid anything queer or inconsistent to achieve success.

What if the cause of my utter confusion and rebellion was the fact I thought my only chance of success was to define myself. But what if I ceased to define myself—what if that was the solution for a better me? To only label one based on their feelings at a specific moment and not to attach that behavior to how they would react during a different situation. What if I was a gentleman but I despised Valentine's day, or any day of the year where I was pressured to buy a gift? What if I decided to draw the blade through that goat's throat but I also agree with PETA?

An insight rushed before me, of course, if another person behaved this way I could take in the delight and approve of their approach in life. A hippie who enjoyed reading Ayn Rand... Why not? Or the writer who just started writing at fifty and worked as a hair dresser for the last thirty years. If I did need a contradictory life, I had to fight clear of posturing. If contradiction was absolute to me, then now I was satisfied and viewed that girl with the book quite fondly. She could have very well been a socialist and only wanted the finer things in life.

One who was too defined could have leapfrogged onto her terrace and eaten that book, that was my first instinct, as I thought she might have been a pretender, a self-proclaimed socialist who indulged in the pleasures of what a capitalist life gives one. The pressure I felt to define myself was why I could lash out at one who made me associate as a Greek or an American or a Greek American or a Caucasian, but too dark to be Caucasian, and not swarthy enough to be ethnic. Was it Dad and Mom who thought I was lost because I hadn't settled and obeyed the traditional norms in life to marry and make a family and keep the same job forever? Bah!

"PETE! There you are."

"MAZZO!"

"Dude, let's go."

"What happened?"

"I got her number. We're going to hang out."

"I knew you were going close."

We found a bar with an open deck and a view of the sea and the beach. Fresh from his conquest, Ricky was all positivity. He had the idea he was going to meet up with Sarah alone that night. I furrowed my eyebrows and, taking a large gulp of white wine, gave him some best friend advice.

"If you meet with her alone, you might totally freak her out. However, I don't know what she's about. I only remind you that we are in Mykonos. To party! Not to fall in love. I think if you meet her alone you might as well tie your dick in a knot and call it a night."

We drank steadily throughout the night, becoming more intoxicated as Ricky waited eagerly for Sarah to text him. I wanted every girl I saw, each and every fine piece of ass. Good God—every girl that crossed my path was the prettiest I'd ever seen. There were too many girls to count, all here in front of me. I gulped more wine, longing for the mellowing, courage-enhancing effect of alcohol, hoping it would help.

At just past one o'clock in the morning, Ricky finally received a message from Sarah. She recommended we meet at a bar called Balthazar at two o'clock. "Fuck yeah!" Ricky sputtered. He wanted us to find Balthazar and arrive before her.

After making a few circles through Little Venice, we eventually found the bar, where the host greeted us and allowed us to settle on a cement ledge because all the tables were occupied. We enjoyed fancy cocktails and watched fancy people. The place had an aura of glamour and unrestrained indulgence. I could tell Ricky was preoccupied with thoughts of Sarah. My thoughts remained free and light, and sipping a Moscow Mule in a crystal glass did not make me any different than the person I was sipping *tsikoudia* with Dad from shot glasses with stained brown bottoms.

We agreed that if things moved in the right direction with Sarah, Ricky would nod his head and I'd disappear leaving the hotel room to them.

Ricky spotted Sarah as soon as she appeared, emerging around a bend in the cobblestoned pathway. As she approached, I turned my head in the opposite direction. When I looked back Ricky had his hands raised like he'd made a touchdown and was shouting her name. He hugged and kissed her and promptly ordered her a drink.

The time rolled past two-thirty; the bar was building energy. There was a bunch of really cool people partying on the patio. I sipped my Moscow Mule, watching people come and go. There were all sorts, young mostly, stylish, well-travelled, well-heeled people, folk who cared about their image and were comfortable in their bodies. I noticed very little attitude, nobody telling you where you could stand or sit, or shoving you into a corner to make you feel second-class; despite the crowd, the people massing in the street outside, the atmosphere was happy and relaxed. I went with it, bobbing from side to side, making soft eye touches on all the pretty girls I picked out.

I looked over at Ricky, who was standing on his own. "How's it going?" I asked.

"It's four o'clock. I'm exhausted. Let's get out of here."

"What about Sarah?"

"Forget about her…"

"What did you say?" I said with a straight face.

"She's not that hot."

"You *really* want to leave?"

"Yeah. Let's go. Tomorrow the beach. There will be so many hot as hell chicks there. Let's get some rest. Get ready for tomorrow."

"Where did she go?"

"The restroom. Let's bounce…"

"Oh, Mazzo, this is women for you. They raise you up and knock you down."

"There are so many hot chicks here that she might have hurt me only a fraction of an emotional point."

"An emotional point?"

"I'm built with a string of a million emotional points."

"Did you just pull that string out of your ass?"

"Dude!" He cracked a big smile. "We're on Mykonos! Two guys from Ohio. This is fucking awesome."

"I climbed another rung on my journey to being a better person today. While you were working on Sarah, I unlocked a big piece of how I'd like to live my life. A way that'd I've been too blind or stubborn to understand."

"This is getting deep."

"Let me finish. I found that life is not absolute. The journey is not a formulaic pattern that we must all abide by to achieve success. And we shouldn't feel intimidated by convention or afraid to embrace the challenge of a different way of life. Even if everyone tells you no or thinks you're delusional or lost or silly… Are you listening to me?"

"She's talking to another dude now!"

"Let's get out of here," I said.

We left our empty drinks on the whitewashed ledge and headed off through the square, skirting around tables before disappearing behind a line of palm trees.

CHAPTER FIFTY

The last time I'd had a woman in bed was October. Now it was July. It had been a cold winter, followed by a musky spring of masculinity inside the army base. My only chance of sex in Chania was if I wanted to pay thirty euros for fifteen minutes in the red light district. To my ongoing dismay, every girl I saw appeared to walk within an impenetrable forcefield. Trying to break through this invisible shield, I'd discovered, was only wasting your life. So, yes, it had been nine months of cold turkey and now here on the island of Mykonos, surrounded by so many attractive people, the pheromones were mixing me up and my blood was boiling below my waist.

Paradise Beach, aptly named, was crowded. We scoured the sand hastily, greeting every girl we passed. We paid twenty euros for two sun beds. After we'd settled in, Ricky ordered a bucket of Mythos. I pulled off my shirt and experienced a surge of alpha male power that I'd never felt before. I had the urge to conquer. It could have been the three B's, Beer, Beach, and Babes, that brought it out in me. Even my language was odd.

"I'm going hunting," I told Ricky, as he was lathering his chest.

"Bring back something good—I'm hungry."

I strolled across the beach with a beer in my hand. I tried to walk with a swagger, tried to look suave and important, flicking down my Persol sunglasses to exchange glances with passing people. A lot of men were checking me out, I noticed.

I stood at a bar enclosed by a dance floor. The rhythm of the music energized me. Before I dove into the scene, I wanted Ricky with me, so I returned to get him. He had made friends with another American, Jack from Boston. To my amazement, they were discussing life. Jack was twenty-years-old, with a typical all-American look. Ablaze with ambitions, aspirations, and determination, he spoke as if he had the answers to everything. He was naive and I admired that in him. He seemed so eager and enthusiastic about everything. It made me wonder if that was what I was missing in my life. Somewhere along the way I had stopped being overzealous, I thought. I wondered if reading too much had contributed to it. I wondered if reading books made me unwilling to be naive. Somehow I needed to get back my youthful eagerness. Naiveté was a great quality for one to possess on many occasions.

Jack was eager to drop names. His best friend, he said, was dating a DJ who was performing tonight. And he himself was dating a Sports Illustrated swimsuit model. He liked to talk about himself. He told us he had left Harvard after his first semester to attend Miami University in Florida.

"What! Why?"

"I want to create my own opportunities. I don't want a degree to do it for me," he said.

He was only a sophomore and he was working for a hedge fund. He traded corn futures. His ambition was overpowering.

I caught sight of women dancing on platforms at the bar. I kept my attention in the other direction. The scene had turned wild.

"Savage!" Ricky said.

"Let's go party!" I declared.

The host rallied the crowd. Bottles of champagne were popping everywhere. I saw Grey Goose bottles the length of my leg. The music had a good beat and there was a swarm of girls in tiny bikinis and sexy one-pieces. I dove into the crowd with a great big smile on my face. I danced with girls from Spain, Italy, Australia. Ricky handed me a shot of tequila. Jack stood on a platform with a bottle of Moët.

"Jack!" Ricky shouted.

I danced, unencumbered by the person I'd been before Mykonos or what I would become afterwards; it felt like the ultimate state of liberation. My only concern was for the moment and, more particularly, the remarkable girls dancing on the platform.

"Ricky! Ricky!" I shouted. "Look up…"

Ricky hesitated for no more than a second before he went and grabbed the girl's hand and helped her down from the platform. I was very proud of him. *That's my boy. That's the Memorable Mazzo I know*, I murmured under my breath. He turned and waved me over to the bar. I approached with a smile.

"Can you buy the drinks?" he asked.

"Are you serious?"

"Dude, I have no cash—they don't take credit card."

I ordered a vodka cranberry for the girl, a tequila for Ricky and a vodka soda for me. Ricky's girl was from Switzerland, a beautiful blond with a well-defined jaw and a muscular stomach. Her name was Angelina. Her friend appeared and introduced herself to me. Her name was Carmela. She was German-born, she told me, from a Turkish father. She had an annoying way of smiling at everything I said. It occurred to me she was on ecstasy. I wanted to ditch her for someone else, but I hung in there out of my sense of obligation to Ricky. I told Carmela I was Greek. She smiled. I told her she had a nice rack. She smiled. I asked her if I could clasp onto her rack with my hands like two leeches. She smiled. I smiled back.

Ricky and Angelina disappeared. I danced with Carmela, waiting for the right time to disappear myself. I almost got my chance when an Italian man started talking to her. But before I could escape she gave him a parting smile and latched back onto me. Taking me by the arm, she dragged me across the sand to the sea. At last we could actually hear each other.

"What did the Italian guy ask you?" I said.

"He asked me if I wanted to have sex," she replied, smiling.

She grabbed my hand and pressed her lips against mine. I felt nothing.

"Let's go find our friends," I said.

We walked along the shore and found them sitting on sun chairs. Ricky was brushing sand off Angelina's thighs. She looked relieved to see Carmela. "We need to catch the bus," she said. As they gathered their stuff, I glanced at Ricky, disappointed for him.

"Let's meet up later tonight," Carmela said.

Neither Ricky nor I replied and the girls walked off.

"What the hell?" I asked. "Why did you pull her away from the dance floor?"

"We went somewhere quiet, so we could talk."

I pushed him over a sun chair.

"What the fuck! You're on Mykonos. This is not the place to lay rose petals."

Back in Little Venice, the evening passed fast and smooth. Ricky had taken an Adderall and his energy level was high. I passed on the Adderall he offered me because I'd never taken one before and I wasn't sure what it would do to me. At a club I tried to make conversation with a girl sitting next to me, but she found me dull and left to sit somewhere else. It was only two in the morning and the club was only now getting crowded, but my energy was depleted. I tapped Ricky on the shoulder.

"I'm going back to the hotel," I said.

He was fine. He was next to a girl, in conversation.

As I left the club, I noticed a Louis Vuitton store across the street right next to a church. I laughed because it seemed so odd.

I woke up next morning and saw Ricky's bag of vitamins on the desk and heard the shower running. It was 11 a.m. Ricky appeared and he was fine.

"Did you get laid?" I asked.

He shook his head. "Dude, you should have stayed though—it was awesome," he said.

Up to this point, neither of us had come close to getting laid. It was easy to meet girls; everyone was friendly here, even the Greek girls. Only if we were to get laid, it was going to take some luck. We also had to be prepared to put in the time; achieving our goal could take the best part of a night, but even then, I felt, it was in the lap of the Gods.

On our way to Super Paradise beach I kept teasing Ricky.

"Suuuuper Paradise. It's going to be Suuuuuuper fun!"

"At least it's going to be clean," he quipped.

"We're going to fit right in," I said.

The crowd was classier and more sophisticated than at Paradise beach. We found sun chairs right away. Ricky lathered. I stared closely at the people around us. A blond with a pretty face approached us. Her breasts looked soft, bulging from her white tank top. She was promoting a club called Cavo Paradiso, and wanted us to purchase tickets to see a big-time DJ. When she smiled I saw her braces; she looked about twenty-one. She wore white cotton shorts that choked her ass crack. The lower half of her ass cheeks swelled in front of my face as Ricky flirted with her. I stared without shame.

She pushed Ricky's sunglasses down to see his eyes and, smiling, said with a shortness of breath, "Yum."

Ricky was excited. He looked over at me because he didn't want to say no. She looked at me. She asked me where I was from. I told her I was Greek. She didn't believe me. I told her we'd think about the tickets. Ricky shook her hand and she complimented him on the softness of his skin. Ricky showed her the coconut lotion he used. He offered her some and she rubbed a gulp onto her hands.

"This is very nice," she said. "I take care of myself. And I like a man to do the same."

Ricky couldn't stop smiling and I couldn't stop giggling.

"Forget her," I said, after she left.

"Dude, she was hot and she was digging me."

"She's doing her job!"

"I'm still going to try and get her number," he said.

A pretty woman is a powerful force when she wants to sell you something, I thought. If she was good, men fell to their knees before her. Just as Ricky had.

Ricky and I walked across the beach toward the Jackie O bar. We passed loads of glamorous people on the way: some with grand and elaborate tattoos, others with small sexy tattoos, many proudly showcasing what a year's commitment at the gym and endless protein shakes could do for your body.

The bar overlooked the beach. We ordered beers which cost eight euros a piece. We watched a delightful brunette lying by the pool, sandwiched between two men. Then I spotted two girls across the bar and signaled to Ricky. We introduced ourselves to them. They were Greek. I spoke Greek with them. They laughed at my accent.

One of the girls was named Anastasia. She was from Athens. She taught Greek and had straight, dyed blond hair and brown eyes. She showed great interest in everything I said. We chatted for a half-hour or so; I could've chatted with her longer, but I saw Ricky was growing restless, since we were talking in Greek, so in order to be kind I ordered four shots that we threw down before Ricky and I moved on.

We settled down back at our sun chairs. I closed my eyes and my mind began to roam. *What's next?* I pondered. No great answer came back to me. I felt vaguely restless and unhinged, quietly desperate to assuage the urge that was niggling at me. I thought back to the last time I had sex. Nearly nine months had gone by since then and I felt the longing to bring sex back into my life. If it were to happen here, on Mykonos, I'd be delighted. However I was fine to return to Crete with nine months without sex under my belt because Ana was there. I'd begun to hope we'd be able to kindle some romance, maybe date and find out if we had a connection with each other.

At the mere thought of having Ana, my groin tingled and I felt a faint shiver of anticipation run up my spine. Which was strange, I thought, because I was actually very hot. The sun beat down on the beach with unrelenting force. Faintly buzzing with alcohol, I squinted away the sweat that rolled down my face, stinging my eyes.

Eventually, broiling, I got up and without a word to Ricky went and plunged into the sea, swimming far out, until I was all alone and the music from the bar could only be faintly heard.

I swam some laps, exerting myself, amazed that while the beach was packed there were few people in the sea. The water was delightful, the color a deep and profound cobalt, and utterly clear. It ran off my skin like silk, flashing silver in the sun.

When the sun sank and dusk arrived, Ricky and I made the smart decision to return to the hotel for some rest. I was wasted and knew that, if I was going to continue partying, I needed to fight my intoxication. I ran a warm tub and climbed in, settling back in the soothing water and lathering myself with fresh aromatic oils. Slowly but surely I felt my energy rebuilding. It was like I had taken some reviving drug. Ricky said something about a girl who was going to meet us for dinner. I tried to throw up, shoving my fingers way down my throat, but to my chagrin nothing would come out.

"Give me the fucking Adderall, you cocksucker!" I shouted from the tub.

Ricky left the packet of Adderall on the sink counter.

"Dude! If I was a girl, I'd give you the greatest blowjob, right now."

"Dude, shut the fuck up!"

"But we're on Mykonos, baby, loosen up."

Under the circumstances, the only dinner I could eat was gyros. And it had to be the greasiest, juiciest, freshest, and most succulent pork gyros on Mykonos. We ate like drunkards at a place called Souvlaki Story. Our plates were a mass of fries and salad and *tzatziki* with a pile of carved pork on top. The food helped me sober up. Then the Adderall took affect and suddenly I felt very sharp. I stopped telling people I was Greek, deciding I wanted to be an American again for a change. "I'm American!" I told the four Greek girls eating next to us.

I felt completely free, unhindered by self-doubt or embarrassment. I had reached that point where I felt like I had nothing left to lose. I had stopped thinking and was no longer analyzing every move I made. I talked to every girl I could. As we walked along, jostling with the crowd in the narrow lanes, I grabbed girls by the hand and danced. I had to yank Ricky to catch up.

We returned to the Louis Vuitton street, where we entered a party in one of the buildings. Large ice buckets containing empty magnums decorated the tables on the porch. Elaborate flower arrangements draped the balcony railings overhead. Inside, the place was packed with people, everyone drinking and dancing to the music that was playing somewhere out back.

From the porch, I could see the stars above the harbor. *The stars will be my witness*, I thought. I chugged a glass of water before ordering a vodka. Ricky hastily leaped for a girl. I remained amazingly calm and alert, scanning the space, watching faces. I sat down at one of the tables. I crossed my legs and, purposely, rested my wrist with my watch and its smart leather strap over my knee. Three girls asked to sit down next to me. They were all cute and they looked very young and lovely, each with a tanned glow that drew me to them.

"Where you girls from?"

"We're from Paris."

"I thought you were speaking Italian."

"We speak French and Spanish."

"All of you?"

"We're all sisters."

"I'm going to need to see some identification."

They laughed. I thought, *keep up the energy, make them laugh, keep them talking about themselves*. I was sure that, eventually, one would fall into my arms and, whispering in my ear, tell me to take her away. Their names were Charlotte, Chloe, and Claire. They spoke three languages and were educated and cultured. I told them I was American. I asked them about Paris. They thought I was an investment banker. It was something about my clothes, they said. I didn't disabuse them of the notion.

Chloe said she was a student. She was dark and had a dreamy look in her eyes. She told me that she loved the stars. She desired the unimaginable, she said, asking me to see a color that did not yet exist. She was young, innocent, prepared to make a mistake, I felt. I was falling in love with her by the minute. Her curiosity intrigued me. She was bursting with ambitions, ideas, a sweet zeal about things she wanted to do. She was elegant and pretty and tall, with a face you would show to your mother who would resoundingly approve. I didn't think of sex. I thought of my future with her. She said she loved to travel. She wanted to see the world.

And then… the stars blinked. Anastasia appeared before us. It was as if God had provided me with light and grace and then the devil had appeared and pulled the ground from beneath my feet. Anastasia didn't just say hello. She grabbed hold of my arm. I looked to Chloe. Anastasia pulled me closer to her. She had a nerve. It was the first time a Greek girl had shown interest in me. Almost one year in the country and this was how it happened. I failed to react. Chloe excused herself. Every word Anastasia spoke felt drawn out. I looked over at Chloe standing with her sisters. I went back to her.

"Sorry about that," I said.

"She's a really pretty girl."

"No. It's not what you think. She's just a friend."

"How do you know her?"

"I just met her!"

The shooting star I had lassoed was slowly dying. I looked for Ricky. I eventually found him across the patio talking to a girl. Anastasia glared at me. I found her sweet. I wanted to please both her *and* Chloe. Telling Chloe I'd be back, I went to the restroom to straighten up. By the time I'd returned, there was no sign of Chloe. Anastasia grabbed my arm. As Anastasia talked, I scanned the patio for Chloe. I wanted to at least exchange numbers with her, to leave a WhatsApp greeting. I saw Ricky was now alone and I left Anastasia and went to him.

"What happened?" I asked.

"I told her to look up at all the stars and she told me I was so annoying," Ricky said.

"I finally had a Greek girl come talk to me. And she ruined it! She ruined it all for me. I met the most wonderful twenty-year-old French girl and that stupid Greek girl from the Jackie O bar ruined it."

"Fuck it, man. This was an amazing trip. I had an amazing time. We talked to so many chicks. I met so many different people. It's four o'clock. Let's call it a night."

"What a kick in the gut. I just wanted her number at least."

"Mykonos, baby!"

* * *

In the morning, I couldn't find our tickets. I was sure they'd been in my bag and thought the housemaid had stolen them. The tickets were transferable, and Ricky freaked out so we skipped breakfast and went straight to the port to buy new tickets. We had a few hours before departure, but Ricky did not want to return to Little Venice so we ate at a café next to the port.

The port was crowded with a lot of depleted faces waiting to get the hell out of there. Then, when the boat arrived, hordes of fresh and excited faces poured onto the island just like we had a couple of days previously. I imagined how they would experience the same craziness we had. I wondered how those people who worked here all summer put up with it.

On the ferry back to Heraklion, we sat outside on the deck and I digested what Mykonos had done to me. Despite our greatest efforts, neither of us had succeeded in getting laid. Yet even allowing for this failure, Mykonos revealed the restricted way I viewed life. I had believed that all success was based on an absolute focus. Black and white. A single path that was the one and only direction. A mutually exclusive journey. One career, one pursuit. A singular focus. One set of beliefs and values. One definite way to live. But now I came to see that the essence of life was the relative! And I finally felt happy, relieved.

Beside me Ricky looked tired and defeated, but he had a nice tan.

"I'm really happy you came to visit," I said.

"Dude. This was an unbelievable time," he said.

I clasped the railing and gazed out at the sea and the islands jutting from it and I watched the ship's propellers churn the water into a gleaming white froth that turned turquoise and then blue as it settled back into the depths. I looked over at Ricky and he was doing the same.

"Are you going back to the US anytime soon?"

"Yes… I think I have to."

CHAPTER FIFTY-ONE

A few days after Ricky left, I began exchanging text messages with Ana. One afternoon we arranged to meet up at a beach club in Agia Marina.

She approached me gingerly and we exchanged a timid hug. She appeared nervous, her head tilted thoughtfully. Her gentle manner helped me feel slightly calmer than usual. I asked her if she wanted to eat anything and she said she'd had toast that morning. Eventually I ordered a fruit smoothie for myself and Ana ordered a fresh-squeezed orange juice.

I was nervous. Part of me still didn't know why I had called her. But the experiences on Mykonos had me wanting to finish the summer strong and maybe there was something with Ana that could turn into something serious.

I apologized for my drunkenness on the night we'd met. By way of excuse I explained that my best friend had been in town. This opening segued into a discussion of our lives. Ana had been in Crete all summer. Over the years she had often visited the island with her family. Now that she was older and had finished her studies, she thought it might be fun to experience it on her own. She was unhappy with her waitress job. The owner of the place was a Norwegian and they were pseudo friends. I almost lost my wits when she told me she only made three euros an hour and no tips.

"What's the point of even working?" I said.

She didn't reply.

"It must be fun?" I continued. "You have your days off and after eleven you can go out… and you're in Greece. What's your dream job?"

"What do you mean?"

"What would you like to be doing if you weren't a waitress?"

"I don't know."

"What are your dreams?"

She said nothing.

"You do have dreams, right?"

"Not really…"

"How can you not have dreams?"

"I don't think about it."

"What! I'm a dreamer… That's what keeps me going."

"What are your dreams?"

"Being in love. A career as a writer. Have you ever been in love?"

"Yeah."

"When was the last time?"

"I'm not telling you."

Everything about her gave me the impression we were unfit for each other. She did not express any emotion. She remained at one level throughout the entire date. I knew she was the type I'd have to continuously spin my mind with figuring out if she really liked me or if she was really happy. I'd have to sift through a large dose of subtext. But at the same time she appealed to me, because she was cute and she was a blond living in Greece and I was horny. And she liked me for no particular reason I could grasp at this point. Moreover, I believed in a presumptuous way I could mold her to my need.

I told her I was glad Karina had invited her and that I did not think Karina had such pretty friends. She said she only knew Karina from a job she'd had earlier in the summer at a jewelry store. When we finished our drinks, she did not want anything more. I asked her if she had been to Sfakia and invited her to go there with me on the weekend.

"It's on the south coast of Crete. It's very beautiful. My father has a cottage there."

"I only get one night a week off."

"You can take Saturday off and we can drive in the morning and you can take the bus back on Sunday. Sound like a good plan?"

"I have to ask for Saturday off."

"Well let me know. I'd like for you to be there with me. It's a very lovely area. I'd like to show you Loutro."

When we hugged goodbye Ana appeared slightly more enthusiastic. I offered to drive her home, but she insisted on walking. Later that night she sent me a text saying she'd like to come to Sfakia. I hoisted myself off the day-bed and stood in front of the mirror and patted myself on the back.

I picked her up at the bus station at ten on Saturday morning. After arriving at Chora Sfakion we got the ferry to Loutro. During the journey I wanted to impress Ana with my Greek so I chatted up the captain who was steering the boat next to us. He asked me where I was from.

"I'm from Greece. What do you mean?"

"You're not from here?"

"You think I don't speak Greek properly?"

"No. You don't speak properly."

Ana only understood a small amount of Greek, but she was very observant and aware and she understood what our conversation was about.

"He says my Greek is no good," I told her. "But I think my Greek is pretty good."

"It's all Greek to me," Ana said.

Loutro looked as amazing as ever; the white buildings clustered on the edge of the deep blue sea beneath a wall of towering cliffs. I noticed Ana taking in the scenery as we sailed into the bay, but she didn't say anything so I couldn't tell whether she was impressed.

From the dock, we headed straight to the beach, walking straight through the middle of waterfront cafés and restaurants, commenting approvingly on those that we liked. At the beach, we settled on sun chairs shaded by tamarisk trees. I watched Ana strip to her bikini and suggested we take a selfie together. She puckered her lips and I unbuttoned my beach shirt and wore my Persol sunglasses. Then I went for a swim, while she relaxed on her sunchair. The sea was heavenly and I lingered for some time, treading water and enjoying the surroundings and the feeling that I was here at Loutro with a girl.

A bit later we went for lunch at a taverna above the beach. Ana said she did not want any food. I told her it was my treat. We shared a small carafe of white wine and a Cretan salad but she only ate a few bites. She listened quietly to me talking the entire time. At one point I stopped myself and asked her to say something because I wanted to hear her speak.

"What do you want me to say?" she asked.

"Anything. You make me feel like a chatty-mouth."

"I don't know what to tell you."

"You can tell me anything! There's no secret to it."

"I have a confession to make... I like the beach but I don't go into the water."

"Really? This is the best place to swim. The water here is fresh and clean and safe."

"I can't really swim."

I widened my eyes and took a tender interest in her plight.

"Let's go for a swim," I said, grabbing her arm.

"I already told you."

"Are you setting up a situation for me to be a proper man?"

"If you were a gentleman, you'd respect my concern."

"Of course not! You're in Crete—a part of the world floating in water."

After lunch, I led her by the wrist to a large rock lying offshore in a deeper part of the bay. We cast off from the rock. Ana flapped about with her hands like a fly that had dropped into a glass of wine. I squeezed her by the waist and she latched her arms around my neck.

"I don't like this."

"Relax. Take a deep breath. I'm here. I'm not going anywhere. And if I do someone from the beach will come and rescue you."

"Stop it!"

It felt like a special moment. Ana made me feel needed and I've never felt truly needed or depended upon by anybody in my entire life (except perhaps for Lucky, but he was a dog and I wasn't so sure he really needed me).

"Sway your hips and your legs. And sway your arms in the same rhythm as your legs but in the opposite way."

I let go of her.

"I don't like it!"

"You're being hysterical. Let go of me."

"Why are you making me do this?"

"Because I'm a sadist."

"What?"

"Sway your legs. There you go. See. You're swimming! Not gracefully but you are swimming…"

She latched onto my arm as her body writhed. As soon as she could feel the stones beneath her feet, she released her grasp and held my hand, and I walked her back to our sun chairs.

"I enjoyed that very much," I said.

"I'm embarrassed."

"That was one of the most endearing moments of my life."

That night we went for dinner in Fragokastello and she ate a full meal. Afterwards we went back to the house at Patsianos and stared out at the sea and the stars from the veranda.

"Will you come sit on my lap, please?" I asked. "I feel awkward with you next to me."

She got up and did as I asked. I wrapped my arms around her body and her arms felt very soft and she was still stiff.

"You didn't have a chance to do any writing today, I'm sorry."

"This day was better than any day of writing. I'm very happy with you here now. All year, I've only ever been here in front of this beautiful view by myself. And the whole time all I ever wanted was to share it with a pretty girl like you, like we are now, in each other's arms."

Finally, Ana relaxed, laying her head on my collarbone, and I tilted her chin up toward my face with my index finger and kissed her for a delightful few seconds. Afterwards we went inside and she squealed as I lifted her onto the bed. She said that she'd like to have sex, but only if I had a condom, so I reached into my backpack for the only one I had left.

The next morning, when I drove her to the bus stop, I told her I wanted to see her every day of the following week when I got back. I kissed her. "You're very sweet," I said. I grabbed her again and kissed her.

* * *

Over the following few weeks we saw each other regularly. Ana always stayed at my place whenever she came to see me in Chania, and I would usually stay at her place whenever I visited her at Platanias.

Then, at some point, my desire for her waned. I didn't like how she refused to show any affection in public—even a tiny peck on the lips embarrassed her—or that she exhibited a coldness in her behavior that, try as I might, I failed to understand. I did my best to activate the spirit within her but she remained unable to open herself up to me and express her feelings.

When we weren't together, I would write for a few hours starting in the late mornings. As soon as the afternoon arrived, I couldn't write anymore. I usual went to the stadium then and played basketball, followed by a calm and leisurely swim. At this time I read mostly in Greek, to improve my language, but some English literature, too. I spent very little time on the internet and never read any articles in the news.

Most days Ana would take the bus after work and be in Chania by eleven. Often we went to the harbor and hung out over a drink or two. She preferred visiting me, rather than the other way around. She also knew I did not like to sleep at her apartment, on account of the mosquitoes that ravaged me and her roommate who was always bringing different men home. Despite our ups and downs, I enjoyed Ana's company. With her I didn't have to pretend to be someone I wasn't. She didn't care that I was neither settled nor rich. She didn't mind staying at my unimpressive apartment. She enjoyed staying with me at Dad's cottage at Patsianos, which I enjoyed too. My only extravagance was paying for our meals and drinks out, as I felt bad she was only making three euros an hour.

Yet after a while my feelings of dissatisfaction with her returned. All at once, I began to worry about what was going to happen next. Feeling pressured by this, I cancelled several dates in a row, telling Ana I was busy writing. She appeared not to mind, replying that it was okay if I didn't want to go out. But then one night, when I asked her to meet me for dinner, she finally revealed her emotions in a text.

"No," she said.

"Why?"

"I have my life too and I'm not just waiting around for you."

My evenings without Ana were lonely and depressing. But at the same time I felt badly conflicted. If I thought of us as a couple, in the moment, things were splendid. However whenever I tried to enlarge the picture and consider the future it bothered me that I didn't see her in it. I could not get over the fact that she didn't have dreams. Or rather I was certain she did have them, but she kept them, along with her emotions, tightly guarded. But whatever they were, I believed that her dreams and my dreams were different and, more to the point, incompatible. For one thing, at some point in the not-too-distant future I wanted to return to the US. I was also preoccupied with trying to comprehend all that had happened to me in Greece.

On the other hand, I found Ana's way of just living, without thinking too much or over-analyzing situations, refreshing. She had also made me reconsider my notion that all a pretty girl wanted was a man with money. Maybe that was true in Los Angeles or New York City or San Francisco, but not necessarily elsewhere, and the world, I was learning, was a vast and multifarious place offering more than a life of eternal questing and grasping.

I decided to try and make it up to her with a trip to Palaiochora. She accepted my invitation, but in a guarded manner. We took the bus there. I hopped on in Chania and she got on at Platanias. There was a moment when I saw her waiting at the bus stop as we drove up. She looked very sweet and simple, wearing a summery dress, her blond hair tied back.

The hotel I had reserved was overbooked, so the owner made it up to us by sending us to a five-star place called the Libyan Princess. "This is a very nice hotel," Ana whispered to me as we entered the spacious and luxurious foyer, walking arm in arm like a well-heeled couple on an illicit weekend.

After we had settled into our room, we went to the beach. Ana made no effort to leave her sunbed and bathe in the sea. She was doing fine lying in the sun, she said. In the afternoon we returned to the hotel. I collapsed onto the bed and closed my eyes. Ana lay next to me. She laid her hand on my chest and said, "Should we do what we do best?"

I opened my eyes and glanced at her before turning her over onto her stomach. Then I pulled her to the edge of the bed. I slowly peeled off her shorts and her bikini bottom. I pressed my lips softly onto her, starting at her waist, and I continued with kisses until I reached her lips and could feel she was very wet.

Afterwards we slept for a half hour. Then we both showered and went out for the evening. A kid I'd met in the army, Marakis, whose family owned a café in town, spotted me and called out. We sat down and ordered beers. He sat with us for a few minutes and we reminisced about the army. I told him that his village, Palaiochora, was a solid place. He would not let me pay for the drinks, so I made sure I tipped him well. By then it was getting on for sunset so Ana and I explored another bar next to the sea. It was divine.

"How beautiful is this scene!" I said.

Ana said nothing. I broke out in theatrical chatter to try and overcome her muteness.

"What more could you ask for in life than to be a part of this moment with mother nature. Look how clear the orange sun is framed above those mountains… The sea is as calm as I've ever seen it… Don't you just love it?"

"It's nice."

"Nice? That's it?"

"What do you want me to say?"

"It's better than nice. Try remarkable… marvelous… splendid… spectacular…"

"I don't say words from the movies like you."

I calmed down and we went silent for a while before I asked, "Why do you like me?"

"What do you mean?"

"Could I be more clear? Why do you like me is not an obscure question."

She tensed up.

"What's going to happen to us at the end of the summer?" I continued. "I'm going back to the US and you're returning to Norway. And I'm not sure when I will be back, if I will ever be back. I really like being here, but I feel in many ways like an outsider and that I've left it too late—I should have been here my whole life. Basically I'm very much an American and I don't know if I can ever detach myself from my American way of thinking. I'd say, consider this a favor, cause if you stay with me… I don't know…"

She didn't respond, so I continued.

"You can't say a word to me. Is the only thing we have in common the fact that we both live in Crete? You never tell me anything about yourself. Is this the Norwegian way, to close off and hide your emotions?"

"I've told you about me."

"I don't care that your parents are truck drivers and your brother is on his second marriage. What do you think of me? I just want the truth."

She straightened and her diaphragm expanded and then she unleashed. "I think you're bipolar and vain and materialistic and very selfish and full of yourself."

"It's about time!"

I squeezed her hand and she turned her head away from my lips. "Tell me more."

"And you keep looking at the girls at the next table. Why don't you go talk to them and fuck them?"

"Now you're going too far. I like watching people. I'm a writer. I discern my surroundings. Is that such a bad thing? I saw you check out the handsome young bus driver. I didn't say anything. You could've asked for his number."

"I made a mistake."

"Listen… I'm unsure if one ever has that feeling of completeness, but I've never had it. And maybe it's love that I want and can never find. I was with this girl for a handful of months back in LA… I left the relationship unfinished. It's probably why I'm ruining what we have now… Ana… Let's just have fun tonight? I shouldn't have brought it up. I'm messed up, you see. You don't want to be with me anyways. I'm saving you from future suffering."

We went for a walk in the quaint streets. Nothing could correct our disconnect, but I found peace in our surroundings, taking a keen interest in ordinary things like the well-tended plants and the shops and the different decorations of each café and restaurant we passed. Ana walked less close to me, but I did not feel bad about it. Then, suddenly, she stopped and looked straight ahead at a tall Greek with a full head of hair and a clean face who was walking toward her and the expression on her face lightened. He glanced at me, before looking back at Ana.

"I see life goes on," he said, before moving on.

"Who was that?" I asked.

She went after him. I went into a restaurant and sitting at a table I could see them having a serious conversation. When she returned I asked her immediately who it was.

"Someone," she said.

"I know that! It was a very important someone."

"Why do you care?"

"Why are you being strange—just tell me. Was that your ex-boyfriend?"

Her eyes fixed on me, but she still didn't say anything.

"It was! Now I know why you never wanted to hold my hand. You've been going through all the Greek guys this summer."

"He was my boyfriend and I loved him for a time."

"What happened?"

"I stopped loving him."

"How can that be?"

"He had weird things about him that bothered me."

"Like what?"

"You don't have to know."

"When and how did you meet?"

She would not speak, so I strengthened my tone. "Is he the backup now? And am I just a fill-in until your next suitable candidate comes along? You're going to tell me, right now!"

"We met in the spring. He was visiting from Athens."

"Should we invite him to sit with us? For direct comparison purposes, my queen."

"You're so mean."

"I don't mind. Should I go find him."

"Sit down. Oh, gosh! He probably thinks we're in love and happy. I don't feel well."

"He doesn't care."

"He does care—unlike you! He actually has feelings and a heart."

"You're really laying into me tonight. Bring it all. Anything else you've got to bring me down. What else?"

"You asked for all this?"

"That must be the *tropo tis zois*, the way of life, for all women. To love a man and forget about him. And maybe that's why you think I'm mean. That's why I can never love, 'cause if I love someone I love them forever, not for convenience or to pass the time."

"You're an idiot."

"Thank you! You think I don't have feelings and a heart? Well, you're completely wrong. I'm sorry for making the night turn out this way, but I'm not sorry for saying how I feel. Which you can't do for some reason. Do you want to be with your ex now? I know you do. This is fate. A sign from God. Here. The card to the hotel. I'm serious. I'm fine alone. The night is ruined with me."

"You haven't ruined it."

"Look at your face…"

"You want me to go?"

"I don't want you to do anything you don't want to do. Life is too fleeting to live constrained. Take the card. I'll get another from the desk. If you do come back it better not be with him."

"Oh my God!"

"You should leave, or I will."

I finished dinner alone, then I went for a glass of wine next door and watched everything with intense curiosity, but I couldn't help worrying. When I returned to the room, past midnight, Ana lay in the bed with her back turned to me. I heard sniffles. I said hello. She didn't utter a word. I learned over her and kissed her on the forehead and I saw her cheeks were red and moist. I felt like a really shitty person.

* * *

A few days after our trip to Palaiochora, Ana texted me asking to see me one more time to try and make sense of it all. I agreed. We met at a bar. She wore a colorful dress and looked pretty and tender and fragile. I apologized for my behavior. She cried and I sat there, emotionless. I knew the pain she was going through. This was why falling in love was dangerous. How did one find it? I had no idea.

By the time we were on our second drink, the mood had improved and we spoke more frankly. Ana said she was finished with Greece. We shared a healthy chuckle when she said she would never date a Greek man again. I asked her where she would go next. She said Australia. I walked her to the bus station and hugged her goodbye.

CHAPTER FIFTY-TWO

In late September, I told my landlord I'd be leaving at the end of the month. I was glad to leave the small and dark confines of the apartment and I was looking forward to spending my last couple weeks in Sfakia in the open countryside with a calming view of the sea.

A sense of *ataraxia* wafted over me the moment I arrived at Kallikratis. Spirto was nowhere to be seen. I whistled. Nothing. On the plastic table, under the mulberry tree, lay a revolver. The door to the house was open. The day was balmy and sunny. I stared at the revolver for I moment, uncomprehending, before grabbing it. I flipped open the cylinder. Empty. Dad appeared in the doorway.

"What's the gun doing on the table?"

"I was training the dog, so it isn't afraid," Dad said. "We have a lot of grapes."

Finally I caught sight of Spirto, tucked away behind the shrubs next to the front door.

"I'm happy for you."

"Are you hungry?"

"Yeah. Do you have food?"

"You want me to fry you two, three pieces of meat?"

"I don't want meat."

"You don't want meat... I can make *fasolia*."

"Okay. Good."

We sat at the small table next to the wood stove. Dad commented on the salt I added and I ignored him. We ate in silence, until halfway through our meal when he expressed his concerns about my plans.

"And what are you going to do in America?"

"What I'm doing now."

"You can stay here and open up a restaurant. What do you think?"

"What?! What do I want to open up a restaurant for... *Maybe* a hotel."

"A hotel would be good. We can build a hotel."

"You and I building a hotel together—*very good idea.*"

"You can build it how you like. I'm seventy-years-old! I'm not doing it for me."

"I have my work."

"You can't do that job here?"

"I'm thirty-two-years-old. I want to see the world—to travel. I can live anywhere in Europe with an EU passport."

"You have to settle somewhere. How are you going to have a family like that?"

"So I can stay in one place for the rest of my life?"

"Yeah. What's wrong with that?"

"Greece is not the only beautiful place."

"Where do you want to go?"

"I could go to Spain."

"Spain? And what are you going to do there?"

"The same thing that I'm doing here."

"Enough with your foolishness... you want go to Spain!"

"Spain is a wonderful country."

"Greece is the best country."

"For the nature and landscape... maybe."

"And how are you going to make money?"

"I don't care about money."

"You need money to live."

"I'll figure out a way."

"You can see all the world from the internet."

"*Malakies* you're saying now. You can't understand what I'm trying to do because the life I'm trying to live has never breached the consciousness of anybody in our family. Can't you see that I'm trying to do something that no one in this family has ever done? Make a living with my head. Do you understand? There are people who write for a living. They have very good lives. They make money."

"Forget your *paramythia*, fairy tales, now."

"I'm too tired to have to explain it to you."

"Why did you come to Greece then?"

"For the grapes. To you help you gather the grapes."

"You can stay a couple months longer and help with the olives."

"Bah!"

* * *

All next morning we toiled at filling baskets with grapes and dumping them into plastic crates, then carrying the crates to the wagon. By one o'clock we were only halfway done. The temperature had risen; it stultified us and made us lazy. We went for lunch and did not start back up until after the sun's power had subsided. We would not have finished in one day if not for some friends of Dad's who stopped by and helped. We filled thirty-five crates of grapes and five large plastic bags.

Throughout the day we worked with an ease and respect for each other that I hadn't experienced before. Somehow the tension between us had lessened, if not vanished completely. For the first time I actually felt a connection to Dad and understood what he was getting at. Maybe the chaos and hostility that had characterized our relationship had finally, by some mystical process, evolved into something positive and good. Possibly, too, the time we had spent apart allowed us both to develop, heal, and ultimately move on from our antagonism. I know that I had grown more understanding of Dad's character and of the world that made him. I appreciated his qualities more. I no longer judged him so harshly.

Though we continued to clash over my plans for the future, on topics such as the land we conversed simply and in harmony. We talked about the vineyard, the olive trees, the orchards and the bees. Now, it seemed, we were actually thinking as one. None of this, I realized, could have happened all at once—as perhaps we had expected at the start. I knew now that I had needed this time with Dad to enable him to reveal his life to me. And, like any father and son who had never seen eye to eye, we needed a certain amount of latitude to allow us to grow into each other.

As I gradually learned more about Dad, I came to learn a great deal about myself and to understand how I am very much like him.

I spent a couple of weeks in Patsianos and most of it was good. Now and then I took some time off and went to Kallikratis. There the thing that struck me was how Dad had finally realized that, when I was writing, he could not bother me and ask me to help him fix this or lift that. I don't know how many times I had to tell him, "Dad, writing is not a thing I can stop *all at once* and return back to where I left off," but at last he got my point. He came to respect my routine and left me alone until the late afternoons.

The day before I was to catch the ferry to Athens, Dad took me on a trip through Sfakia. He recommended and insisted we go. And it was during this trip, on a crisp, clear day, that we substantiated our relationship.

We set out around ten in the morning. From Kallikratis we drove westward, passing through the sleepy village of Asfendos before reaching the main road. We passed the village of Imbros where restaurants advertised the starting point for the Imbros gorge, offering tourists a morning meal before they hiked down to the sea. We curved around the mountains and Dad pointed out the spot high up on the slopes where, during the Second World War, the Germans had held a post that commanded the surrounding countryside. Dad drove slowly, taking everything in, staring at our surroundings as if for the last time. We descended the mountain with a view of the glowing blue sea in front of us. Even after many trips down this road I found the scenery captivating. At the bottom of the mountain we turned back west and cruised along the coast. I could see that Dad's mind had wandered off somewhere unknown to me. *The sea is good to have next to you*, I thought. The moment we entered Mom's village, Chora Sfakion, Dad made a sharp right and shifted to first gear so we could make it up the steep road. There were cement houses scattered on each side of the road—a few of them were modern-looking while others looked so old and decrepit you had to wonder if anyone stilled lived in them. At the top of the ascent, we passed a weather-beaten shepherd standing by the roadside with a flock of sheep. He held his *katsouna* behind his back and his black shirt was unbuttoned. The sweat on his tanned skin glistened in the warm sun beating off him.

Eventually Dad pulled into a rocky cul-de-sac, parking next to an unfinished cement church with square windows and a naked entranceway.

"We're going to see your mother's grandparents' tomb," Dad said. "Bring your camera."

I didn't answer. I simply got out of the car with languor, compatible with how the day felt to me.

Just up a tiny slope by the side of the church stood a large marble tomb. I looked closely at the upper part where there was a box-shaped headboard with a little opening enclosed by a glass window. Through the glass I could see a black and white framed photograph of my grandmother and grandfather dressed in their traditional black garb. Beside the photograph was an unlit oil candle. Engraved on the tomb were their names, their dates of birth, and the year each of them died. It was a serene moment in which I became lost trying to understand what this meant to me. Grandpa lived to eighty-five, I calculated. Grandma lived to eighty-seven.

"This is a Kallikratis church," Dad said.

"What do you mean?"

"It is a Kallikratis church!" he said.

I did not probe any further because I did not want to start an argument.

"I'll give money for them to rebuild the church."

"Why don't you give money to build a school?" I said.

Dad ignored my comment and walked back toward the car.

We drove back down the hill and all the way down the road until we reached the town center of Chora Sfakion. We walked down to the harbor where Dad greeted some people he knew. An arcade of restaurants overlooked the harbor, but we went around it, passing through the rear of the waterfront hotels until we came to the far end of the arcade. Here Dad slowly and carefully looked around before sitting down at a table.

"Why didn't we go to Nikos' taverna," I asked.

"Because his brother's restaurant is next door and they don't talk. And if we go to one the other will be upset."

I ordered *moussaka* for old time's sake and Dad ordered fish. We remained relatively quiet as we enjoyed our meal. I was glad to be in the shade next to the sea. The arcade was quiet with only a few tourists scattered at each of the restaurants. At the end of our meal the owner of the restaurant came to our table and introduced herself to Dad. She was an older, stout lady with a hard-looking face. They remembered each other from when they were young. Back then Dad brought grapes to her village to sell, apparently. They talked of the old life in the villages. He told her how many years he'd been in America. Their conversation was odd to me, because Dad had only driven down from Kallikratis—a hundred years ago this would have been a big trip, but nowadays it was only a twenty-five-minute drive. Dad introduced the woman to me and said I was his son.

"What work do you do?" she asked me.

I hesitated.

"He writes," Dad said. "For movies."

"Really? Very good," she said. "It's a pleasure to meet you."

I furrowed my brow in wonder. Not because of the woman's reaction, but on account of Dad. His comment had come way out of left-field, leaving me almost speechless. I suddenly remembered an odd incident that happened many years ago. At the time I was surprised that such a thing had come from Dad, but it immediately made me think differently of him. I remembered we were eating dinner and, as we ate, talking about the American elections and evaluating who'd been a good president and who hadn't been so good. Dad was gnawing on a bone of some sort, but suddenly he stopped and said, "That Martin Luther King. Him. He wanted to help the poor and they killed him. That's how they do it in America."

It was the same feeling today. Dad's words took me completely by surprise. But they made me realize that he possessed an acute perspicacity and the ability to grasp the essence of situations, like his own son's, that I hadn't previously credited him for. He showed me that he wasn't an ignoramus; at times he'd even proved I was the one whose awareness was lacking. My admiration was such that it hadn't mattered to me that Dad thought Martin Luther King had once been president of America.

After we finished the desert the owner treated us to, we got up to leave. We wished the woman well and she wished me well and told me to return to her restaurant some time. Then we passed by a bakery and met Markos, the owner, before we left the village. He treated me to an espresso as Dad and he talked about village politics. He handed Dad a couple bags of *paximathia,* which Dad refused, so he gave them to me.

Afterwards, in the car, I said I was unsure of Markos' last name.

"Is his name Douroundakis?"

"You still don't know?"

"I'm asking you. I think it's Douroundakis. I just want to be sure.

"How many times do I have to tell you?"

"You have never told me."

"You don't remember anything."

"I don't know why you're upset. I just asked. Maybe I forgot."

"You said I never told you.

"So it is Douroundakis?!"

"Do you know your mother's last name?"

"Douroundakis."

"He's Douroundakis. They're cousins."

"Okay! You tell me a name and you expect me to know who they are. 'He's Manolis,' you say, 'he's Manoussos,' but there are a hundred Manolis and Manoussos in Sfakia! You never tell me their last names."

Our bickering subsided and we were quiet and when we approached the road to Kallikratis, Dad drove past it.

"You want to see your grandmother's house in Argoules?"

"Argoules?"

"Yes. Where we have the olive trees. We have a house there. You don't know that?"

"No."

"Let's go see it."

"I'm tired. Next time."

"You're leaving tomorrow."

"I've seen Mom's grandmother's house. It's the same, no?"

"You say you want to be a writer. If you are a writer, you have to experience how the old life was. To spend time with the old people and listen to them and hear them. The young kids at the cafés in Chania know nothing."

"Fine! Let's go."

We reached the village of Argoules and Dad parked the car on the side of the road next to a one-story cement house where locals were resting on the porch. They invited us to sit down and have coffee with them, but Dad graciously declined, telling them we were just here to take a look at the house. We passed around the back of their house and followed a lane that dipped and snaked around a patch of olive trees and climbed a path that was rough and a stony underfoot. Observing the landscape, I instinctively grasped that living here must have been rough. After twenty meters or so we came to a one-story stone building, with jagged walls, standing beside a pile of rocks. To call it a house, as Dad did, was inaccurate. A shack maybe, but even that was a stretch. There was no yard or space to sit outside. The wooden door was weathered and cracked. There was a sizable hole near the top of it. Dad used a rock to break the rusty padlock. Crossing the threshold we entered a small rectangular space that was very cool and lit only by the light coming through the door. I walked carefully, afraid something would jump out at me. As I circled around to take it all in, I wondered how anyone could live like this. I could reach up and touch the ceiling that was layered with sticks. There was a bed in one corner and pottery next to the head of the bed and a place to cook in the corner opposite of the bed. On the wall were pictures of Dad's kids and Dad's brother's kids.

"I went through hell to build this," Dad said.

"Did you put those pictures there?"

"No. Uncle Dee sent them."

There were a couple of water vases and old pots and pans by the sink. Cobwebs hung in the corners. The floor was laid with a coarse layer of cement. A calmness came over me as I absorbed the scene. Floor to ceiling I was confronted with the detritus of a way of life that was remote and unfathomable to me.

"Both of you lived in here?"

"Yeah."

"Where did you go to the bathroom?"

"Outside in the corner."

"How did you shower?"

"We warmed up a pot of water."

Adjoining the shack was a pen for sheep and chickens. Everything was built with stones, uneven, of all different sizes, and sealed with cement. Dad closed the door behind us and secured it with a couple of large rocks. I smirked, but I wasn't surprised by Dad's behavior anymore. Turning back, I gazed at the house wondering what life had once been like for Dad.

At the car, I asked Dad, "You only lived in this house in the winter?"

"Yes. It took me three hours to come here with the donkey. I went by foot. I went to Rodakino and Chora Sfakion to sell grapes…"

I looked at Dad, noting his brown eyes and creased, weathered skin. In the pit of my stomach I felt a falling sensation.

"You don't understand what I went through," he continued. "I didn't know my father. It made me a tough man. I got experience on how to live. After the army I worked in the ships as a crewman. I went to Miami. A lot of men left the ship and didn't return. I called Uncle Dee. I asked him if I should stay. He told me he had taken care of the paperwork for me to be legal and I went back on the ship."

"When did you go to America?"

"In March 1970. I left Miami in August."

"You were on the boat for six months?"

"No! One month. It was six months by the time I got the papers. Until the papers were ready, I was in Greece. You don't understand…"

"I understand."

I could sense within Dad that those six months were the longest of his life. Almost as if he had regretted not jumping ship with the others in Miami.

"We didn't have lights when I left for America! And you don't appreciate it."

"What do you want me to do? Give you a gold medal. You're not the only American who came from nothing."

"You had a lot."

"We were a working-class family."

"You like to make fun of me because I don't speak English. But I didn't go to school like you. I worked. I did not talk with anyone. I only said hello and goodbye. Your mom knows English because she's a woman and she talked with people who spoke English."

We sat in silence as we drove back along the coast towards home. When Dad said I didn't appreciate what he'd done, he was wrong. I was just unable to properly show my appreciation. I couldn't bring myself to say the words, *Dad I appreciate what you did with deep sincerity and all my heart. To set up the situation for me to live in Greece and serve in the army and to test me ceaselessly. The vineyards. The olive trees. The orchards. The ways of goats and lambs. The rooster. For Spirto. The panagiria. The parties you hosted for me. I appreciate the old life you shared with me on this journey. I appreciate it. I do. I appreciate it!*

I know if I had said how much I appreciated him, it would have been a relief to both of us—only I couldn't do it. I think it was my Sfakian lineage, stitched deeply into me, that would not let me show weakness. Only this was one of my greatest weaknesses. The inability to praise the talents and accomplishments of others and to recognize the hardships they faced—simply because I felt that I had never received due praise my entire life.

An intense emotion overtook me. Dad must have known that I appreciated what he'd done for me, because I came here and lived with him and learned my culture and my ancestry.

My experience here fed me a drop of nectar from the gods. I had tasted the experience with a deeper and more profound consciousness than any other in my life, and the result revealed to me how disproportionate I was once living with no real tangible perspective to lean on.

The question arose: why return to the US? Now that Dad and I had achieved a breakthrough in our relationship, it seemed fitting that I should stay and become a partner with him and maybe even build a hotel. However my time with Ana had showed me I couldn't extricate myself from my American way of thinking, even though I did not like the way that this American mentality forced me to consider money as of tantamount importance in most decisions.

At the same time, I did miss America. I missed the dreams. I missed the passion in pursuing those dreams. The opportunities that gave a person from terrible circumstances, like Dad's, the chance to make something better of their life. I respected America as much as I respected Greece. I had a flicker in my heart to return to the US and see it through the prism of what I now knew. Yes. I had hated myself because I had hated my inability to resist the natural flow of those around me and, in the pursuit of my dreams, go my own way.

I also realized that if I stayed in Greece, my life would be static—i.e. I would still be in the same spot ten years from now. This idea of not progressing wasn't in my DNA; it was where my American nature ultimately won out. I had to return to America. Give it my all in whatever I did. Pursue my ambitions truthfully and faithfully. My American idealism convinced me I should return.

A rush of courage overcame me. Having seen the raw conditions in which Dad had lived as a child emboldened me to pursue my greatest life. And to never be quiet. I was armed and prepared to return to America and find great success. I thought of Eleftherios Venizelos, the former Greek statesman, who was integral in uniting Crete with the rest of Greece. I remembered a quote of his that inspired me, when he said to the royal family of Greece when they were negotiating the terms of the union between Greece and Crete: "Speaking as one of the three hundred thousand Cretans, I do not surrender you the right to negotiate, without reference to others, the national interests of my homeland… We cannot entrust our national future into the hands of just one family."

I was imbued with forthright convictions about how I would live the rest of my life. I would live free of restrictions and never lack the courage to challenge existing paradigms or change my way of life if it could be improved.

Just before we reached the road back to Kallikratis, I told Dad I was going to stay down here, because I wanted to take one last swim.

"I'll come in the morning," I said.

"And how are you going to come?"

"I'll hike the gorge. I haven't done it yet."

"You haven't hiked the Kallikratis gorge?"

"No. Not yet."

"It's the best gorge… You have to do it."

Dad left and afterwards I walked down to the beach, my thoughts swirling. There was only one thing that I did not need to hear from Dad nor had I ever heard from him. For him to say "I love you" would be facile, a mere formality, I thought. I knew how he felt about me and I appreciated everything he had done and to say it would only be contrived. *Ennoeite*, I already know that, as the Greeks would say.

I stepped onto the sand and dug in my toes. I was taken by the splendor of the scene. The land and the sea and the setting sun and the moon appeared all at once. This was the kind of moment I loved because I felt that I was human and I was at one with mother nature, connected to it and present with everything it offered me.

I removed my shirt. My bathing suit was unnecessary.

Desolate Gavdos lay in the distance. I turned around and Fragokastilo rested peacefully on the edge of the land. The mountains rose beyond, unchanging. All I knew just then were the mountains and the sea and the sun and color of the sun as it changed when it dropped and the water which felt good all over my body. I inhaled deeply. Then slowly let the air out. It felt good. There was a man sitting next to his bicycle on the beach. A flock of goats grazed on the land beyond him. I was naked. I turned my head back toward the sea and thought, *damn I'm lucky*. Touching land and feeling water and seeing the moon and sun with a breeze wafting over my face. I felt in the midst of a natural uninhibited routine like the breaking of the sun on the horizon when the light canvases the land and the sea turns a few shades lighter.

ΤΕΛΟΣ

ACKNOWLEDGMENTS

I'm grateful to so many people for helping get this story into readers' hands.

To my editor Ian Smith, who I found on the Reedsy platform, who took a genuine interest in my story and really helped pull it out of the gutter and encouraged me on the right direction. To John Knight for reading the almost-finished draft and sharpening it up.

I'm grateful to my girlfriend, Natasha, who saw the potential in me, even when I was unemployed and broke. To my good friends—Denis and Praneet—who were an integral part in helping me to see the forest for the trees, as well as for financial support during troubled times. To Dan and Rahul, my first friends when I moved to New York City at twenty-two-years-old, who have always been there for me as genuine friends, no matter the circumstances. To Donnie, who's never been short on positivity, ensuring I would get this book done. To all the writers I met on this journey who inspired me to never give up on writing, and for the mutual connection we shared that comes in the lonely pursuit of a career as a writer. To my Greek comrades in the Army who embraced me as their own even though I was from America.

To Joey, my brother, this book is truly meant for you. To Georgia, you have been a bedrock of emotional support on this bumpy road. To Demetria and Nick, who have enlightened me on their own perspectives on growing up in this world. To Uncle Dee who immigrated to America at the age of ten and helped bring Dad. To the original George Manouselis who immigrated to America in 1916 and was the conduit through which the rest of the family used to immigrate.

To my parents for their enduring love and allowing me to roam the world freely and discover it for my own.

ABOUT THE AUTHOR

Peter Manouselis is a Greek-American writer. He holds a degree in finance from Ohio State University. He worked as an investment banker on Wall Street for four years after college before he embarked on a career as a writer—finding his passion for writing during acting school at the age of twenty-seven. He started off writing screenplays then turning his attention to poems and book writing. He was born and raised in a small town in Ohio, but his curiosity has led him to have lived in Los Angeles, San Francisco, Madrid, and Chania (Crete). Currently, he resides in New York City working as an investment banker over the last year, but he continues to write on platforms LinkedIn, Medium, and Instagram, sharing his perspective on the world for the better.

Made in the USA
Columbia, SC
27 June 2020